METHUEN'S MANUALS OF MODERN PSYCHOLOGY
EDITED BY C. A. MACE

# FRUSTRATION AND CONFLICT

# FRUSTRATION AND CONFLICT

AUBREY J. YATES, Ph.D.

*Senior Lecturer in Psychology*
*University of Western Australia*

LONDON: METHUEN & CO LTD

NEW YORK: JOHN WILEY & SONS INC

# CONTENTS

PREFACE                                                    *page* ix

1  INTRODUCTION                                                   1

2  FRUSTRATION AND FIXATION                                       4

3  FRUSTRATION AND AGGRESSION                                    66

4  FRUSTRATION AND REGRESSION                                   113

5  CONFLICT                                                     139

6  FRUSTRATION, CONFLICT, LEARNING THEORY, AND
   PERSONALITY                                                 174

   BIBLIOGRAPHY                                                204

   INDEX                                                       226

108380

# TEXT FIGURES

2.1  The Lashley jumping apparatus            *page* 6

2.2*a*  A non-frustrating situation involving a barrier    9

2.2*b*  A frustrating situation involving a barrier and pressure to respond    9

2.3  A comparison of mean latencies to the positive and negative cards for rats with position fixations    13

2.4  Part of a maze used in the experiment by de Valois    47

2.5  Percentage of rats fixating their position-responses when an attempt is made to develop a card discriminative response    63

3.1  Strength of aggressive response as a function of strength of frustration    70

4.1  Apparatus used in the experiment by Sanders    129

4.2  Diagram of the elevated maze employed in the experiment by Whiting and Mowrer (the removable barriers are represented by dotted lines)    133

5.1  Representation of an approach-approach conflict    142

5.2  Representation of an approach-avoidance conflict    143

5.3  Representation of an avoidance-avoidance conflict    143

5.4  Representation of a situation involving command with threat of punishment    144

5.5  Representation of a situation involving command with the prospect of reward    144

5.6  Representation of a situation involving prohibition with a threat of punishment    146

5.7  Approach and avoidance gradients under conditions of strong and weak drive    152

5.8  Shift in direction of indiscriminate approach tendency as a function of increased approach drive    153

5.9  A three-dimensional model of conflict and displacement    157

5.10  The wide-white, medium-grey, and narrow-black alleys in which the rats were trained and tested    158

5.11  Parallel gradients of approach and avoidance    162

6.1  Apparatus used in experiments by Amsel    183

6.2  Learning curve and curve of responses to the frustration (white) side for five rats    186

6.3  A conception of approach-avoidance conflict as it affects the attempt to assess the strength of an approach motive from manifest motive-related imagery in thematic apperception    195

vi

# TABLES

2.1   Number of rats developing fixations in soluble and insoluble
      problem situations                                      *page* 8
2.2   Effect of different schedules of punishment on initial responses
      learned in soluble and insoluble problem situations          12
2.3   Description of eight three-window situations                  14
2.4   Persistence of position stereotypes acquired under different
      degrees of frustration                                       18
2.5   Persistence of position stereotypes and position habits       18
2.6   Number of trials to extinction                               41
2.7   Variability in initial training and development of fixations  44
2.8   Number of middle-alley entrances in trials 25–30             48
2.9   Stability of fixated responses following four periods of reward
      for exercising the fixation                                  51
2.10  Design of experiment in study by Knopfelmacher               52
2.11  Logical combinations of reward and punishment in Maier's
      early experiments                                            61
3.1   Latency of crying as a function of time of withdrawal of bottle  68
3.2   Aggression scores in two doll-play sessions                  81
3.3   Changes in frequency of three content categories for two groups  87
3.4   Mean change in favourable and unfavourable traits after frus-
      tration                                                      91
3.5   Covariation of anti-Semitism with three hypothesized causal
      factors                                                      94
3.6   Percentages of more victimized and less victimized Catholic
      subjects who fall into the less prejudiced and more prejudiced
      half of the anti-Negro scale                                 94
3.7   Design of experiment by Berkowitz and Holmes                 96
3.8   Rotated factor loadings for men and women                    99
3.9   Mean percentage aggression in two doll-play sessions accord-
      ing to degree of identification and agent of punishment (boys)  106
4.1   Characteristics of sample in experiment of Barker, Dembo,
      and Lewin                                                    116
4.2   Frequency of various activities in free play and in frustration  118
4.3   Constructiveness of primary play                            119
4.4   Percentage of total experimental time spent in various activities
      for strong and weak frustration groups                      120
4.5   Constructiveness of primary play for strong and weak frustra-
      tion groups                                                  120
4.6   Mean constructiveness of episodes                           121
4.7   Mean Mood Index                                             121

vii

4.8   Patterns of motivation, shock and satiation in five experiments
        by O'Kelly                                                            131
4.9   Percentage of subjects correctly identifying day of birthday and
        Christmas Day                                                        137
4.10  Mean maturational level on Bender Gestalt test under four
        conditions of regression                                            138
5.1   Average strength of pull in grams on test trials                      156
5.2   Percentage of responses in different categories as a function of
        type of conflict                                                    164
5.3   Percentage of responses in different categories in avoidance-
        avoidance conflict situations as a function of absolute
        strength and equality of responses                                  166
6.1   Aroused motivation to achieve (approach) and to avoid failure
        (avoidance) as a joint function of motive (M), expectancy
        (P), and incentive (I), where $I_s = (1 - P_s)$ and $I_f = (-P_s)$   194

# PREFACE

The idea of writing this book arose out of a number of seminars held in 1957–8 at the University of New England in Australia. It seemed to the writer that a systematic examination of the accumulated knowledge in the areas of frustration and conflict might facilitate the development of theories which would assist in overcoming some of the confusions which presently exist concerning the relationship of frustration and conflict. The book does not, however, constitute an original contribution with respect to theory. It is hoped that it will prove useful to advanced students who have a particular interest in frustration and conflict or who are doing research in these areas.

A special debt of gratitude is extended to Professor Duncan Howie, of the University of New England, where most of this book was written. His constant encouragement and stimulating critical comments were of the greatest value. In a more indirect way, the author is also indebted to his former teachers, Professor L. S. Hearnshaw of the University of Liverpool; and Professor H. J. Eysenck, of the Institute of Psychiatry. The final chapter of the book was written at the University of Western Australia.

For permission to reproduce the tables and figures, the author is indebted to the following individuals who kindly gave their consent: G. W. Allport; A. Amsel; B. G. Andreas; J. W. Atkinson; R. G. Barker; F. A. Beach; J. S. Brown; A. H. Buss; R. L. de Valois; P. Ellen; I. E. Farber; R. S. Feldman; F. K. Graham; F. Knopfelmacher; H. Levin; B. A. Maher; N. R. F. Maier; N. E. Miller; E. J. Murray; J. F. Rosenblith; N. M. Samelson (Morse); R. R. Sears; J. W. Thibaut; R. M. True; J. W. M. Whiting; H. C. Wilcoxon.

The American Psychological Association granted permission to reproduce tables and figures from: *Journal of Comparative and Physiological Psychology*; *Journal of Abnormal and Social Psychology*; *Journal of Consulting Psychology*; *Journal of Experimental Psychology*; *Psychological Review*. For permission to reproduce other tables and figures the author is indebted to: *American Journal of Psychology*;

ix

*Child Development*; Iowa Academy of Sciences; The Journal Press; *Science*; State University of Iowa, Studies in Child Welfare; McGraw-Hill Book Company; D. Van Nostrand Company; Williams and Wilkins Company. Special thanks are due to Dr Brendan A. Maher and Dr John Atthowe for very generous assistance in various ways.

AUBREY J. YATES

*September 1961*
  *University of Western Australia*

# Chapter 1
# INTRODUCTION

In the past thirty years an enormous amount of research has been carried out in the field of study covered by this book. The study of frustration and conflict has proved to be a source of perennial interest to psychologists working both with normal and with abnormal subjects.

We shall be concerned here primarily with the *experimental* work which has been carried out in this area and will have little to say about the clinical aspects of frustration and conflict. This emphasis is not intended, of course, to belittle the significance of work carried out on a clinical basis, nor indeed to deny that the experimental researches largely constitute attempts to formalize more rigorously, and thereby to test, the hypotheses resulting from clinical insight and experience. Ultimately, however, clinical experiences or hunches can be validated, or invalidated, only if they are expressed in a form which makes them amenable to disproof, and even then only if that form is such as to enable the hypothesis to be tested experimentally.

A restriction to the field of experimental studies still leaves a very wide scope for any survey of frustration and conflict, since, as we shall see, these terms have been used to refer to almost any situation prior to goal-achievement. Thus, any learning situation could be regarded (and has been so regarded by some psychologists) as a frustrating situation until the required response has been mastered to the point at which further errors do not occur. Clearly, therefore, even within the experimental field, some further restrictions had to be imposed if the survey were to be kept within reasonable bounds. For this reason we have chosen a limited number of well-explored fields, within each of which a coherent, if sometimes contradictory body of knowledge has accumulated.

In the second chapter we will discuss the controversial experiments of Maier and his colleagues on frustration and fixation. One of the most irritating features of present-day psychology is the tendency for

1

topics to be taken up enthusiastically for a few years and then forgotten. Equally irritating is the reluctance of psychologists to acknowledge their debt to earlier workers in the field or to work out the full implications of particular systems before going on to devise new systems. The classic example is, of course, the work of Hull, whose system has never been fully explored and is now regarded as outmoded and outdated by many psychologists. Yet Hull's system, particularly in its latest formulation (1952), contains literally hundreds of precise predictions concerning behaviour in given situations. The importance of Maier's contribution therefore lies in the persistence of application over a long period of time and the attempt to work out in detail the full implications of the system. In this respect Maier is almost unique in modern American psychology. A good deal of attention has been devoted to Maier in this book because there is no doubt that the lasting value of his work has been obscured by sheer prejudice and *a priori* convictions.

In the third chapter we review the very large amount of experimental work carried out on the relationship between frustration and aggression. The systematic formulations of the Yale school of psychologists, working within the general framework of early Hullian theory, have resulted in a significant increase in knowledge in this field but also in an equal number of problems, such as the relationship between overt and fantasy aggression, the generality of aggressive behaviour, and so on. The important point, however, to notice is the way in which systematic experimental investigations lay bare ever more clearly the precise nature of the particular problem.

In the fourth chapter the work on frustration and regression will be reviewed. Curiously, although the original experimental assault in this area resulted in one of the most famous investigations in psychology, very little work has been reported in this field since. The phenomenon of 'regression', however, is not unitary and learning theorists have devoted a good deal of attention to forms of regression other than the primitivation studied by Lewin and his colleagues.

In the fifth chapter we shall consider the extensive work of Miller on conflict, with some backward glances at other approaches. Miller's work is comparable with that of Maier in extensiveness, covering as it does a similar period of time.

Finally, in the sixth chapter we shall consider in some detail some of the problems glossed over in earlier chapters, such as the problem of the relationship between frustration and conflict. We shall also here consider the general relationship between frustration, conflict, and learning theory; and some work by Atkinson in the field of choice behaviour.

The topics mentioned above undoubtedly represent a somewhat arbitrary selection. We have chosen them in preference to other possible topics (such as frustration and repression) largely on the grounds that the experimental evidence is sufficiently great to warrant some fairly general conclusions. It would, however, be entirely premature to expect any great degree of certainty or body of knowledge within this general field of study at the present time.

# Chapter 2

# FRUSTRATION AND FIXATION

The study of stereotyped or fixated behaviour has a long history. One of the earliest studies to demonstrate the occurrence of fixated behaviour was that of Hamilton (1916). He used as apparatus an enclosure from which animal or human subjects could escape by choosing the correct exit door from a choice of four. Hamilton, however, varied the correct exit door in random order, except that the same door was never correct on successive occasions. Under these conditions subjects showed various kinds of adaptive or non-adaptive behaviour, including repetitive, stereotyped behaviour. With animals in particular Hamilton found 'many instances of persistent re-entrance of an alley during a given trial when as many as ten successive punishments therein failed to direct the subject's activities toward the untried alleys' (Hamilton, 1916, p. 30). Stereotyping of response was particularly likely to occur if the subject became very emotional or excited.

In a later study Patrick (1934) placed human subjects in a very similar situation, involving an insoluble problem, strong pressure to respond, and no possibility of escape except by finding the correct door. Under these conditions (which meet Maier's later criteria for insoluble problem situations very closely) he too found a marked increase in stereotyping of response. The work of Maier, however, marked a new phase in the study of such fixated behaviour

Maier's book on frustration, which was published in 1949, derives its significance both from the wealth of experimental evidence on which it is based, and the fact that it purports to describe a type of behaviour which is difficult to explain in terms of orthodox learning theory. Maier points out that the appearance of a new response has traditionally been accounted for in one of four ways. The response may be conceptualized in terms of associative learning (conditioning); reward satisfaction (trial-and-error); perceptual re-organization; or problem solving (insight). After discussing the implications

4

of each of these theories for therapeutic intervention he gives a number of instances of maladaptive behaviour which do not appear to fit satisfactorily into any one of the above categories. With regard to enuresis, for instance, he points out that the response of wetting is usually severely punished, rather than rewarded, by the parents, yet it persists in spite of the punishment. On the other hand, if the child is given love and special attention, the response may disappear, although it was successful in achieving what the child presumably desired (love and affection) and was therefore rewarded. Maier concludes from these considerations that 'the major weakness of the approach that makes past learning an explanation of present unadaptive behaviour . . . resides in the fact that it fails to account for the persistence of such a learned response despite its repeated failure on later occasions' (Maier, 1949, p. 18).[1] It was Maier's purpose in his book to demonstrate a type of behaviour which he believed could not be subsumed under the rubrics of ordinary learning theory. Furthermore, he believed that the distinctions he made would have important practical implications for therapy and training (teaching) methods with children and adults.

Maier's work may conveniently be treated in three sections. We shall first consider his major conclusions prior to the publication of his book; then review the principal criticisms of his work and the accompanying experiments; finally we shall review Maier's replies to his critics, his work subsequent to 1949 and the significant changes which have more recently occurred in his orientation.[2]

## I. MAIER'S SYSTEM (TO 1949)

### 1. General experimental design

#### a) APPARATUS

In the experiments with which we are here concerned Maier made use of the Lashley jumping apparatus. This is shown in Fig. 2.1. It consists essentially of a small stand from which the rats jump. Facing the animal on a stand are two 'windows' in which are placed cards, with a design printed on them. The rat is required to choose one of the two cards by jumping at it and striking it with his body.

[1] Mowrer (1950) has drawn attention to the same phenomenon and called it 'the neurotic paradox'.

[2] The pre- and post-1949 division will not be adhered to rigidly – in some instances the later work serves merely to confirm the earlier conclusions and in such cases will be referred to in the appropriate place.

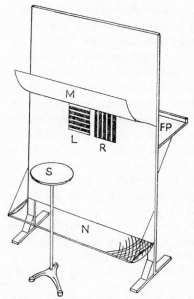

If the choice is correct, the card falls over when struck and the animal lands on a platform behind it on which is food (the reward); if the wrong card is chosen, on the other hand, the rat receives a bump on the nose and falls into a net below (punishment).

b) THE PROBLEM

Two types of problem may be set. Within the *soluble* type of problem, the rat may be required to learn to jump to a particular side, either left or right (position-response) irrespective of which card is in that position; or it may be required to jump at a particular card (symbol-response), whether it appears on the left or right side. Most rats are able to solve these two problems without any difficulty.[3] The

Fig. 2 1. The Lashley jumping apparatus. (Source: Lashley, K. S. 'The mechanism of vision: I. A method for rapid analysis of pattern vision in the rat'. *J. genet. Psychol.*, 1930, *37*, 453–60.)

second type of problem is the *insoluble* one. In this case the cards are latched and unlatched in a random sequence so that no response can be learned which will always be rewarded and escape punishment. In this case the animal usually refuses to jump after a short experience of this insoluble situation. When this happens, Maier forces the rat to jump by directing at it a short blast of air.[4] If the rat is unable to make *abortive* responses (such as jumping right over the cards or directly into the net, etc.) it will be compelled to react to the cards.

c) SUBJECTS

Maier invariably used rats in this problem, but as we shall see later attempts have been made to place human beings in similar situations.

[3] The rat may be allowed to learn a position-reward response which corresponds with its 'natural preference' (i.e. its first free jump); or it may be required to learn a position-reward response *opposite* to its 'natural preference'. The latter problem has been used only once, by Maier, Glaser, and Klee (1940).

[4] Maier and Ellen (1952) substituted tail-tapping for the air blast; and this technique seems to have been used in all subsequent studies.

## 2. Types of behaviour elicited in Maier's discrimination problem situation

a) SOLUBLE PROBLEM SITUATION

In this situation, two kinds of response could be readily elicited:

i) *Position-reward responses.* The rat learns to jump to either the left or right window, irrespective of which card is placed there.

ii) *Symbol-reward responses.* The rat learns to jump to one or other of the cards, irrespective of the side on which it is placed. Maier terms these *goal-oriented* or *goal-motivated* responses, since the behaviour of the rat is clearly determined by whether or not reward results from making a particular kind of response.

b) INSOLUBLE PROBLEM SITUATION

When the problem is made an insoluble one, the behaviour of the animal is quite different from that elicited in the soluble problem situation. Three kinds of responses are found:

i) *Position-stereotype responses* in which the animal always jumps to the same *side*, irrespective of whether it is rewarded or punished.

ii) *Symbol-stereotype responses* in which the animal always jumps to the same *card*, again irrespective of whether it is rewarded or not.

iii) *Abortive responses.* These responses represent the animal's attempt to withdraw from, or escape, making a response to the problem. Thus the rat may try to jump over the apparatus, or directly into the net. As far as possible Maier tried to eliminate such responses.

The stereotyped responses are so called because they are highly resistant to change. The same jump will be repeated consistently and without exception over hundreds of trials. Maier found that position stereotypes were more commonly formed than symbol stereotypes (80% as against 20%) and that stereotyped responses tend to be highly specific in execution.

Maier found that after 160 trials of training in either the soluble or insoluble situation, all animals would develop a consistent mode of responding *either* to the same side *or* to the same card. Outwardly the behaviour of the two groups could not be distinguished.

Suppose now that animals which have developed stereotyped responses in the insoluble problem situation are given the opportunity of developing an adaptive response, i.e. the experiment is now changed so that the problem is a soluble one, of the kind the animal

B

would have had no difficulty in learning in the past. Table 2.1 contrasts the behaviour in one study of animals initially developing

TABLE 2.1

NUMBER OF RATS DEVELOPING FIXATIONS IN
SOLUBLE AND INSOLUBLE PROBLEM SITUATIONS

|  | Number | Per cent |
|---|---|---|
| Soluble (position habits) | 1/10 | 10 |
| Insoluble (position stereotypes) | 7/11 | 63·6 |

Source: Maier, N. R. F., Glaser, N. M., and Klee, J. B. 'Studies of abnormal behaviour in the rat: III. The development of behaviour fixations through frustration'. *J. exp. Psychol.*, 1940, **26,** 521–46

position-reward responses in the soluble problem situation with animals developing position stereotypes in the insoluble problem situation. Both groups are required to change to a symbol-reward response.[5]

From the results of this and other studies, Maier (1949) concluded that about 75% of animals with position stereotypes are unable to change their responses when the problem is made soluble, whereas only 25% of animals with position habits are unable to change from one type of rewarded response to another.

Stereotypes are called *fixations* if the animal is unable to switch to a new response (when the test situation changes from insoluble to soluble) in 200 trials.

### 3. Maier's definition of frustration

Maier clearly distinguishes in his work between a *frustrating situation* and a *frustrated organism*. It is important to note that whether or not an animal is frustrated cannot be deduced from either the experimental situation as such or from the existence of a stereotype.

The essential components of a *frustrating situation* are:

(a) That the animal be faced with an insoluble problem;

(b) That a response to the problem be imperative (i.e. the animal is not permitted to escape or leave the field in any other way);

[5] The positive symbol was a *white circle on a black background*. It is unfortunate that Maier did not keep consistently to this plan in his later studies, since a change to a *black circle on a white background* as the positive symbol changes the nature of the problem (as Maier himself has demonstrated) and makes comparison among studies difficult. For this reason, no consolidated table of results can be meaningfully presented.

(c) That the animal be highly motivated to respond.

Maier's definition of a frustrating situation is important because it is very clear cut, relatively restrictive, and would lead him to reject as frustrating many situations which are commonly regarded as such. This may be shown by reference to Fig. 2.2. Fig. 2.2a shows a situa-

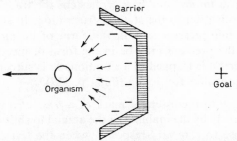

Fig. 2.2a. A non-frustrating situation involving a barrier. (Source: Maier, N. R. F. *Frustration*. New York: McGraw-Hill, 1949.)

tion in which an organism is prevented from reaching a goal by a barrier. *The barrier* is *insurmountable*, and the organism moves towards what was initially a lesser attraction and now becomes a substitute goal. For Maier, such a situation does not constitute a frustrating situation, since a minor goal is present, and hence escape is possible. As he says: 'In order for positive and negative attractions to function in this manner, one must presuppose that the situation does not frustrate the organism. If frustration occurs then the behaviour must be explained by different principles' (Maier, 1949, p. 125). A frustrating situation in the sense in which Maier conceives it is shown in Fig. 2.2b. Here the organism is unable to attain its goal, is unable to leave the field, and is under great pressure to respond. In this situation, he says:

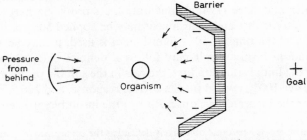

Fig. 2.2b. A frustrating situation involving a barrier and pressure to respond. (Source: Maier, N. R. F. *Frustration*. New York: McGraw-Hill, 1949.)

When escape or the choosing of substitute goals is prevented, the situation becomes more stressful and frustration may be made a more likely condition. The animal's methods of avoiding the unpleasant effects of barriers may be further prevented by forcing the animal towards the barrier. Thus any pressure exerted that drives the organism *towards* the barrier, hastens the transition from the state of motivation to the state of frustration. In some of the experiments this pressure was in the form of an air-blast. In life situations the pressure may be in the form of meeting deadlines. When a person is trapped in a situation, he is surrounded by barriers and pressures for action (ibid., p. 127).

Turning now to the essential mark of a *frustrated* animal, this is determined solely by the inability of the animal to shift from a stereotyped response to a reward-response, when the test conditions are changed from insoluble to soluble. A stereotype, therefore, does not indicate frustration – it may be a *normal* response to an insoluble situation. In such a situation, it is impossible to determine from the animal's behaviour whether the stereotyped response is normal or abnormal. *A stereotype is a sign of frustration only if it is shown to be fixated when the animal has an opportunity to change it.*

### 4. General characteristics of fixations

It is claimed by Maier that fixated behaviour manifests certain characteristics which differentiate it clearly from ordinary learned behaviour. These characteristics will be considered in turn.

a) THE UNIQUE EFFECTS OF PUNISHMENTS[6] ON FIXATIONS
Maier's work on the role of punishment constitutes the critical contribution of his studies and must be considered in some detail. In this section, however, we shall confine our attention to his earlier views. As Maier and Klee (1943) point out: '. . . problems may vary in degree of difficulty, and punishment may be applied 50% of the time or 100% of the time. If 50% punishment is used, it may be applied in a random fashion or it may follow a definite pattern' (p. 378). Taking the initial situation first, the rats in the soluble problem situation receive 100% reward for the correct response, and 100% punishment for the incorrect response. Rats in the insoluble problem situa-

---

[6] 'Punishment' is here quite objectively defined as the occurrence of an incorrect response by the rat which leads to a bump on the nose, absence of food, and falling into the net below the jumping stand.

tion, on the other hand, are rewarded and punished an equal number of times *whatever* response they make, i.e. reward and punishment are administered *randomly*. Yet *both* groups of animals develop highly consistent responses, in spite of differing schedules of reward and punishment.

When rats in both groups are required to *change* their responses, the situation becomes quite complex. Thus, the rat (of either group) with a left-position or left-stereotype response may be required to *reverse* its initial response (i.e. change from a left-position to a right-position response), in which case the left-position response will be punished 100% of the time; or it may be required to *shift* from its initial response (i.e. change from a left-position response to a symbol response), in which case the left-position response will be punished 50% of the time *in an orderly fashion*. Put in another way, this means that the rat developing a left-position response in the insoluble problem situation (50% reward/50% punishment in a *random* order) could either be placed on a schedule of 100% punishment for expression of its fixation or on a schedule of 50% reward/50% punishment *in an orderly fashion* for the expression of its fixation, when the situation is changed from soluble to insoluble.

Maier and Klee (1943) carried out a complex experiment to investigate the effects of these various schedules of punishment and reward. They were especially concerned to note the effects on (i) the number of fixations; (ii) the speed with which the initial response was abandoned;[7] (iii) the additional number of trials to learn the new response *after* the old response was abandoned.[8] Three groups were used: (i) position-reward; (ii) symbol-reward; (iii) insoluble problem. Each group was subdivided into: (*a*) rats required to *shift* from their initial responses; (*b*) rats required to *reverse* their responses. The results are shown in Table 2.2.

It is clear that for all three groups 100% punishment of the initial response (when this response is required to be changed) produces more fixations than 50% orderly punishment (17/30 compared with 6/30). If we now look at the two sub-groups of animals in the frustrated group, however, and consider those animals which did *not* fixate, then 100% punishment is *more* effective than 50% punishment

[7] Measured by the number of trials before the animal made its *first* response opposite to the initial response.
[8] The new response was considered learned when it was practised without error for 30 consecutive trials but the additional trials did not include these 30 criterion trials.

in inducing these animals to give up their initial response (18.5 trials versus 86.2 trials). Maier explains these results by postulating that punishment may *either* itself act as a frustrating agent *or* as a nega-

TABLE 2.2

EFFECT OF DIFFERENT SCHEDULES OF PUNISHMENT ON
INITIAL RESPONSES LEARNED IN SOLUBLE AND INSOLUBLE
PROBLEM SITUATIONS

|  | Groups | | | | | |
|---|---|---|---|---|---|---|
|  | Frustrated | | Position habit | | Symbol habit | |
|  | Reverse | Shift | Reverse | Shift | Reverse | Shift |
| Pattern of punishment | (100%) | (50%) | (100%) | (50%) | (100%) | (50%) |
| No. rats fixating | 8 | 5 | 3 | 0 | 6 | 1 |
| No. rats not fixating | 2 | 5 | 7 | 10 | 4* | 9 |
| Av. No. trials to abandon 1st response | 18·5 (16–21) | 86·2 (30–148) | 8·6 (4–21) | 34·2 (13–50) | 47·8 (40–57) | 14·2 (8–20) |
| Av. No. trials to learn 2nd response | 16·5 (4–29) | 2·6 (1–12) | 4·3 (0–9) | 10·4 (0–46) | 43·3 (0–105) | 1·1 (0–3) |

*These animals all formed position habits.
Figures in brackets indicate range of scores.

Source: Maier, N. R. F., and Klee, J. B. 'Studies of abnormal behaviour in the rat: XII. The pattern of punishment and its relation to abnormal fixations'. *J. exp. Psychol.*, 1943, **32**, 377–98

tive incentive. In the former case it may itself produce fixations;[9] in the latter case it will facilitate learning a new response

b) THE COMPULSIVE NATURE OF FIXATIONS

Maier's analysis of his experiments led him to conclude that 'the fixated animal actually has learned which card punishes and which does not . . . the animal has made the required differentiation but is unable to practice the required response. This property of the fixation makes it appear as a form of compulsion' (Maier, 1949, p. 43).

Four lines of evidence may be cited in favour of this contention.

i) When exercising the fixated response, the behaviour of the rats differs when the positive card is exposed on the side of the fixation, as compared with the exposure of the negative card. This is shown

[9] As shown by its differential effects on the two groups *not* subjected to the insoluble problem situation in this experiment.

by the fact that the animal is more reluctant to jump when the negative card is exposed. Fig. 2.3 shows the mean latencies to the positive and negative cards for rats developing position fixations in a study by Feldman (1953). In the insoluble problem situation (Stage 1)

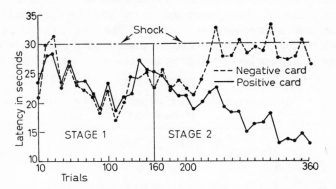

Fig. 2.3. A comparison of mean latencies to the positive and negative cards for rats with position fixations. (Source: Feldman, R. S. 'The specificity of the fixated response in the rat'. *J. comp. physiol. Psychol.*, 1953, **46**, 487–92.)

there is no preference for either card. When the problem is made soluble, however (Stage 2), the latency of response is much greater when the response is made to the negative card than when it is made to the positive card.[10]

ii) Rats which do abandon their fixations adopt the required response very rapidly, sometimes immediately, showing that they have learned the response but cannot exercise it because of the compulsive nature of the fixation. Thus, Maier and Klee (1945) found that 19 animals which fixated 'were then given 30 guidance trials.[11] As a result of this guidance . . . 13/19 rats (68·4%) which failed to solve by trial-and-error immediately found the solution after 30 trials of guidance' (pp. 144–5). This may be compared with the data in Table 2.2 above, where 10 rats with position habits took an average of 34·2 trials to abandon the initial response, and a further average of 10·4 trials to adopt the new response.

[10] The phenomenon was originally called the 'resistance behaviour' of the rats and was related to the amount of air-blast required to induce the rats to jump (Maier, Glaser, and Klee, 1940). It has been reported also in studies by Neet and Feldman (1954) and others.
[11] The meaning of this term will be discussed shortly.

iii) Fixated rats also show differential abortive behaviour to the positive and negative cards when exercising their fixation.[12]

iv) Finally, a brilliant experiment by Ellen (1956) showed that rats with fixations could show clearly that they would exercise their learning, provided this was not incompatible with their fixation. To demonstrate this, Ellen converted the two-window situation used by Maier into a three-window situation. Ellen used all eight possible combinations of positive and negative windows (Table 2.3), with the rat placed either between the left and centre, or between the centre

TABLE 2.3

DESCRIPTION OF THE EIGHT THREE-WINDOW
SITUATIONS

| Situation | Window | | |
|---|---|---|---|
| | 1 | 2 | 3 |
| 1 | +* | + | + |
| 2 | + | + | − |
| 3 | + | − | − |
| 4 | − | − | − |
| 5 | − | − | + |
| 6 | − | + | + |
| 7 | + | − | + |
| 8 | − | + | − |

* A plus sign indicates a positive card in the window; a minus sign indicates a negative card.

Source: Ellen, P. 'The compulsive nature of abnormal fixations'. *J. comp. physiol. Psychol.*, 1956, **49**, 309–17

and right, windows. Now if a rat with a left-position fixation is placed between two windows, with the left window negative and the right positive, it will, as we have seen, usually jump to the left negative window. Suppose, however, we now introduce a third window to the extreme left and make it positive (situation 7 in Table 2.3), according to Maier's theory the rat should now jump to the far left positive window rather than to the near left negative window since by so doing it can now perform the correct (rewarded) response which will not, however, conflict with the exercise of the fixated response, since this is a left-position fixation.

While some of Ellen's results are puzzling, he did find that the rats

[12] The question of abortive behaviour will be discussed in more detail later.

preferred the *positive* card to the *negative*, provided the jump to the positive card did not interfere with the expression of the fixated response. Furthermore, at the end of the day's training on the three-window situation, when Ellen retested the animals on the two-window situation, the fixated response was still present, i.e. expression of the learned response *per se* (which was, of course, rewarded) did *not* serve to destroy the fixation. These results are by far the most convincing evidence that rats with fixations do learn the correct response when the problem is made soluble, but are unable to exercise it except in certain favourable conditions.

c) THE PERMANENT NATURE OF FIXATIONS

Maier and Klee (1941) reported a series of experiments in which they attempted to interfere with the fixated response by putting the animals through a series of other activities. This, of course, is the classic method of interfering with the stability of ordinary learned habits. However, a large variety of methods tried by Maier and Klee were largely unsuccessful in breaking these animals of their fixations. Using 11 animals with symbol-reward habits and 10 with position fixations, they subjected them to the following procedures:

i) A vacation period of at least 4 months during which no testing was carried out;

ii) Training on a symbol-reward problem (100 trials);

iii) Training on the one-window situation in which only one card is presented and the animal is forced to respond to it irrespective of whether it is the positive or negative card (100 trials);

iv) Various combinations of the above three techniques;

v) Convulsions, induced by metrazol.

In spite of these determined efforts, 7 out of 10 rats completely retained their position fixations. The symbol-reward rats, on the other hand, all easily relearned that response following vacation.

Later experiments by Neet and Feldman (1954), and Feldman and Neet (1954, 1957) have shown that electro-shock convulsions do not affect the stability of fixations. The use of ECS was, of course, based upon the assumption that it disrupts recently learned habits. Since the number of ECS treatments was varied, these results again lend support to Maier's contention that the fixation is not simply a strong habit.[13] However, Murphree and Peters (1956) reported that

---

[13] A recent study by Feldman *et al.* (1959) reported a similarly negative result for chlorpromazine.

a course of 18 ECS treatments after induction of fixations did markedly increase the variability of behaviour in the animals when retested for persistence of fixations (these 'fixations' should more properly be referred to as 'stereotypes'). A possible explanation for the discrepancy in these results compared with those obtained by Feldman and Neet lies in the fact that the latter massed the post-shock trials at 10 per day for 20 days, whereas Murphree and Peters spaced their post-shock trials.

d) THE SPECIFICITY OF FIXATIONS

An unpublished experiment by Maier[14] showed that the fixated response adopted in the insoluble problem situation did not generalize to other situations where a response incompatible with the fixated response was learned. Thus, using his three-table reasoning test (Maier, 1932), he found that rats which had developed *right* position fixations in the insoluble test situation were able to learn a *left* position response in the maze situation as rapidly as non-fixated rats.

The specificity of the fixated response was confirmed in a later experiment by Feldman (1953). He took a group of rats with position or symbol fixations which were unable to adopt a new response and taught them the new response by giving them *walking* instead of jumping trials (using guidance alternated with trial-and-error). At the same time that they were learning the walking response, the rats were given interspersed free jumping trials to see if the acquisition of the walking response led to the abandonment of the fixation. Although it will be clear from what has gone before that the rats had learned the jumping response (though unable to exercise it), nevertheless, actually practising and learning the *same* response by walking instead of jumping had no effect on their fixation. The rats could still not *jump* to the correct window.[15]

e) THE TENSION-RELIEVING ASPECT OF FIXATIONS

Mainly as a result of his experiments on the induction of convulsions in the rat in the insoluble problem situation, Maier concluded that performance of the fixated response results in what he calls tension relief. 'The abnormal fixation gives the animal a way of responding to insoluble problem situations – a way without which such situations would have remained highly stressful' (Maier, 1949, p. 52). He is, however, careful to emphasize that 'it must not be supposed

---

[14] Reported in Maier (1949, p. 47).
[15] This experiment, of course, also supports positive findings on the permanent nature of fixations.

. . . that this adjustment value of fixations is a factor in determining the appearance of fixations. Any adjustment accomplished must be regarded as purely incidental and not as a factor that contributes to the development of fixations' (ibid., pp. 52–3). Maier is here, of course, arguing that such tension-reduction accompanies the performance of the fixated response, but is at pains to emphasize that the tension-reduction is not a rewarding situation, i.e. the fixated response is not learned because it is drive-reducing.

f) THE ALL-OR-NOTHING CHARACTER OF FIXATIONS

The main evidence in favour of the all-or-nothing character of fixations is derived from the bimodal distribution of the stereotyped animals when the insoluble problem situation is made soluble. Maier found that the stereotyped animals tended to fall into two clear-cut groups—a small group which was able to change to a position-reward or symbol-reward response in less than 200 trials (usually much less than 200 trials), and a group of animals which was unable to modify its fixated response within 200 trials.

Thus, Maier and Klee (1943) found that '. . . for the 37 rats which abandoned the old response,[16] 148 trials was the maximum score. The 23 rats which did [not][17] abandon the response continued to make the old response for 200 trials each' (p. 386).[18]

g) VARIABILITY IN STRENGTH OF FIXATIONS

Although fixations either occur or fail to occur, nevertheless, established fixations can vary in strength. Maier and Feldman (1948) report an experiment which throws some light on this problem. One group of rats was divided into three sub-groups, each group being given 8, 16, or 24 days' training in learning a position-reward response. The other group was similarly divided into sub-groups which practised position-stereotype responses for 8, 16, or 24 days. All groups were then required to learn a symbol-reward response, using guidance plus trial-and-error. The predictions were that increasing the amount of time spent under frustrating conditions would increase the time necessary to learn the new response in all groups; and that for each period of training the position-stereotype group would have greater difficulty than the position-reward group in changing to a symbol-reward response. The results, as shown in Tables 2·4 and

---

[16] This includes rats trained in both the soluble and insoluble problem situations
[17] The word 'not' was inadvertently omitted in the paper.
[18] Similar results have been reported by Maier, Glaser, and Klee (1940), Maier and Klee (1945), and Maier and Ellen (1956).

TABLE 2.4

PERSISTENCE OF POSITION STEREOTYPES
ACQUIRED UNDER DIFFERENT DEGREES
OF FRUSTRATION

| Frustration period | No. of rats | Av. No. of trials to abandon position-response | Av. No. of additional trials to learn* | Av. total trials |
|---|---|---|---|---|
| 8-day | 37 | 30·1 | 32·8 | 62·9 |
| 16-day | 37 | 49·0 | 30·8 | 79·8 |
| 24-day | 37 | 44·4 | 22·9 | 67·3 |

\* Criterion trials not included.

Source: Maier, N. R. F., and Feldman, R. S. 'Studies of abnormal behaviour in the rat: XXII. Strength of fixation and duration of frustration'. *J. comp. physiol. Psychol.*, 1948, **41**, 348–63

2.5, are highly interesting. Combining sub-groups (Table 2.5), the average number of trials required to abandon the initial response is more than doubled for the position-stereotype animals compared with the position-reward, thus confirming earlier results. Once the initial response was abandoned, however, the position-stereotype animals learned the new symbol-reward response much more quickly than the position-reward animals. With regard to the degree of practice of the initial response (Table 2.4), for the position-reward animals, 8 days' training was no different than 16 or 24 days' in terms of its effect on the animals' ability to change; but for the position-stereotype animals, 16 or 24 days' practice in the frustrating situation is apparently more hindering than 8 days.

TABLE 2.5

PERSISTENCE OF POSITION STEREOTYPES
AND POSITION HABITS

| Group | No. of rats | Av. No. of trials to abandon position-response | Av. No. of additional trials to learn | Av. total No. of trials |
|---|---|---|---|---|
| Frustrated | 111 | 41·2 | 28·8 | 70·0 |
| Motivated | 42 | 20·7 | 43·4 | 64·1 |

Source: Maier, N. R. F., and Feldman, R. S. 'Studies of abnormal behaviour in the rat. XXII. Strength of fixation and duration of frustration'. *J. comp. physiol. Psychol.*, 1948, **41**, 348–63

Maier and Feldman concluded that there are two degrees at least of fixation and that the results also support Maier's contention that punishment itself may be frustrating.[19]

h) ROLE OF GUIDANCE IN ALTERING FIXATIONS

One of the most important points put forward by Maier is that although fixated responses cannot be altered by any of the methods commonly found useful to extinguish *learned* responses, they can, nevertheless, be changed relatively easily by the use of appropriate techniques. The method utilized by Maier is that of 'guidance', as he calls it, and is described as follows:

Two fixated animals unable to adopt the symbol-reward response in 460 trials were presented with an open window on the side opposite the fixated position preference and the negative card on the side of the position preference. The experimenter then prevented them from jumping to the negative card . . . and, instead, pushed them towards the open window. At first it was almost necessary to carry them to the open window, but gradually the experimenter was required to use less and less interference. By the end of 20 trials the rats chose the open window themselves. The positive card was then placed in the open window and it was chosen by both rats. Thereafter, the positive card was chosen regardless of its position. The position fixation had been successfully broken (Maier, 1949, p. 53).

Essentially, the method of guidance requires only that the animal be prevented from expressing its fixated response and be induced to practise an alternative. Subsequent experiments, however, led Maier to some important qualifications concerning its role in the breaking of behaviour fixations. Most importantly, guidance *is not a learning technique*. Its main usefulness is in inducing the animal to abandon its fixated response. Once this has happened, the usual trial-and-error reward situation is reinstated and the animal then proceeds to *learn* the required new response in the usual way. Maier concludes that 'the method of guidance weakens the response the animal practises, but it does not materially aid in the learning of an alternative.

---

[19] Feldman and Neet (1957), using 8-day and 12-day training periods in the insoluble problem situations, found much more rapid abandonment of the initial response and learning of the second response (using guidance plus trial-and-error) in their non-shock groups. However, the results are not strictly comparable as the discrimination problem (second response) in their case was a light versus a dark window.

For this reason it is an excellent procedure for altering fixations since these maintain themselves because they are strong and not because alternative modes of behaving are absent' (Maier, 1949, p. 58).

Most of the evidence concerning the role of guidance comes from an early study by Maier and Klee (1945). In the first experiment they compared position-reward and position-stereotype groups when required to switch to a symbol-reward response under conditions of guidance alone, or trial-and-error alone. Thirty successive trials of guidance on the new response were followed by 70 free trials (both windows unlocked) and 170 trials of 50% orderly punishment. They found that only 2/28 animals adopted the new response during the 70 free trials, i.e. guidance did not assist learning. On the other hand, fixated rats failing to adopt the new response in 200 trials did so immediately after being given 30 guidance trials, i.e. they had learned the new response during the 200 trials but were unable to express it until the old response was broken by guidance. In the second experiment the guidance trials were alternated with the usual trial-and-error trials. The results showed that rats given guidance *and* trial-and-error abandoned the first response more quickly than rats given only trial-and-error (average of 32·7 trials as against 90·3 trials) but took considerably longer to adopt the new response (average of 69·2 trials as against 13·0 trials). It will be noted that the *total* number of trials to adopt the new response is similar for both groups (101·9 trials as against 103·3 trials). Thus guidance appears to facilitate the abandonment of fixations but does not facilitate the learning of the new response.

The second principal role of guidance is the *prevention* of fixations. Thus, in the same study by Maier and Klee no rats failed to learn the second response when given guidance alternated with trial-and-error (this applies both to position-stereotype and position-reward rats).[20]

Haslerud, Bradbard and Johnston (1954) used three different techniques in attempts to break fixated responses. In addition to Maier's usual technique they used mechanical guidance in which the fixated response was prevented by the use of a transparent screen; and

---

[20] Similar results were obtained by Maier and Ellen (1952) and by Maier and Feldman (1948). Feldman and Neet (1960) have also shown that the development of fixations can be prevented if ECS is given during the insoluble problem training at the conclusion of each day's training. Similar results were not obtained with reserpine (Feldman and Liberson, 1960), nor with meprobamate and phenobarbital (Liberson et al., 1959).

'handling' in which the animal received emotional soothing for 30 seconds. There was no difference between the three techniques in the number of trials it took to break the fixation, nor in the number of additional trials to learn to a criterion, while the correct response, once achieved, was equally well retained in subsequent free trials by all three groups. The role of guidance in the breaking of fixations appears from these results to be rather more complex than Maier's own results indicate.

i) THE EFFECTS OF PREVIOUS EXPERIENCE ON THE FORMATION OF FIXATIONS

Not very much work has been reported on this aspect of fixations, but two studies are relevant. Maier and Klee (1943) took groups of rats which had been placed in the soluble or insoluble problem situations and subsequently required to shift. One group shifted from position-reward to symbol-reward responses; one group from symbol-reward to position-reward responses; and the third group, which consisted of fixated rats, adopted either position-reward or symbol-reward responses by guidance plus trial-and-error. Supposing now that all three groups are exposed to the insoluble problem, what will be the effect of the previous training? Will any or all of the rats fixate? And if they do, will they fixate the earlier response, the current response acquired in the insoluble problem situation, or some new response?

When the insoluble problem was introduced 54/60 rats persisted in the current response adopted just before the introduction of the insoluble problem situation. There was no disorganization of the response in progress, and no tendency to return to previously acquired responses.

When the animals were now required to *shift* from this stereotyped response to a new response under 50% orderly punishment, 34/60 (57·6%) fixated the ongoing response. Maier and Klee were also able to show that when animals which had fixated in the earlier experiments were compared with those which had not, the former showed *fewer* fixations in the present situation – in other words, a history of previous fixations, which have been broken by guidance, confers some degree of immunity to subsequent frustration.

In another experiment, Maier and Ellen (1952) required rats to learn a difficult discrimination with or without the aid of guidance. Although guidance did not facilitate learning of the discrimination, only 10% of the guidance group failed to learn, whereas 35·6% of the non-guidance group failed to learn. The animals which did learn the discrimination were then placed in the usual insoluble problem situation followed by the soluble problem situation. Maier and Ellen found that only 6·2% of the guidance group fixated, whereas 35·7% of the non-guidance group fixated. Learning a difficult discrimination (which may itself constitute a frustrating situation) under guidance appears to protect the animal from fixating when it is later put in an insoluble problem situation.

## 5. Types of response to frustration

So far we have discussed only the general characteristics pertaining to *fixated* responses. In the experimental situation devised by Maier, the number of ways in which the animal could respond in the frustrating situation were very limited. Maier, therefore, has not a great deal to say about the types of response which may manifest themselves in such a situation.

Maier does, however, attempt to relate other work on frustration to his own system. He questions, for instance, the Miller–Dollard thesis that *aggressive* responses to frustration are always goal-seeking and that the aggression disappears when the goal is reached (drive reduction). He quotes instances from their book in which the aggressive behaviour resulting from frustration clearly was not directed towards the blocked goal. Furthermore, the aggressive response persisted even if the barrier to the goal was so strong that it could not be overcome. Thus, for Maier, aggression is frequently the *endproduct* of frustration, not a means to an end, i.e. it is behaviour without a goal. The aggression may, of course, incidentally overcome the barrier and the goal may in fact be reached, but this is not necessary. The subject, after all, cannot be sure he will attain his goal when he begins his aggressive behaviour. Aggression, like fixations, is essentially tension-relieving. In this way it is, Maier claims, possible to account for such activities as revenge. 'Revenge relieves tensions and this relief makes revenge sweet and satisfying. No problem is solved, however, and no wrong is corrected by revenge' (Maier, 1949, p. 106). The above analysis would, perhaps, be more appropriately applied to such behaviour as cursing and swearing, or backbiting and tale-bearing, but the general point is quite clear.

Maier attempts to interpret *regressive* behaviour, as described by Barker, Dembo and Lewin (1941), in similar terms. Regressive behaviour is behaviour without a goal and is tension-relieving. Such responses appear without learning and disappear when the frustrating situation is removed. Maier's discussion of regressive behaviour is relatively weak and he fails to make any reference to at least one point which strongly supports his system, namely, the persistence of barrier behaviour in the frustrated children, in spite of the fact that it is never rewarded, i.e. the usual laws of extinction do not apply.

The same analysis is applied to behaviour commonly termed *resignation*. Under extreme and prolonged frustration a subject may simply resign himself to his fate and refuse to perform any positive action. While this phenomenon manifested itself in a number of Maier's rats, he is careful to point out that this mode of behaviour presents difficulties for frustration-theory, in that it does not describe a type of action that is an end in itself. He considers it may represent a terminal condition of repeated and prolonged frustration.

Thus a state of frustration may lead to aggressive, regressive or resigned behaviour. All of these responses Maier terms 'symptoms' of frustration. Whether all of these responses represent different types of fixations or whether a fixation is a mode of response which may have different characteristics is not very clear. However, in discussing instances in which these frustration-characteristics *interact*, he says that: 'for the present it seems desirable to retain the four classes of behaviour: aggression, regression, fixation and resignation as the characteristics of behaviour induced by frustration', and continues: 'At present all types have been observed' (Maier, 1949, p. 113). Again, as an example of their simultaneous interaction, he says: 'Fixation and regression frequently are combined with aggression in racial prejudice. Such prejudices persist regardless of facts and consequences (fixation); the reasons for believing are frequently unsound and go back to childhood, and there is a failure to make obvious distinctions (regression); and finally racial prejudice is associated with destructive behaviour towards some group or individual (aggression)' (ibid., p. 114).

In this analysis, fixation appears to refer simply to the fact that a response persists, whereas the two other concepts (regression, aggression) define the *content* of the persisting response. If this is so, then clearly the term fixation is of a different order to the other two and is possibly superfluous.

C

## 6. Distinction between frustration-instigated and motivation-instigated behaviour

So far we have discussed only the general characteristics of that behaviour which Maier calls frustration-instigated behaviour. Maier is, however, concerned to show how this kind of behaviour may be distinguished from what he calls motivation-instigated behaviour. He does, in fact, list twelve such differentiating criteria (Maier, 1949, pp. 159–61). However, these are clearly not all independent and may conveniently be reduced to six:

(1) Frustration-instigated behaviour is characterized by its stereotyping, i.e. its fixedness and compulsiveness; whereas motivation-instigated behaviour is characterized by its plasticity and variability.

(2) The effects of reward and punishment are different for the two types of behaviour. Reward has no effect on frustration-instigated behaviour and punishment is either ineffective or intensifies the behaviour by increasing the degree of frustration. On the other hand, reward and punishment are selective factors in motivation-instigated behaviour, i.e. they help to determine which responses will be strengthened and which weakened.

(3) The frustration-instigated behaviour may be destroyed by the technique of guidance; but this technique is of no value in changing motivation-instigated behaviour.

(4) The degree of frustration can be relieved by the expression of the fixated response, regardless of whether or not the response is adaptive, whereas responses expressed by a motivated individual are satisfying only when the responses are adaptive.

(5) Frustration-instigated behaviour tends to be non-constructive in nature, involving primitivization and regression, whereas motivation-instigated behaviour tends to be constructive in nature and to involve selective adaptation, i.e. learning.

(6) The response actually utilized during frustration tends to be a function of its availability to the organism, whereas the response expressed in a state of motivation, while it may initially (i.e. before any experience of consequences) be determined by availability, will readily be influenced more by anticipated consequences.

In view of what Maier considers to be the above clearly differentiating characteristics of the two types of behaviour, he proposes that the laws governing the appearance and disappearance of these two types of behaviour must be different, and that only confusion will result if the two types of behaviour are not kept separate. Accordingly, he defines motivation as characterizing 'the process by which the expression is influenced by consequences to which such behaviour leads' (Maier, 1949, p. 93). Frustration is characterized by the fact that 'the selection of behaviour is determined by forces other than goals or mere neural connections' (ibid., p. 94). The crucial differentiating characteristic then would seem to be the effect on future behaviour of the consequences of a particular response.

## 7. Applications of Maier's distinction between motivation-instigated and frustration-instigated behaviour

The distinction between these two kinds of behaviour, if sustainable, would clearly have important practical implications and applications, and indeed half of Maier's book is devoted to spelling out in considerable detail some of the ways in which such a distinction operates. In particular, he tries to show that some common forms of misbehaviour may result from *either* frustration *or* motivation and that, from the point of view of correct treatment, it is important to determine which type of behaviour is involved. Only a brief reference to some of these applications of Maier's system is possible.

a) NEUROSIS AS FRUSTRATION-INSTIGATED BEHAVIOUR
After a brief review of the well-known experiments of Pavlov, Gantt, Liddell, Masserman and others on the induction of experimental neuroses in animals, Maier comments that a common factor running through all of these studies is 'the appearance of a kind of behaviour in the animal which seemed not to be demanded by the motivating and learning conditions of the test situation, and which at the same time seemed to be caused by the test situation' (Maier, 1949, p. 140). This situation is paralleled in human neurotics by what Mowrer (1950) has called the 'neurotic paradox', i.e. the paradox that the behaviour of the neurotic seems to be at once self-defeating (i.e. punishing) and self-perpetuating (i.e. fixated). The neurotic frequently feels compelled to perform in some particular way even though past experience has taught him that such actions are likely to be followed by punishment rather than reward and even though the neurotic often *knows* the correct response for the given situation. As a result of these considerations, Maier concludes that frustrating situations and neurosis-producing situations are essentially the same. The responses in experimental (and human) neurosis are:

i) non-goal oriented

ii) compulsive

iii) fall under one of the four types of response to frustration, i.e. are either fixations, regressions, aggressions, or resignations.

Maier goes somewhat beyond this simple analogy, however, and presents a tentative theory of neurotic behaviour. According to him, the crucial identifying characteristic of a neurosis is its 'spread of effect', i.e. its generality. The effects of frustration may generalize and this may be accomplished in two main ways:

i) By increased generalization (i.e. the subject reacts to stimulus elements which formed part of the original total situation);

ii) By a reduction in the frustration threshold.

It may be noted in passing that for Maier the crucial characteristic of the neurotic is his frustration, not his behaviour. The behaviour cannot be tackled directly, since it is merely a symptom (determined largely by the availability of response at the time of frustration). Maier's theory of neurosis is, however, very sketchy and need not be discussed further here.

b) SOME COMMON ABNORMALITIES OF BEHAVIOUR

Maier points out that some behaviour deviations may result from one of *two* causes, i.e. they may be *motivated* by a desire for a particular goal (in which case treatment involves the provision of the desired goal in a legitimate manner) or they may be the result of *frustration* (in which case the correct treatment involves treatment of the underlying frustration). In this way, Maier discusses two types of stealing, thumb-sucking, destructive behaviour, whining and delinquency and their appropriate methods of treatment. Let us look at three of these briefly.

i) *Two types of stealing.* Stealing may be motivation-instigated, i.e. the boy may simply have a very strong desire to own a watch since all the other boys in the neighbourhood have one. In such instances, the most effective method of treatment will be the provision of the desired goal, either by giving him a watch or helping him to save up for one. The stealing may, however, be frustration-instigated, i.e. the boy may steal to gain attention from his parents, who show pronounced preference for his younger sister. In this case, according to Maier, the treatment is not the provision of a watch but the provision of attention, i.e. the removal of the frustration the boy feels because he is neglected.

ii) *Two types of destructive behaviour.* Destructive behaviour may be due to failure on the part of the parents to provide appropriate opportunities for the child, e.g. taking a watch to pieces and trying to put it together again may be *constructive* from the child's point of view. Treatment here would consist in the provision of appropriate materials which the child can regard as his own to experiment with. On the other hand, destructive behaviour may be symptomatic of frustration and represent a desire to hurt the parents. In this case, the treatment would clearly be different (though, as Maier points out, destructive behaviour under controlled conditions, as in play therapy, may be beneficial for the frustrated child, in that it will be tension-relieving).

iii) *Two types of criminal behaviour.* Maier makes a distinction between one kind of criminal behaviour (theft, fraud, kidnapping, tax evasion) which is motivated behaviour and seems to be a function of the subject's relative evaluation of possible consequences (success and failure). On the other hand, there are certain kinds of crimes (especially sex crimes and murder) which frequently seem to bear the marks of being frustration-instigated behaviour and which the most severe punishments (anticipated or actually previously experienced) do not seem to influence.

c) THE EFFECTS OF REWARD AND PUNISHMENT ON BEHAVIOUR
We have already discussed the effects of punishment in Maier's experiments and pointed out some instances where punishment may be completely ineffective and others where it may exercise a selective effect. It is now time to make some general remarks about Maier's position with regard to the effects of punishment. Clearly, from what has already been said, Maier's basic contention is that *the effects of reward and punishment depend upon whether the behaviour to which they are applied is frustration-instigated or motivation-instigated.* The withholding of reward is not necessarily the equivalent of punishment. Maier distinguishes between anticipated rewards which are then withheld (which would be equivalent to a punishment) and rewards which might have been given, but are not. Similarly, he distinguishes between anticipated punishments which are withheld and a punishment which might not have been given but is.

The important points which Maier makes may be summarized as follows:

i) In motivated behaviour reward and punishment exercise selective effects; in frustration-instigated behaviour they have no differential effect, since the behaviour is an end in itself (the important practical consequence of this would be that punishment is justifiable if, and only if, the behaviour being punished is selective and if alternative modes of response are available. In such cases, punishment will serve as a negative incentive. A most important qualification, however, would be that even in such a situation, the punishment itself must not induce frustration. See below.).

ii) Punishment may itself constitute a frustrating situation in which case it will (a) increase the strength of frustration-instigated behaviour, if this is prevalent; or (b) transform a motivated state into a frustrated state. 'Punishment can only serve as a negative incentive when the organism is in a motivated state and when its intensity is not great enough to excite the frustration process and cause it completely to dominate over the motivation process' (Maier, 1949, pp. 196–7).

iii) Reward *may* reduce a state of frustration if it satisfies the need which is being frustrated. It may also work in an important manner by raising the *level of aspiration*. Hence it may be important to reward people who feel inferior and compensate for it by boasting and bragging. Our natural tendency is to try to punish these people by ridiculing them, but, as already pointed out, punishment merely strengthens such behaviour. Rewarding such behaviour on the other hand may permit such a person to direct his activities elsewhere and thus afford opportunities for new learning.

iv) Reward may serve the important function of raising the frustration threshold and hence help to prevent frustration in the future. This function of reward may be particularly important when punishment (frustration) is anticipated in the near future. Maier illustrates this point with an example – it is more important to give a child rewards *before* going to the dentist, than after. 'Present rewards may serve to prevent future frustrations' (ibid., p. 199).

v) Rewards and punishments may generalize in their effects.

vi) Whether or not punishment will induce a condition of frustration will depend on the subject's frustration threshold, the degree and duration of the punishment and the subject's perception of the situation. Punishment 'may be perceived as an insurmountable barrier or obstacle to need satisfaction' (Maier, 1949, p. 201). Maier believes that the most frustrating form of punishment is that given by one individual to another, since such punishment will be seen as degrading or rejecting, whereas 'inanimate' punishment (e.g. an insurmountable obstacle) may be objectively recognized and accepted.

It follows from Maier's analysis that reward is *always* preferable to punishment as a method of training. If punishment becomes necessary, 'it is then important to make the punishment only severe enough to produce avoidance behaviour and it should be so administered as to avoid the degradation of the individual. When one person punishes another there is always the danger of directly depriving the punished individual of self-respect' (ibid., p. 205). This danger is present even when the behaviour is motivation-instigated.

d) METHODS OF PSYCHOTHERAPY

The most important application which Maier makes of his distinction between motivation-instigated and frustration-instigated behaviour is in the realm of counselling and psychotherapy.

Maier emphasizes that there are two quite distinct phases in psychotherapy. The first phase corresponds to 'guidance', and Maier emphasizes in particular that frustration must be 'relieved' by expression *before* the second phase, that of trial-and-error techniques of retraining can be successfully employed. In other words, the situation of the patient is exactly parallel to that of the rat on the jumping stand. However insightful the *therapist* may be with respect to the patient's problems, his insights will be useless to the patient himself until the latter's frustration-instigated responses have been disrupted by expressing themselves under guidance. Once this is achieved, the normal processes of trial-and-error will assert themselves. Equally important, however, with respect to the trial-and-error behaviour of the patient, is the fact that the solution of the patient's problem must be 'discovered' by the patient himself; indeed, a solution 'imposed' by the therapist may well constitute a form of punishment (degradation) and constitute a new frustration.

Maier's views on the importance of the expression of frustrated behaviour in a permissive situation as tension-relieving and as necessarily preceding trial-and-error behaviour is similar to Freud's notion of catharsis and is clearly distinguished from behaviour which is drive-reducing. The expression of frustration-instigated behaviour may be tension-relieving even though the response itself is punished. This catharsis, then, sets up the conditions under which motivated behaviour can reappear.

These two fundamental aspects of the process of psychotherapy (tension-relieving expression paving the way for new learning by trial-and-error) led Maier to the conclusion that the initial role of the psychotherapist is essentially a passive one; later, his task becomes primarily that of assisting the patient to obtain new insights by helping him to restructure his field. Thus Maier is led to the conclusion that non-directive psychotherapy, particularly as practised by Rogers (1939), is that which is most in accord with his theoretical deductions and he finds, indeed, that Rogerian technique does contain the two essential elements outlined above.

## II. CRITICISMS OF MAIER'S WORK

First, we shall consider some general criticisms which can be made of Maier's work up to the time of the publication of his book in 1949. Then we shall look at the various alternative explanations of Maier's results which have been proposed.

### 1. General criticisms

#### a) METHODOLOGICAL CRITICISMS

i) *Reliability of the phenomenon.* There is considerable doubt concerning the percentage of rats which might be expected to develop fixations in the insoluble problem situation. Maier himself, in summarizing the results of three experiments, concludes that approximately 70% of rats will develop such fixations when trained in the insoluble problem situation. Such an average is virtually meaningless, since the percentage may range from 50% to 92%.[21] This unreliability, of course, does not in any way invalidate the phenomenon, since it refers only to the percentage of animals likely to develop fixations, and not to the reliability of the fixation, once induced. Such a phenomenon might be important if only two rats in every hundred develop fixations. It does indicate, however, that the phenomenon is influenced by variables which Maier has not brought under control. Most important of these, presumably, would be the variable of neuroticism. Since Maier equates neuroticism with frustration, it is possible that the percentage of rats developing fixations is largely a function of the percentage of neurotic rats in each sample (when the experimental conditions are comparable in all other respects).

ii) *Failure of experimental control.* Originally, Maier attempted to determine the differences in behaviour between groups of rats faced

---

[21] Maier (1956) has listed at least nine reasons why the percentage of fixations may vary from one study to another. This does not, however, account for the variability found in *strictly comparable studies.*

with a soluble and an insoluble problem respectively. In all other respects, the experimental conditions were identical for the groups. However, he quickly found that the group of rats faced with the insoluble problem withdrew from the experiment, i.e. refused to jump. He therefore introduced a technique which compelled the rats to make a jump, by means of a blast of air (later he used electric shock, hunger, and tail tapping). To be consistent, however, Maier should also have applied the forcing stimulus to his soluble problem group, since otherwise it is impossible to determine which factors are influencing what the rat does.[22]

b) SURREPTITIOUS INTRODUCTION OF CONCEPTS OF LEARNING
   THEORY

A careful reading of Maier's book leaves the reader in no doubt that Maier has at various points introduced some concepts of learning theory by the back door, as it were. Some examples of this will be given.

i) *Generalization.* The most striking example of such use is to be found in Maier's discussion of neurosis. According to Maier, the crucial identifying characteristic of a neurosis is its 'spread of effect', i.e. its generality, its all-pervading character. Now, he goes on to say that 'there seem to be two ways in which the condition of frustration established in a problem situation may become so general that it becomes a condition of the individual, rather than one aroused by the situation' (Maier, 1949, pp. 151–2). The first way is through increased generalization.

> The various aspects of the frustrating situation become symbols of the situation so that many of them appearing in isolation produce behaviours that the original situation induced . . . there seems little doubt that the animal studies suggest that the carry-over from the frustrating situation to outside situations is partly one of transfer by the medium of equivalent stimuli. Thus if an individual is frustrated in connection with PWQ he may show his symptoms when he sees any of the following symbols: WXYZ; WAS; XX; $\gtrless$; W; $\diamond\diamond$; $\vee\vee\vee\vee\vee$. For him all contain W (ibid., pp. 152–3).

ii) *Factors determining response fixated.* In his discussion of this point, Maier indicates that the most important factor determining

---

[22] Maier and Klee (1945) apparently used guidance in conjunction with airblast when altering fixations.

which response will be fixated under frustration is the *availability* of the response. The availability of a response, however, seems to be determined largely by previous experience. Thus, if animals are taught two mutually exclusive habits in succession, they will tend to maintain the most recently taught response, when the insoluble problem situation is introduced. The experiment reported in this connection by Maier and Klee, however, can readily be interpreted in terms of straightforward learning theory. Thus, if a symbol-reward response is taught initially, and then replaced by a position-reward response, clearly the former will be extinguished by non-reinforcement and the latter will therefore be the most available response when frustration is introduced.[23]

iii) *Psychotherapy*. In his discussion of psychotherapy, Maier discusses the way in which the expression of frustrated behaviour influences the growth of insight. In the first place, familiarity is gained with all aspects of the situation; secondly, new proximities (i.e. associations) are gained; thirdly, reversed relationships are discovered. But it is clear that all of these notions involve familiar concepts of learning theory.

Maier's reply to these criticisms would probably be that he is far from denying the influence of learning on (*a*) the availability of responses in the frustrating situation and (*b*) the generalization of these responses to other situations. What he would deny is that behaviour in the frustrating situation (once evoked) is affected by learning.

c) INCONSISTENCIES

Few modern psychologists, having carried out a series of significant experiments in a particular area, have been able to resist extrapolation from these results to a much wider area (the single notable exception has been the work of Hull). Maier is no exception to this rule and although his speculations are undeniably brilliant and provoking, nevertheless certain inconsistencies arise in the application of his experimental findings to a wider field.

i) *Generality vs. specificity*. In his *experimental* work Maier is at pains to insist upon the specificity of the frustration-instigated response. We have already referred to the experiment in which a position fixation did not interfere with the acquisition of a position response in a different experimental situation. Yet in his application

---

[23] The question of response-availability in relation to fixation will be considered further in part III of this chapter.

of his findings, Maier frequently contradicts this principle. For example, he regards the responses produced by neurosis as essentially similar to those produced by frustration, yet goes on to assert that the effects of frustration generalize, i.e. that situations similar to the frustration situation (even if identical in only a few respects) may call out the frustration-instigated response. This is clearly inconsistent with his notion of specificity.

ii) *The effects of tension-reduction.* In his experimental work, Maier points out that animals which develop fixations maintain these fixations indefinitely. The expression of these fixations, however, may be beneficial to the animal, since it will relieve tension. Now it follows clearly from these two points that tension-relief can exercise no influence whatever on the fixation itself, i.e. it cannot lead to the development of adaptive behaviour. Nevertheless, it is explicitly asserted that such tension-relief may influence the development of adaptive behaviour in the sections dealing with the applications of Maier's system. In discussing non-directive counselling, for instance, Maier writes, 'the relief given often is sufficient to permit the person to return to the same situation and view it in a constructive manner' (Maier, 1949, p. 129). As an example, he cites the work of Baruch (1941), who found that children who were able to dissipate their frustrations by mutilating clay models of their parents become better adjusted at home. As another example, Maier cites his own work in industry, where an important factor in maintaining industrial morale is the provision of facilities for the worker to 'blow off steam'. It is clear that these applications do *not* follow directly from Maier's experimental results, and are indeed in conflict with them.

iii) *The role of guidance.* Closely allied to the immediately preceding criticism is Maier's *extension* of the role of guidance from the experimental to other situations. In his experimental work, the role of guidance is quite clear. Its purpose is simply to prevent the occurrence of the frustration-instigated response. Thus, the experimenter, as the rat is about to perform its fixated response, places his hand so that the rat is compelled to jump to the rewarded side.

Maier concluded from the results of his experiments (discussed above) that guidance did *not* aid the learning of *new* responses directly, but only indirectly by creating appropriate conditions in which such learning might take place. In his discussion of psychotherapy, however, the role of guidance is not so clear cut. Maier quite clearly states that the expression of the frustration-instigated behaviour (catharsis) sets up the conditions under which *motivated* behaviour can reappear – but this would be true only if the behaviour were expressed under guidance. Yet Maier explicitly stresses that at this stage of therapy, the role of the therapist must be *passive*, i.e. that the patient should not be guided at all at this stage. In fact, in psychotherapy, guidance is given only during the later trial-and-error behaviour, when the therapist attempts to help the patient in restructuring his perceptual experiences. But we have already seen that in the animal experiments guidance has no effect on trial-and-error behaviour, but is effective only at the stage of catharsis.

d) MISCELLANEOUS

Finally, we may consider some other difficulties which arise from a perusal of Maier's work.

i) Maier's results, if valid, are mainly important in constituting a clear disproof of the effect theory of learning, i.e. that responses are acquired and extinguished on the basis of their consequences. He has, however, very little constructive to offer in the way of explanation for his own results.

(*a*) Maier pays little attention to the anomaly of the fact that about one-quarter of the animals which are trained in position-reward responses are unable to change those responses when required, i.e. fixations can occur in situations where reward and punishment are exercising selective effects. Maier offers no explanation for these odd results, except to say that these animals must have become fixated in some way!

(*b*) Maier's 'explanation' of the tension-relieving characteristics of frustration-instigated behaviour is odd, to say the least. He says that 'if it is assumed that frustration is a process that temporarily dominates an individual's condition and that frustration tensions are relieved by the reactions they produce, we are able to supply a psychological mechanism to account for the relief' (Maier, 1949, pp. 218–219). But this psychological mechanism turns out to be no explanation at all. Maier continues: 'In expressing frustrated behaviour the condition of frustration is reduced, and the motivation process may again become dominant and be permitted to function' (ibid., p. 219). Apart from the fact that this is not an explanation at all, it is open to the same objection as raised before, namely that in the experiments, expression of the frustrated response *by itself* had no effect whatever on subsequent tendencies to repeat the response. The whole point of Maier's experiments was that once a fixated response was established, it was unaffected by any subsequent events, except guidance.

(c) Most importantly, having rejected an explanation of the appearance of frustration-instigated behaviour in terms of learning theory (in any of the four forms outlined at the beginning of this chapter) Maier at this stage could offer no explanation at all for such behaviour. All he says is that it happens, but does not happen in accordance with the orthodox laws of learning. He can state only the *conditions* under which frustration-instigated responses are most likely to appear and some of the *factors* influencing such responses – for example that the responses are essentially dependent, not on punishment *per se*, but upon the *random* nature of the punishment. Such descriptions, of course, constitute a low-level form of explanation, but Maier suggests no mechanism which determines the subject's response, except that of availability, which has a distinct flavour of being determined by learning principles.

ii) Maier's treatment of *conflict* and *anxiety* must be mentioned in passing. Originally Maier applies the term conflict to any learning situation, i.e. any situation in which choice behaviour is involved. Conflict in this sense involves different competing motives, though in some cases the conflict may scarcely be apparent. Later, however, Maier introduces a new meaning of the term conflict in connection with his treatment of the nature of anxiety. Anxiety, according to Maier, can indicate frustration in two ways. 'Insofar as the term anxiety indicates a state of generalized fear . . . it fails to be goal-oriented and thus appears as a product of frustration.' On the other hand, 'when fears become highly specific, as in the case of phobias, a behaviour fixation is indicated'. Hence 'some of the characteristics of anxiety seem to be reducible to a condition of frustration' (Maier, 1949, p. 131). On the other hand, anxiety may represent a situation in which 'frustration has not taken over sufficiently to produce action, such as an attack on the object feared' and in which 'the person remains motivated by fear and compelled by frustration', i.e. anxiety may be a condition intermediate between motivation and frustration. Thus, tensions will persist in such a situation and as a consequence the anxious person is less able to obtain the reliefs that dissipation of the tension will bring. Maier, in other words, considers the anxious person as intermediate between the normal and the neurotic. He is, as it were, undecided whether to be frustrated or motivated. This, then, is what Maier understands by the use of the term 'conflict'.

He uses this term to indicate a region where motivation-instigated and frustration-instigated forms of response are evenly balanced.

> The extent to which this stage of conflict can exist will depend both upon individual differences in thresholds to frustration and upon differences in the tenacity with which individuals can maintain the motivation process. Undoubtedly, situational factors also can be discovered that tend to promote an oscillation between the two processes (Maier, 1949, p. 134).

This new notion of conflict as being characterized by a tug-of-war between frustration-instigated and motivation-instigated behaviour is not worked out in any detail by Maier and indeed is not essential to his system. It is, in fact, difficult to see how it can be fitted in to his system, since the notion of conflict clearly clashes with the all-or-none characteristic of fixations, i.e. they either appear or do not appear – there is no period when they are slowly establishing themselves in competition with motivation-instigated responses.

## 2. Alternative explanations of Maier's results

It is an extraordinary fact that Maier's work has mediated very little research outside his own laboratory, either by way of confirmation or refutation. On the one hand his work has been flatly ignored; on the other hand, its importance has been minimized.[24] Fortunately, such little experimental work as has been carried out has been so carefully and ingeniously designed as to merit careful consideration for its bearing on Maier's work.

The reinterpretation of Maier's results in terms of learning theory can be conveniently considered in three parts. First, there is the attempt to account for fixations in terms of responsiveness to the acquired drive of fear. Secondly, an attempt has been made to ac-

---

[24] The treatment accorded to Maier's work by American psychologists has been such as to make even a tough-minded Eysenckian start thinking in terms of defence mechanisms! His work on fixations is not discussed at all in Stevens' (1951) Handbook, is dismissed perfunctorily in Osgood (1953, pp. 454–5), and is given equally scanty, though more respectful, treatment by Hilgard (1956). McClelland (1950), in his review of Maier's book, contemptuously dismisses all his work as easily explainable in terms of the fixation as an anxiety-reducing response. One would never guess from McClelland's review that Maier and Schneirla (1942) were among the earliest proponents of a two-factor theory of learning. It is ironical that less than 10 years after McClelland's review, the drive-reduction theory of learning should itself have been sunk without trace as a mechanism for learning (see the final salvoes recently fired by Young (1959) and White (1959)).

count for fixations in terms of partial reinforcement. Thirdly, Maier's results have been explained in terms of responsiveness to the primary drive of pain. These will be considered in turn.

a) FIXATIONS AS ANXIETY-REDUCING RESPONSES

It is well known that, historically, there have been two major points of view among learning theorists concerning the conditions essential for the occurrence of learned responses, or the change from one learned response to another. One theory, exemplified by the work of Pavlov, may be said to descend from the associationistic tradition. In this tradition, learning takes place when the conditioned and un-conditioned stimuli are contiguous – by reinforcement Pavlov means, in fact, the occurrence of the unconditioned stimulus. The second type of theory is descended from hedonistic traditions and is exem-plified by the work of Hull (1943). It is most easily demonstrated in the Skinner box in which the rat learns to press an originally neutral bar because each time it does so it is rewarded by food. Reinforce-ment in this type of experiment refers to the fact that giving the rat food leads to drive-reduction, i.e. the dissipation of hunger. Alter-natively, the situation may be regarded as one of escape from an unpleasant primary drive.

Now the question arises whether these two kinds of experiments can be subsumed under the same set of principles of learning, or whether separate laws are necessary. Naturally, in the interests of parsimony, psychologists have attempted to unify the field, the most serious attempt to do so being the monistic theory of Hull (1943). Hull tried to show that Pavlov's classical experiments did involve drive-reduction and that it was Pavlov's very restricted experimenta-tion which had led him into error.

Hull's position has, however, been rejected by a number of theorists in the field of learning, most notably by Mowrer, who has expounded his two-factory theory of learning in a number of papers (see Mowrer, 1950, Chaps. 9 and 10 especially). Mowrer's argument rests essentially on a distinction between *escape* from noxious stimulation and *avoidance* of the same situation. It has been shown experimentally that in a conditioning situation the avoidance response may be com-pletely unlike the original escape response. From his analysis of a large number of such experiments, Mowrer concluded that there were two distinct forms of learning. One form of learning is mediated through the autonomic nervous system, involves drive-*induction*, and depends on contiguity. This form of learning Mowrer calls 'conditioning'. The other form of learning is mediated through the central nervous system (via the skeletal musculature), involves drive-*reduction*, and depends on reward. The most important aspect of Mowrer's theory, however, concerns the relationship between these two forms of learning. Logically, conditioning, or drive-induction, is prior. By contiguity the animal learns a secondary drive, such as fear. This learning sets the animal a problem, which it then proceeds to solve by trial-and-error, the skeletal response being learned on the basis of its efficacy in reducing the secondary drive. Thus, Mowrer calls the second type of learning *problem-solving*.

A considerable amount of experimental work has been carried out in an effort to demonstrate the validity of Mowrer's two-factory theory. This work has been reviewed by Mowrer (1950, Chaps. 9 and 10; and 1956 for a more recent review) and by Miller (1951). Miller's experiment (which was not designed to support Mowrer's position but is now generally conceded to do so) is perhaps the best-known example. The apparatus used by him consisted of two compartments, one white, with an electrifiable grid as the floor, the other black, with a smooth solid floor. In the white compartment were a wheel and a bar, which, on being respectively turned and pressed, would open a door separating the two compartments. Initially, the rats showed no preference for either compartment. They were then shocked in the white compartment and quickly learned to escape from the white compartment to the black, a response which persisted after the shock treatment was stopped. If the door between the compartments was now shut, the rats, when placed in the white compartment (with no shock) exhibited signs of fear and quickly learned to turn the wheel to escape from the white compartment to the black. Since they were no longer motivated by shock, it was a reasonable inference that they were motivated by learned fear, which had become attached to the original neutral cues of the white compartment. Furthermore, Miller was able to train the rats to abandon their wheel-turning response (by arranging for it to fail to open the door) and adopt instead a bar-pressing response, which was now successful in opening the door. In other words, in such a situation, the rat learned a fear response to the white box (contiguity learning). This fear response then served as a *stimulus* to the rat, setting it a problem (how to reduce the learned anxiety) which, with the door locked and the original escape route blocked, impelled the rat to trial-and-error behaviour until it solved the problem by learning to turn the wheel or press the bar (reward learning).

Even more impressive was May's (1948) study. Using an apparatus similar to that of Miller, he first trained rats to jump from the white to the black compartment by means of shock. He then placed the rats in the white compartment and restrained them from jumping while shocking them. At the same time he sounded a buzzer. He argued that the buzzer would become connected to the postulated fear reaction and by mediation to the jumping response. This in fact happened. When the buzzer was sounded without shock the rats jumped into the black compartment, *although the buzzer had never before been connected with the jumping response.*

These two experiments offer convincing evidence that fear can be learned and serve as a stimulus for further learning (Mowrer points out that the use of hunger and thirst as motivating conditions appears to be an historical accident), and much other work supports their position. Before passing to a consideration of the relevance of this work to Maier's position, however, brief mention must be made of an important extension of Mowrer's contiguity principle. In his experiments, Miller had found that the escape or avoidance response would extinguish fairly rapidly, if the fear response were not periodically reinforced by the unconditioned stimulus of shock (as Mowrer puts it, the rats 'reality tested' from time to time by delaying making the instrumental response). However, Solomon and Wynn (1954), in a series of studies, have indicated that a fear response may persist for many hundreds of trials, provided the original shock situation is a very intense one. This phenomenon they call *traumatic avoidance learning.* Under such conditions, they have obtained behaviour which is as persistent as any found by Maier and which is resistant to all the usual methods of extinction.

Only one study has been reported which is directly intended to show whether or not fixations can be explained within this framework of *secondary* drive reduction. This study was carried out by Farber (1948). According to Farber, the anxiety-reduction theory of avoidance learning involves three assumptions:

i) Intense stimuli such as shock can produce an internal drive state, probably mediated via the autonomic nervous system;

ii) External stimuli (cues) present at the time of shock acquire the capacity to evoke these autonomic responses, and thereby the

D

drive, which, when elicited in this manner, is termed 'anxiety';
iii) Removal of these cues (e.g. by the animal escaping) reduces
the anxiety and hence constitutes a reinforcing state of affairs.

It follows from these assumptions that (a) even after shock has
been removed, the secondary reinforcement resulting from the reduction of anxiety following escape from the cues eliciting it may materially retard the extinction of any response closely associated with
these cues; (b) the elimination of anxiety in this situation should pre-
clude the possibility of maintenance (by means of secondary reinforcement alone) of responses which are no longer adaptive. It was
considered that feeding in a situation in which anxiety had been
developed would remove the anxiety state and thereby decrease the
resistance to extinction of any non-adaptive response.

Initially, two groups of rats were given 40 training trials in a
single-unit T-maze, with food reward in the goal-box on the preferred side (a non-correction technique being used). For the next 60
trials one group was shocked in the arm leading to food; the other
group continued as before. Not unexpectedly the shocked group
initially began running to the opposite side, where they were also
shocked. Farber found that very quickly they returned to the side
on which food was placed and continued to run there. At the end
of 100 trials, half of the shocked group and half the controls were
fed in the *arm* of the maze leading to food; the other halves were not.
Following this, extinction trials were begun, all rats being required
to shift from their original response to the opposite goal-box.

Farber's principal hypothesis was that feeding in the area where
shock was administered would eliminate the anxiety and that these
animals would then be able to shift successfully; whereas the shocked
but not fed animals would continue to run to the original goal-box
because such behaviour would continue to be drive-reducing. Half
the control group were also fed in the arm of the maze to demonstrate that the feeding did not interfere directly with the running
habit, but rather with some mechanism which was maintaining the
habit.

In the extinction series, the criterion used was two successive
responses to the non-preferred side, which now led to food. Table 2.6
shows the means, medians, and SDs for the four groups to reach the
criterion.

It will be seen that there is no difference between the two control groups, indicating that feeding in the arm of the maze does not interfere with the habit directly. When, however, the two experimental groups are compared, it is seen that the shock group which was fed extinguished much more rapidly than the shock group which was not fed. Indeed, the former group behaved essentially like the two

## TABLE 2.6

### NUMBER OF TRIALS TO EXTINCTION

|  | Experimental | | Control | |
| --- | --- | --- | --- | --- |
|  | Shock | Shock/fed | No shock | No shock (fed) |
| Median | 33 | 10 | 8 | 8 |
| Mean | 61·12 | 15·04 | 9·71 | 9·50 |
| SD | 74·09 | 19·24 | 3·83 | 5·75 |

Source: Farber, I. E. 'Response fixation under anxiety and non-anxiety conditions'. *J. exp. Psychol.*, 1948, **38**, 111–31

control groups. Farber concludes that 'the feeding procedure not only reduced the degree of fixation in the shock-fed group, but *on the average* prevented fixation entirely' (p. 123).

Certain similarities and differences between this experiment and Maier's should be noted. Farber, like Maier, forced his animals to respond in the situation, if necessary by shocking them in the alley leading to the arms of the maze. Secondly, the problem was insoluble in the sense that the rats could not escape shock in the maze, whatever they did. Thirdly, the rats could not withdraw from the situation. The differences are equally important, however. Firstly, the situation did not constitute an insoluble problem in the sense in which Maier uses that term.[25] Allied to this is the point that punishment was given on every trial. From this, it follows that punishment was not random, as in Maier's insoluble problem situation. Finally, if Farber's theory is correct, the rats in trials 41–100 (i.e. the shock trials) were in fact being rewarded *twice* on every trial – once for escaping from the shock, once by finding food in the goal-box.

Admitting these differences, Farber appears on the face of it to have produced important evidence indicating that fixations developed in a frustrating situation are responses to the anxiety induced

[25] Because although shocked whichever side they ran to, they could run 'through' the shock to reach food (reward) on one side.

by shock, that these responses will be maintained when no shock is given because they are anxiety-reducing, but will disappear if the anxiety is removed directly, when the animal will be able to reverse its original habit. Farber summarizes his experiment by saying that 'it would seem appropriate to conclude that the continuation of acts under conditions which might be expected to result in their extinction is, in fact, due to factors operating in ordinary learning situations' (p. 129).

Applied to Maier's experiments, Farber's results would indicate that the rats in the insoluble problem situation fixated a particular response because this response was successful in getting them off the jumping stand, i.e. it reduced the anxiety associated with the jumping stand, the latter having been associated with the fear induced by the air-blast.[26]

b) FIXATIONS EXPLAINED IN TERMS OF PARTIAL REINFORCE-MENT

The term 'partial reinforcement' 'refers to reinforcement given at least once but omitted on one or more of the trials or after one or more of the responses in a series' (Jenkins and Stanley, 1950, p. 194). As Jenkins and Stanley point out, until about 1940 most experiments dealing with the effects of reinforcement used either 100% or 0% punishment/reward ratios. It is clear however that the response-to-be-learned may be reinforced to any degree from 0% to 100%; similarly, competing ('incorrect') responses in the same situation may be punished in the same way. Furthermore, the actual amount of reinforcement given may be given either randomly over the total number of trials; or it may be given regularly, e.g. every fifth trial. Thus, reinforcement may vary in frequency and pattern.[27] (The situation is actually more complex than here represented, since partial reinforcement may be applied in a correction or non-correction situation, and may refer to reinforcement at regular or irregular intervals of *time*, or to reinforcement after a regular or irregular

[26] Moltz (1954) has repeated and confirmed Farber's experiment, and additionally has shown that the extent to which 'therapy' (feeding in the shock area) reduces anxiety is related to the similarity in stimulus condition between shock and therapy. If the maze colour in the therapy area was different from the colour during training, the number of trials to extinction increased significantly. Moltz also showed that simple confinement of the rat was as effective as feeding it.

[27] Although as we have seen Maier and Klee (1943) discussed these problems and actually carried out detailed experiments on the effects of reward/punishment patterns, their paper is not mentioned by Jenkins and Stanley in their review (cf. note 24).

number of *responses*.) As a result of an extensive survey of the literature, Jenkins and Stanley arrived at the following conclusions:

i) *Acquisition of responses*. 'Acquisition proceeds somewhat more
rapidly and reaches a higher final training level under continuous
reinforcement than under partial reinforcement' (p. 209).

ii) *Maintenance of acquired responses*. 'All other things equal, performance under a partial reinforcement schedule tends to be somewhat lower than that under a continuous reinforcement one as
measured in terms of single responses' (pp. 213–14).

iii) *Extinction of acquired responses*. 'All other things equal, resistance to extinction after partial reinforcement is greater than that
after continuous reinforcement when behavior strength is measured
in terms of single responses' (p. 222).

It is clear that the experiments of Maier reported earlier involve
partial reinforcement. For example, in his earlier experiments he made
use of a 50/50 random schedule of reinforcement/non-reinforce-
ment in his insoluble problem situation, whereas for the soluble problem the schedule was one of 100% reinforcement/0% punishment
for the correct response in the case of the position- and symbol-reward
groups (e.g. Maier and Klee, 1943).

Wilcoxon (1952), however, pointed out that Maier's method differed in important aspects from the usual partial reinforcement situation. The main difference lay in the fact that in the insoluble problem
situation Maier rewarded and punished *every* response the rat made
an equal number of times. In the usual 50/50 partial reinforcement
method, however, the *correct* response is rewarded and punished on
a 50/50 basis, but the *incorrect* response receives 100% punishment.
Wilcoxon argued, therefore, that Maier was omitting consideration
of an alternative explanation of his results in terms of partial reinforcement. Wilcoxon argued that a greater percentage of fixations
would be expected with partial reinforcement than with Maier's
insoluble problem technique (which he calls non-differential
reinforcement).

Using three groups of rats, Wilcoxon trained them to adopt a
consistent response under conditions identical with those used by
Maier. Group 1 learned under conditions of continuous reinforcement for the correct response; group 2 under conditions of partial
reinforcement (correct response rewarded 50% of time: incorrect
response always punished); group 3 under conditions of non-selec-
tive partial reinforcement (position- or symbol-response rewarded

randomly an equal number of times). All three groups were then required to change their response under conditions of 100% reinforcement for the correct new response, and 100% punishment for the incorrect old response.

The principal results are shown in Table 2.7. In the initial training situation Wilcoxon found that the rats in the insoluble problem group showed more variability (i.e. took longer to adopt a consistent

TABLE 2.7

VARIABILITY IN INITIAL TRAINING AND
DEVELOPMENT OF FIXATIONS

| Group | N | Initial training | | | | Test training | |
| | | Trials before first consistent response series | | Trials before final consistent response series | | % Fixated | % Not fixating |
| | | Mean | SD | Mean | SD | | |
| I. Continuous reinforcement | 15 | 7·4 | 8·06 | 7·4 | 8·06 | 38 | 62 |
| II. Partial reinforcement | 13 | 25·3 | 21·44 | 25·3 | 21·44 | 92 | 8 |
| III. Insoluble problem | 12 | 59·8 | 47·22 | 75·0 | 55·57 | 58 | 58 |

Source: Wilcoxon, H. C. ' "Abnormal fixation" and learning'. *J. exp. Psychol.*, 1952, **44**, 324–33

response) than rats in the other two groups and contrasts this with Maier's contention that '. . . the inconsistent administration of punishment in the insoluble problem is recognized by the rat and cuts short the variability in behaviour that normally occurs in a problem situation' (1949, p. 69).[28]

[28] This finding of Wilcoxon is mentioned here because of the puzzling nature of the quotation from Maier. In fact, in all of the experiments of Maier which contain appropriate data, the rats in the insoluble problem situation showed *more*, not less, variability than rats in a comparable soluble situation. Thus in the first experiment of Maier and Klee (1945) groups 1A and 1B (both adopting position stereotypes in the insoluble problem situation) took an average of 28·5 (range 0–100) and 53·8 (range 0–370) trials to establish the response consistently (*not* including the final 160 criterion trials) compared with groups 2A and 2B (both groups learning position-reward responses) which took only 2·7 (range 0–10) and 2·0 (0–20) trials respectively. Similar results are found in Maier, Glaser, and Klee (1940), Maier and Klee (1943), Maier and Klee (1945, 2nd experiment), and Maier and Ellen (1952). It is also clear from the above that Wilcoxon's charge (1952, p. 327) that Maier's comparisons were illegitimate ones, is quite incorrect.

More striking than this is Wilcoxon's finding that under continuous reinforcement 38% of the rats fixated; under insoluble problem conditions, 58%; and *under partial reinforcement conditions, 92%*. These results were in line with Wilcoxon's predictions on the basis of learning theory.

Wilcoxon made three other important contributions to the controversy. In the first place he showed that both fixated and non-fixated animals showed differences in latency between correct and incorrect jumps long before the animals made correct choices. Since such differences applied to both groups, they cannot be taken as constituting evidence for behaviour not amenable to the principles of learning. Secondly, he showed that animals which learn abortive jumps during acquisition of the initial response are quite unlikely to learn the subsequent test discrimination. From a learning theory point of view the jumps would be regarded as learned responses of escape from hard bumps on the nose; and, as such, would be expected to interfere with the acquisition of new responses, because they would decrease the effectiveness of punishment. When Wilcoxon divided his animals into Learners and Non-learners, he found that the former made on average 3·9 abortive jumps, compared with an average of 29·2 jumps for the latter. Finally, Wilcoxon showed that fixations could be broken by techniques derived from learning theory but owing nothing to 'guidance' as described by Maier. Two techniques were chosen: (*a*) the animal was forced to jump repeatedly while confronted with the locked negative card in the fixated window and while an open window appeared on the non-fixated side; (*b*) the open window and the negative card were alternated from side to side, as if the open window were the positive card in a regular discrimination sequence. Both these methods were successful, 13/18 fixated rats abandoning their stereotyped response.

Wilcoxon therefore concludes that 'fixations are not in any way symptomatic of an abnormal condition. Rather, they are strong habits which can be unlearned, if the conditions are made appropriate' (p. 332). Once again, a strong case seems to have been made out for considering Maier's results as explainable in terms of orthodox learning theory.

A rather different explanation of fixations was given by Gladin and Denny (1955). They argued that in the insoluble problem situation a rat which develops a consistent position-response will be maximizing the expectation that a jump to a non-rewarded card will be followed by a rewarded jump. The probability that a rewarded jump will follow an unrewarded jump will be ·61, whereas the probability that an unrewarded jump will be followed by another unrewarded jump will be only ·39. Thus, if the animal learns these expectancies during the insoluble problem period, this tendency to jump to unrewarded cards rather than rewarded cards might interfere with acquisition of the correct response when the problem is made soluble. They tested this hypothesis by predicting that there should be a drop in the latency of a jump on a trial which followed a non-rewarded jump compared with a trial following a rewarded jump in the insoluble problem situation. Their results supported their hypothesis. On the first day of the insoluble problem situation the mean latency difference between responses following falls and successful jumps respectively was 22·5 seconds (the latency being longer following a fall, as would be expected) but by the eighth day this difference was reversed. Hence, it would seem as if the animals are learning to respond to sequential cues in a meaningful way rather than developing non-adaptive responses.

c) FIXATIONS AS LEARNED RESPONSES REDUCING PRIMARY DRIVE

Wolpe (1953) provided an explanation of Maier's findings which differs somewhat from those based on reduction of a secondary drive. He regarded the total situation as one in which the animals were responding, not to the cards themselves, nor to anxiety induced by the air-blast, but to the noxious properties of the air-blast itself. He postulated that the air-blast induces a primary drive and that jumping reduces this drive and hence is reinforced. 'When jumping in a particular way has thus been repeatedly reinforced it becomes firmly established as the habitual response to the air-blast stimulus, and the more firmly it is established the weaker does the competing alternative response tendency become' (p. 114). In other words, the stimulus for the rat is the air-blast and not the cards themselves. It is easy to see how such a response could become established but it is difficult to see how this notion of Wolpe's can be sustained in competition with the anxiety-reduction hypothesis, particularly in view of Farber's results showing that fixations persist even when the noxious primary stimulus is withdrawn. However, Wolpe claims that his theory can adequately account for all the difficulties raised by Maier with respect to anxiety-reduction theories.

Lack of variability has often been found in situations involving strong primary motivation. Indeed, there is a considerable body of evidence which indicates that under conditions of strong motivation behaviour may become less variable in certain learning situations where *the problem is at no stage insoluble.*

The earlier experiments by Hamilton and Krechevsky (1933), Everall (1935), Meunzinger and Wood (1935), O'Kelly (1940), and, from Maier's own group, Kleemaier (1942) demonstrated this phenomenon in which an ongoing response became fixated even though it was shocked both at a choice point, where other choices were available, and in the goal-box as well. A more recent experiment by de Valois (1954) serves to demonstrate the phenomenon. He used a simple maze, of which Fig. 2.4 presents one section. Four groups of rats ran the maze under conditions of either an approach motive (6 or 22 hours' water deprivation with water as reinforcement) or an avoidance motive (light or strong shock while in the maze with escape as reinforcement). During trials 1–24, the rat could turn left or right at each choice point, the centre alley being kept closed. Variability of behaviour was measured by changes in turn on successive trials at each choice point. Beginning with trial 13, each of the four groups of rats was divided, one sub-group continuing under the original motivating conditions, the other switching to a new motivation. For trials 25–36, the centre alley was opened and the number of runs through this alley (now the shortest distance to the goal) recorded.

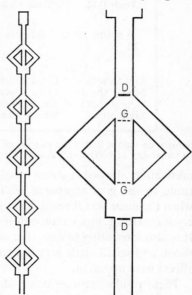

Fig. 2.4. Part of a maze used in the experiment by de Valois. (Source: de Valois, R. L. 'The relation of different levels and kinds of motivation to variability of behaviour'. *J. exp. Psychol.*, 1954, **47**, 392–8.)

The results of the experiment were clear cut. In the early part of the experiment (trials 1–24) high levels of motivation (22 hours' thirst, strong shock) resulted in less variability of behaviour than low levels of motivation. There was a tendency for animals shifted from low to high motivation at trial 13 to decrease in variability compared with animals maintained on constant motivation or shifted to low motivation. The most important results, however, were those concerned with the effects of opening the centre alley from trial 25 onwards. Table 2·8 shows the results. Animals under *strong*

TABLE 2.8

NUMBER OF MIDDLE-ALLEY ENTRANCES
IN TRIALS 25–30

| Motivation | | Number of entrances (Trials 25–30) | |
|---|---|---|---|
| Trials 1–12 | Trials 13–24 | Mean | SD |
| 6 hours | 6 hours | 13·20 | 6·49 |
| 22 ,, | 6 ,, | 12·82 | 7·21 |
| 22 ,, | 22 ,, | 5·45 | 6·71 |
| 6 ,, | 22 ,, | 1·50 | 2·70 |
| Light shock | Light shock | 13·70 | 7·89 |
| Strong shock | Light shock | 1·64 | 2·36 |
| Strong shock | Strong shock | 0·00 | 0·00 |
| Light shock | Strong shock | 0·33 | 0·66 |

Source: de Valois, R. L. 'The relation of different levels and kinds of motivation to variability of behaviour'. *J. exp. Psychol.*, 1954, **47**, 392–8

motivation showed a much smaller tendency to take the shorter route to the goal compared with animals under *weak* motivation when the maze was thrown open. In fact, the animals running under constant strong shock motivation *did not enter the centre alley at all*. It is also interesting to note that animals shifted from strong to light shock on trial 13 made very few entrances, i.e. secondary motivation effects were apparent.

These results seem to place Maier in a dilemma. It is true that results such as those reported by de Valois were also obtained by Kleemaier (1942). Maier, therefore, would presumably argue that these rats were fixated, as he did in the case of Kleemaier's. However, two serious difficulties immediately arise. In the first place, as de Valois points out, rats motivated by strong thirst drive, *and rewarded 100% of the time*, will develop stereotyped behaviour to a much greater extent than rats weakly motivated by thirst. It is difficult to argue that such rats are frustrated, even though their behaviour is fixated. Secondly, if we accept that de Valois' rats are fixated, whether motivated by strong hunger or electric shock, then clearly Maier's definition of the necessary conditions for the development of fixations must be abandoned – *since, at no stage of the experiment was an insoluble problem presented to the rat, nor were the rats motivated by hunger compelled to respond, nor was there any random sequence of reward and punishment.* De Valois concludes that 'variability of behavior is a function of the amount of motivation' and that this theory 'can adequately explain the results of experiments which have shown that Ss exhibit fixated behavior when shocked in mazes, or given insoluble problems and/or air-blasts in a jumping apparatus. These various situations are seen as producing very intense motivation for Ss, and therefore producing less variable behavior than the usual thirst or hunger motivation' (p. 397).[29] Results such as these, of course, pose problems, not only for Maier, but also for theories of learning themselves. The general indications are that in certain situations learned responses become 'frozen' or fixated for reasons which are at present obscure.[30]

It will be convenient to discuss at this point a series of studies which throw further light on the problem of reward/punishment ratios and their relevance to Maier's work.[31] These studies differ in an important respect from those of Maier, in that they made use of a water maze (in which the animal, swimming under water, has to choose one of two doors in order to escape) instead of the Lashley jumping stand. They differ, therefore, in type of motivation employed in the original training situation, degrees of unavoidable punishment inherent in the situation, and type of response required (Knopfelmacher, 1952).

After training animals in the usual way to acquire either position-reward or position-stereotype responses, Russell and Pretty (1951) trained both groups to adopt a symbol-reward response under 50% systematic punishment. Animals failing to learn within 300 trials were placed on a schedule of 100% punishment for the stereotype.

[29] In calling the persistent behaviour 'fixated', de Valois was assuming that opening the centre alley in his experiment was equivalent to requiring the rat to shift from a position stereotype to a symbol-reward response in Maier's experiments. Maier would no doubt reply that de Valois' animals persisted in a very strong *habit* and that they were not fixated in his sense at all.

[30] In accounting for lack of variability in terms of high primary drive, de Valois provides for an alternative explanation of results such as those of Farber, discussed above. De Valois' theory is also similar to that of Wolpe.

[31] These studies are included here because in general they regard the behaviour as a direct response to the punishment rather than to anxiety. It is curious that Maier has never made any reference to this work.

As expected, the position-reward animals all learned both responses quite easily. On the other hand, only one of the seven position-stereotype animals learned the symbol-response under 50% punishment, but the remaining six all shifted successfully under 100% punishment. Russell and Pretty point out that while the reward group learned under 100%, and extinguished under 50%, reinforcement, the stereotype group learned under 50% random, and were then required to extinguish under 50% systematic, punishment (or, subsequently, 100% punishment). They found, in their own experiment, that the actual percentage of rewarded trials (in the acquisition phase) for the reward group was 98%; but for the stereotype group only 49%. In other words, the reward/punishment schedules were practically identical for the stereotype group in both phases, making discrimination exceedingly difficult and presumably, therefore, retarding new learning. These results clearly contradict Maier's contention that increasing punishment either has no effect on fixations or actually strengthens them.

Knopfelmacher (1952) investigated the effect of rewarding consistently the stereotyped response. Four groups of rats which had developed position stereotypes in the water maze were given respectively 0, 60, 120, 180 trials in which the stereotyped response was always rewarded by escape. They were then required to learn a symbol-reward response under 50% punishment and, if this failed, 100% punishment of the stereotype. In terms of Maier's theory it would clearly be predicted that (a) the resistance to change of the fixated response should not be affected by reward or, therefore, by differential amounts of reward; and that (b) under 50% and 100% punishment a bimodal distribution would be obtained of rats which did, and rats which did not, learn the new response. Maier's theory is contradicted on both counts. Table 2.9 shows the number of animals breaking the stereotype under the two modes of punishment. It is clear that the greater the number of rewarded trials prior to the introduction of punishment the more resistant is the stereotype to change. Secondly, every stereotyped animal learned the new response under one or other of the punishment ratios. Both of these results run contrary to expectations based on Maier's system.

In a further study, Knopfelmacher (1953a) utilized the design shown in Table 2.10. Four groups of rats were trained in the insoluble problem situation under two degrees of intensity of punishment (detention following choice in the maze for 8 or 80 seconds before

## TABLE 2.9

STABILITY OF FIXATED RESPONSES FOLLOWING
FOUR PERIODS OF REWARD FOR
EXERCISING THE FIXATION

| No. of rewarded trials | No. of animal | Stereotype acquisition trials | Trials to break | |
|---|---|---|---|---|
| | | | 50% punishment | 100% punishment |
| 0 | 6 | 280 | 120 | |
| | 1 | 270 | | 83 |
| | 3 | 240 | | 80 |
| | 5 | 210 | 262 | |
| | 2 | 200 | | 6 |
| | 4 | 160 | 239 | |
| 60 | 7 | 470 | | 49 |
| | 8 | 420 | | 38 |
| | 9 | 280 | | 28 |
| | 10 | 270 | | 4 |
| | 12 | 210 | 225 | |
| | 11 | 160 | | 36 |
| 120 | 14 | 350 | | 29 |
| | 13 | 300 | | 74 |
| | 18 | 220 | | 47 |
| | 16 | 200 | | 18 |
| | 15 | 180 | | 45 |
| | 17 | 180 | | 15 |
| 180 | 19 | 490 | | 25 |
| | 21 | 420 | 168 | |
| | 23 | 360 | 220 | |
| | 22 | 190 | 223 | |
| | 20 | 190 | | 42 |
| | 24 | 180 | 70 | |

Source: Knopfelmacher, F. 'Some effects of reward on the strength of position stereotypes in the white rat'. *Quart. J. exp. Psychol.*, 1952, **4**, 78–86

final escape was permitted). The two 8-second groups were then required to shift their response under either 50% or 100% pattern of punishment; likewise the two 80-second groups. Those rats which failed to learn the new response under 8 seconds' detention in phase 2 were then put on the 80-second detention routine, and if they still

## TABLE 2.10

### DESIGN OF EXPERIMENT BY KNOPFELMACHER

| Group | 1 | 2 | 3 | 4 | 5 |
|---|---|---|---|---|---|
| Iᴀ | Preliminary training | Insoluble problem 8 sec. detention | Soluble problem 8 sec. detention 50% punishment | Soluble problem 80 sec. detention 50% punishment | Guidance |
| Iв | ,, | ,, | Soluble problem 8 sec. detention 100% punishment | Soluble problem 80 sec. detention 100% punishment | ,, |
| IIᴀ | ,, | Insoluble problem 80 sec. detention | Soluble problem 80 sec. detention 50% punishment | | |
| IIв | ,, | ,, | Soluble problem 80 sec. detention 100% punishment | | |

Source: Knopfelmacher, F. 'Fixations, position stereotypes and their relation to the degree and pattern of stress'. *Quart. J. exp. Psychol.*, 1953a, 5, 108–27

failed to learn were given guidance. The most significant results obtained by Knopfelmacher were as follows:

(1) Learning of the stereotype in phase 1 was unaffected by the intensity of the punishment (8 or 80 seconds);

(2) In phase 2:

(a) With punishment ratio held constant (at 50% or 100%), intense punishment was more significant than mild punishment in breaking stereotypes (as in the previous experiment Knopfelmacher distinguishes between number of trials to abandon the stereotype and number of trials to learn the new response). In fact, no animals in group IA broke the stereotype in 150 trials, and only 2 in group IB; whereas all animals in groups IIA and IIB broke the stereotype in less than 80 trials.

(b) Within the *intense* punishment groups, the stereotype was more easily broken if punishment were given 100% of the time. This was not so for the *mild* punishment groups; but, when the latter was changed to an intense punishment routine, 100% punishment became significantly more effective.

(c) Three rats in group IA and one rat in group IB developed fixations in Maier's sense, i.e. the stereotyped response was unaffected by either intense or mild punishment and was only changed by guidance.

Knopfelmacher's results clearly contradict Maier's thesis that intense punishment may be frustrating. On the contrary, intense punishment given 100% of trials is easily the most efficacious way of breaking the stereotype. Fixations, in particular, and resistance to change, in general, are much more likely to be found under conditions of *mild* punishment.

With respect to the learning of the correct response, after the stereotype has been abandoned, Knopfelmacher claimed that intense punishment accelerates learning the soluble problem, but this conclusion is untenable, since he is comparing changes in the intense punishment groups which could not abandon the stereotype and hence by definition could not learn. Clearly, differences in rate of learning can validly be made only if both groups are able to learn!

Finally, Knopfelmacher found evidence supporting Maier's claim that latency of response to the positive and negative cards in phase 2 showed increasing divergence when punishment was intense even before the stereotyped response was abandoned, i.e. the rats had discriminated the correct from the incorrect card even though still responding to the incorrect card.

Knopfelmacher's experiments therefore qualify Maier's findings in several important respects and support them in others. They also run counter to explanations of the phenomena in terms of partial reinforcement effects, stressing rather the importance of the severity of punishment, not the pattern.

Knopfelmacher is inclined to reject the anxiety-reduction interpretation of fixations and favours an explanation for his own results with respect to differences in the effect of punishment in terms of escape from the noxious stimulus itself: escape from the detention compartment may be regarded as the goal which terminates a sequence of responses in the apparatus. As Knopfelmacher (1953b) puts it, 'Escape reinforces approach behavior towards the escape ladder; detention, interposed between the animal and the escape ladder, weakens it. Since the effect of reinforcement on a response is a negative function of the time interval between them, position stereotypes are more effectively reinforced under conditions of 8 – rather than 80 – seconds detentions' (p. 154). He also puts forward the ingenious hypothesis that in groups IA and IB,

> reinforcement in phase 3, consequent upon a response to the positive door, may not have been sufficiently different from what was punishment consequent upon a response to the negative door to motivate discrimination learning. If differential motivation was absent, the two signs to which differential amounts of reward were attached, did not represent cues of differential incentive value to the animal. It would then follow that 'from the animal's point of view' all responses in phases 1 and 3 were equally rewarded [Note: The original reads, 'phases 2 and 3'] (p. 154).

With respect to the few genuine fixations themselves, he favours the view that they may be the result of 'anxiety *defined in terms of the physiological anxiety syndrome*' (p. 157; italics in original).

In line with Knopfelmacher's finding that *duration* of punishment or frustration is the most significant variable in accounting for resistance to change is the experiment of Jones (1954). He required normal adult Ss to learn a pattern of response over time to a choice between two keys (e.g. LLRL, etc.). The problem was first made insoluble for all groups, but the number of trials in the insoluble situations ranged from 5 to 50 to 100 under incentive or non-incentive conditions. At the end of the insoluble trials, a soluble problem was imposed without warning and the number of trials to reach the criterion of 5 correct repetitions of the sequence L–R–R calculated. The most important finding of Jones was that the time to solve the soluble problem increases up to 50 trials, but does not increase further with 100 trials. As Jones puts it, 'under conditions of prolonged frustration the subject is likely to make some form of adaptation to the frustrating situation' (p. 19). The situation seems to be roughly analogous to Knopfelmacher's 8- and 80-second detention period – the latter leads to variable behaviour, the former to fixated behaviour. Jones found similar results for 'mean duration of stereotypes' (i.e. responding 6 or more times in succession to the same key) and mean proportion of stereotyped responses to total number of responses. In line with Maier's contention and other findings on humans by Marquart (1948) and Marquart and Arnold (1952), Jones also reported that during stereotyped behaviour sequences there was less vacillation as measured by the subject's pressure on the keys; and also that those subjects who developed sequences of stereotyped responding were unaware that they had done so.

d) EXPLANATION OF FIXATIONS IN COGNITIVE TERMS

Eglash (1951) made a valiant attempt to explain Maier's results within a cognitional framework. He argued that when the insoluble problem is made soluble the position-stereotype rat is faced with a much more difficult problem than the position-reward rat. The former must *perceive* that the pattern of punishment has changed from 50% random to 50% orderly. He must then *associate* the positive card with reward on both the fixated and non-fixated side, and similarly, associate the negative card with punishment on both sides. Finally, he must *reason* that the new pattern of punishment on the fixated side also applies to the non-fixated side. Furthermore, Maier's argument from the differential latencies to positive and negative cards that the rat has solved the problem is not conclusive since this finding does *not* tell us anything about the rat's generalization to the non-fixated side. In other words, if the rats 'continue jumping to their habitual window, they can successfully predict the occurrence of reward and punishment, while their experience during the insoluble problem has taught them that if they revert to the other window, they are unable to predict . . . the fixated animal may even learn that jumping at the negative card makes the positive card appear' (p. 427).

The principles of perception, association, and reasoning are applied with much ingenuity by Eglash to some of Maier's most important results. The effects of guidance, for example, in breaking fixations, but not facilitating learning, are explained in terms of the four associations necessary for complete learning of the new response. Before coming to guidance, the animal has learned to associate one card with reward, one with punishment on the fixated side, as indicated by his differential latency of response to them. Guidance teaches him to associate the non-fixated side with reward (third

E

association) and hence breaks the fixation. But the rat has still to learn to associate the non-fixated side with punishment also (fourth association); only when he has done this is learning complete. Unfortunately, after these acute analyses, Eglash found himself forced to abandon his own theory, since he could not explain in cognitive terms either the differential effect on fixation of various *amounts* of frustration (Maier and Feldman, 1948) or the fact that animals would look towards and sniff at food in the open goal-box on the non-fixated side, but still jump to the fixated side – a clear instance where a cognitive response was overborne by a compulsion. Nevertheless, Eglash's analysis of what is involved in switching from an insoluble to a soluble problem remains of considerable value.

e) THE FIXATED RESPONSE AS SUBSTITUTE RESPONSE

Having abandoned his attempt to account for fixations in cognitive terms, Eglash (1954) proposed a quite different explanation. One can either regard a fixated response as a strong habitual response which overrides (inhibits) all possible competing responses; or one can regard the situation as involving essentially the inhibition of a single response (jumping to the correct window) which leads to the appearance of substitute responses. The so-called fixated response, therefore, may be regarded as essentially a *substitute* response *pattern*. In support of this argument, Eglash points out that the so-called fixated response pattern is actually extremely variable, involving as it does abortive responses, etc. The only consistent aspect of the situation is the failure of the rat to jump to the side opposite to the fixation. Eglash agrees with Maier that the appropriate response has been learned but argues that it cannot be exercised because it is inhibited, not because the fixated response is prepotent. In this situation the animal simply performs as best it can and indulges in substitute responses as far as these are permitted.

## III. MAIER'S REPLY TO HIS CRITICS AND HIS MORE RECENT FORMULATIONS

In two papers (Maier and Ellen, 1951; Maier, 1956), published after his book, Maier replied to his critics. In these two papers and in a recent one (Maier and Ellen, 1959) he has also somewhat revised his earlier position and extended his thinking. We shall first briefly review his reply to criticism and then detail the recent extensions of his theory.

a) REPLY TO CRITICISMS

With respect to the proponents of an anxiety-reduction theory of fixations, Maier replied in two ways. Firstly, he agreed that anxiety may be an important determiner of behaviour.

> Because frustration theory does not exclude the learning of avoidance responses, this experiment [i.e. Miller's, 1948] and others of similar nature are not questioned, except in so far as they may be generalized to interpret all experiments which use punishment as a training device. Since Miller has not attempted to generalize his interpretation to include abnormal fixations, his findings and interpretations are not in conflict with this aspect of the theoretical issue. In other words, we do not reject the possibility of the motivated learning of avoidance and approach reactions (Maier, 1951, p. 437).

With respect to Farber's experiment, Maier made two specific criticisms.

i) He criticized Farber for concluding that his results were entirely consistent with an anxiety-reduction interpretation of fixations. The resistance to extinction of the shocked/non-fed group compared with the other groups in Farber's experiment were, argued Maier, largely due to the presence of four animals with extinction scores of over 100; similarly in the shocked-fed group, one animal was clearly differentiated from the remainder. 'It is obvious that these five animals contributed most of the variance within their respective groups, thereby accounting for the major differences between the shocked group and the non-shocked-fed group' (Maier, 1951, p. 439). In other words, Maier argued that Farber's 'fixation' group showed the familiar distribution of scores when the insoluble problem was made soluble. Maier is here, however, undoubtedly on shaky ground, as Farber (1954) effectively showed. Even omitting from consideration all animals which took over 30 trials to extinguish, the mean extinction score of the shocked group was still significantly higher than the means of the other three groups. Furthermore, highly skewed distributions of extinction scores are by no means uncommon in extinction procedures in situations where frustration in Maier's sense could not possibly be present. On the other hand, Maier would probably have been on safer ground had he denied that Farber's experiment involved frustration – since on every trial the animal was twice rewarded – once by escape from shock, once by finding food in the goal-box. Farber's experiment, therefore, is more analogous to that of Miller, which Maier willingly admitted was amenable to anxiety-reduction explanations. In support of this argument is the fact that all but four of the shocked group extinguished in less than 70 trials and only two animals reached Maier's criterion of frustration by failing to extinguish in 200 trials (it is possible of course that a different criterion of frustration would be necessary when using a T-maze).

ii) Maier, however, was too intent on making a more damaging criticism to deny that Farber's experiment was a frustration one. He pointed out that the shocked-fed group which readily extinguished was (a) prevented from exercising its fixated response by being confined closely in the punishment area; (b) not allowed to practise the correct response; and (c) rewarded in the punishment situation. These three conditions exactly parallel Maier's own technique of guidance in the Lashley jumping stand situation. Hence, argues Maier, it is not at all surprising that all but one of these animals learned the new response in less than 40 trials, since Farber had destroyed the fixation by guidance. This criticism is a perfectly valid one. From it, of course, we can draw only the conclusion that Farber's experiment is not a crucial one as between the two theories. It is perfectly possible to argue *per contra* that the essential role of guidance is to destroy anxiety in the test situation, and hence permit the rat to learn new responses.

In general, Maier argued that the anxiety-reduction theory could not explain the following aspects of his findings:

i) The fact that the fixated animals learn the correct response when the insoluble problem is made soluble, but cannot exercise it.

ii) The differential effects of 100% and 50% punishment.

iii) The bimodal distribution of scores.

iv) The compulsiveness of the response, even when an open window with food in it is presented.

v) The effects of guidance on fixations.

Furthermore, if the anxiety-reduction theory is correct, then it would seem that responses based on secondary reward (anxiety-reduction) are stronger than those based on primary reward (food).

Turning now to Wilcoxon's theory that fixations are the result of the effects of partial reinforcement (Wilcoxon acknowledged the importance of anxiety-reduction in the insoluble problem situation, but did not specifically investigate it), Maier points out that animals in Wilcoxon's partial reinforcement group were punished every time they jumped to the negative side and every other time they jumped to the positive side. 'This procedure results in animals being punished on three out of four trials when they jump at random during the early stages of learning, and on two out of four trials when they have mastered the problem' (Maier, 1956, p. 374). Wilcoxon's experiment, therefore, is not a crucial one 'because according to frustration theory the greatest number of fixations should occur in the group that received the most punishment, and this is the so-called partial reinforcement group' (ibid., p. 374). With respect to Wilcoxon's conclusion that abortive jumping may prevent rats from discovering that the problem is soluble and thus may interfere with learning of the discrimination problem, Maier argues that the opposite interpretation to that of Wilcoxon is equally plausible, namely that failure to learn causes abortive jumping. Furthermore, abortive jumping has different characteristics for the positive and negative cards when the rat is in the discrimination situation – 'it declines in frequency for the trials on which the positive card is on the side to which the animal has been jumping, but increases for the trials on which the negative card is on the side to which the animal has been jumping' (Maier, 1956, p. 376). Maier and Ellen (1956) indeed found no difference among fixated rats and non-fixated rats either in terms of percentage of rats jumping abortively in the discrimination situation or in terms of percentage of rats showing the differential abortive jumping referred to above. Maier therefore concludes that abortive jumping is not a causal factor in the phenomenon of fixation.

The apparent demonstration by Gladin and Denny (1955) that rats learn to respond to sequential cues in the insoluble problem situation and that this interferes with subsequent performances of the correct response in the soluble problem situation was criticized by Feldman and Waite (1957). Gladin and Denny had made several alterations in the experimental situation used by Maier, and when their experiment was repeated with appropriate modifications, Feldman and Waite could find no evidence whatever for a differential latency between non-rewarded–rewarded sequences and rewarded–rewarded sequences, nor between those animals which did overcome the fixation and those which did not. They also suggest several artefacts which might explain the positive results of Gladin and Denny.

Finally, Maier rejects Wolpe's explanation of fixation as strong habits learned as responses to the primary drive induced by the air-blast. In the first place Klee (1944) was able to obtain fixations (admittedly with difficulty) by using only the hunger drive to force a response. Secondly, Feldman (1953), as we have seen, showed that rats which had developed jumping fixations would also develop walking fixations if a special path was introduced between the jumping stand and the cards. Thirdly, Maier and Ellen (1954) and Maier, Glaser, and Klee (1940) showed that fixations increased in number as the discrimination problem was made more difficult. Fourthly, Maier and Ellen (1952) and Maier and Klee (1943 and 1945) have shown that rats which have developed fixations once are less prone to develop them in subsequent insoluble problem situations. Fifthly, Feldman (1957) argued that, if Wolpe's theory were correct, it would follow that there should be a positive correlation between the number of air-blasts and (i) the number of trials required to break a fixation under guidance; and (ii) the number of trials required to learn a new response after the fixation is broken. Using the data gathered by Maier and Feldman (1948), Feldman could find no support for Wolpe's contention. Sixthly, in a study by Neet and Feldman (1954) it was found that rats able to abandon conflict-induced stereotypes had received significantly *more* shocks than rats unable to abandon their stereotypes.

All of these findings are incompatible with Wolpe's basic hypothesis, as is the later experiment of Ellen (1956) described earlier. Hence, Maier rejects Wolpe's hypothesis as a satisfactory account of fixation.

b) RECENT DEVELOPMENTS IN MAIER'S THEORIZING

We shall consider four aspects of Maier's theorizing here: the role of punishment, the frustration threshold, the principle of availability, and frustration-inducing situations.

i) *The role of punishment.* We have already touched upon the role of punishment several times and it is clear that both for Maier and his opponents the matter is of crucial importance.

It is clear that the situation is of very great complexity, and it is also clear that this complexity has been fully recognized neither by Maier nor by his opponents. If we confine ourselves for the moment to Maier's earlier experiments, the various combinations of reward/ punishment that can be encountered are shown in Table 2.11. Maier and Klee (1943) investigated the first six of these possibilities, but neglected to explore the final two. It can also be seen from the Table

## TABLE 2.11

LOGICAL COMBINATIONS OF REWARD AND
PUNISHMENT IN MAIER'S EARLY EXPERIMENTS
(FOR CORRECT AND INCORRECT RESPONSES)

| Initial response | | | Subsequent response | | |
|---|---|---|---|---|---|
| Initial response to be learned | Pattern of reward/punishment for | | Required to | Pattern of reward/ punishment for | |
| | Correct | Incorrect | | Correct | Incorrect |
| | Responses | | | Responses | |
| A. *Soluble problem* | | | | | |
| 1. Position-reward | 100/0 | 0/100 | Reverse to P.R. | 100/0 | 0*o*100 |
| 2. Position-reward | 100/0 | 0/100 | Shift to S.R. | 100/0 | 50/50† |
| 3. Symbol-reward | 100/0 | 50/50† | Reverse to S.R. | 100/0 | 0/100 |
| 4. Symbol-reward | 100/0 | 50/50† | Shift to P.R. | 100/0 | 50/50† |
| B. *Insoluble problem* | | | | | |
| 1. Position-stereotype | 50/50* | | Reverse to P.R. | 100/0 | 0/100 |
| 2. Position-stereotype | Reward/punish- | | Shift to S.R. | 100/0 | 50/50† |
| 3. Symbol-stereotype | ment for every | | Reverse to S.R. | 100/0 | 0/100 |
| 4. Symbol-stereotype | response | | Shift to P.R. | 100/0 | 50/50† |

\* Punishment/reward pattern random.
† Punishment/reward pattern orderly.
P.R.—position-reward response
S.R.—symbol-reward response

that the change in the pattern of punishment depends upon whether
the animal is required to *reverse* its response or *shift* to a new response. The situation, however, is even more complex than this, in
two ways. In the first place, the *actual* pattern of punishment which
the animal receives may be quite different from the pattern of punishment to which it is theoretically exposed. The actual pattern of
punishment depends entirely on whether or not the animal learns.
Thus, if we take an animal required to reverse a position-stereotype
response (B1 in Table 2.11) it is clear that it will receive 100%
punishment for expressing its stereotype *only if it unfailingly expresses it*, i.e. if it is fixated. An animal which does not fixate will
receive a pattern of punishment *which will be changing all the time
as it learns* until finally it will be rewarded 100% for its behaviour.
It is most unfortunate that the pattern of punishment actually received by the animals in different groups has never been reported.

Until this is done, it is virtually impossible to evaluate properly the various studies.[32]

In the second place, it will be obvious from Table 2.11 that the patterns of reward/punishment included therein by no means exhaust the possible patterns which could be applied, both for the soluble and the insoluble problem. In this connection, two recent experiments by Maier have thrown new light on this problem and caused a quite radical revision in his thinking. In the first experiment (Maier and Ellen, 1954), three groups of rats learned position *habits* under the usual conditions of 100%/0% reward/punishment schedule. Each group was then required to learn a difficult discrimination habit under a different schedule of reward/punishment for the *initial* response and 100% reward for the new response. Thus, repetition of the position-response was now rewarded on 80%, and punished on 20%, of trials for group A; the equivalent ratios were 50% reward and 50% punishment for group B, and 20% reward and 80% punishment for group C. In the second experiment (Maier and Ellen, 1955), three groups learned position *stereotypes* in the usual way (insoluble problem) and were then required to learn the same difficult discrimination response as in the first experiment. The patterns of reward and punishment matched those in the previous experiment. The usual criteria for abandonment of the position habit or stereotype, and for the acquisition of the new symbol-response, were employed.

The results of the two experiments are shown in Fig. 2.5. The most important finding is that a ratio of 80%/20% reward/punishment *or* the reverse caused *more* fixations in the groups of rats with position stereotypes than did a ratio of 50%/50% reward/punishment. The reverse was the case for the groups with position habits.[33] To explain these results, Maier and Ellen (1955) put forward four hypotheses:

(*a*) An organism becomes acquainted with its surroundings by learning the degree to which its behaviour leads to certain consequences. Environments may range from orderly to disorderly

[32] Wilcoxon (1952) and Russell and Pretty (1951) make a passing reference to this point while Maier (1956), in criticizing Wilcoxon's study, actually makes the point being urged above. However, the actual pattern of punishment for the most part remains a closely guarded secret.

[33] The fact that the 50% reward/50% orderly punishment schedule for position *habits* produced such a high proportion of fixations is explained by Maier and Ellen as due to the fact that a more difficult discrimination problem was used in this experiment (i.e. the positive stimulus was a white circle on a black background).

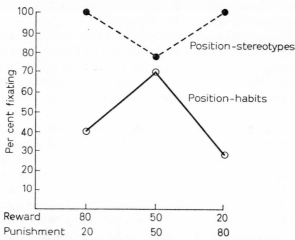

Fig. 2.5. Percentage of rats fixating their position-responses when an attempt is made to develop a card discriminative response. (Source: Maier, N. R. F., and Ellen, P. 'The effect of three reinforcement patterns on positional stereotypes'. *Amer. J. Psychol.*, 1955, **68**, 83–95.)

ones, depending upon the degree to which 'what leads to what' is consistent.

(*b*) Frustration, as an intervening variable, is more likely to occur in an organism when its environment changes markedly in orderliness and conflicts with its expectation of events, pleasant or unpleasant, than when the order in a situation is consistent and expectations are fulfilled.

(*c*) The occurrence of frustration leads to the fixation of a highly available response.

(*d*) An organism with a fixated response can learn 'what leads to what', but it cannot alter its choice because of the compulsive nature of its fixation (Maier and Ellen, 1955, p. 90).

Put simply, Maier is now arguing essentially that whether or not a given reward/punishment ratio produces a fixation, depends upon how far it is different from the pattern which has just preceded it. Thus, for rats initially learning under conditions of 100% reward for the correct response, the change to a pattern of 50% reward/50% punishment is *more* disturbing than a change to *either* of the other patterns, since these are equally *regular*. For rats with position stereotypes, on the other hand, a change from a random to an orderly pattern of 50% reward and 50% punishment is *less* disturbing than the change to *either* of the other patterns.[34]

The interesting point to notice from Maier's analysis is that he appears to have adopted a cognitive or expectancy point of view. Indeed, he explicitly says that '. . . the degree to which a given experience is disturbing, confusing, or frustrating, depends not only upon the situation but also upon the individual's expectations . . .' (ibid., p. 93).

ii) *The frustration threshold and the physiological basis of individual differences.* In the insoluble problem situation, not all animals develop fixations, while in the soluble problem situation, some animals do develop fixations. To explain individual differences in susceptibility to fixations, Maier has recently given increasing attention to the 'frustration threshold' (Maier and Ellen, 1959). The threshold is considered to be an all-or-none affair, i.e. the animal whose 'frustration tolerance' is exceeded develops a sudden, complete fixation (this notion is also used to account for the bimodality of the results). The frustration threshold itself Maier (1956) considers to be physiologically determined and probably mediated through the autonomic nervous system. It may be distinguished from autonomically determined emotional behaviour by the patterning of the various physiological indices. Maier's interest in the autonomic nervous system as a possible basis for frustration is based on the belief that stressful situations may lead to a sudden upsurge of autonomic activity which would tend to inhibit 'voluntary' behaviour. As a possible alternative basis, Maier (1956) has considered Coghill's (1929) concept of individuation which argues for a primitive level of control involving grosser patterns of behaviour which in the normal adult are inhibited by the growth of more complex neural patterns. 'Frustration removes inhibition and permits the grosser responses to take over . . .' (ibid., p. 383). Neither of these notions has, however, been worked out in any detail.

iii) *The principle of availability.* Recently, Maier and Ellen (1959) have elaborated a good deal on the factors which may determine which response is actually fixated. In the insoluble problem situation the actual courses of action open to the rat are somewhat limited by

---

[34] It should be carefully noted that these conclusions are not necessarily at variance with the hypothesis that 100% punishment can induce fixations. We must distinguish between the effects of punishment and the effects of a *change* in punishment schedule.

the nature of the experimental conditions. Among the factors postulated as influencing which response is fixated are: 'Physical nearness, biological ease (including the response in progress), natural or unlearned preferences, primitiveness or simplicity of response, previous experience or training, and cultural or sociological influences' (ibid., pp. 201–2).[35] We need not consider these further at this point, since no direct experimentation has been carried out on the problem.

iv) *The frustrating situation.* In an earlier section, a careful description was given of what constituted a frustrating situation by Maier. The criteria of insoluble problem, inability to leave the field and pressure to respond were cited. The notions of insolubility and inability to leave the field have, however, now been virtually abandoned. Thus, Maier and Ellen (1955) describe as frustrating the following situations:

(*a*) an insoluble problem;
(*b*) pressure from behind;
(*c*) barriers preventing escape;[36]
(*d*) persistent or severe punishment;
(*e*) consistency or inconsistency of results that conflict with expectations.

In general, they lean toward the generalization that a frustrating situation is frustrating when it involves *the experience of failure* – and this, of course, is a far cry from the original very rigid definition of a frustrating situation.

The above account has been given in some detail because of the general neglect of Maier's work by American psychologists and it indicates clearly the extraordinary richness and provocation of Maier's studies, extending as they do over a period of 20 years. In spite of weaknesses and many puzzling features, Maier's results and formulations must clearly be taken seriously in any attempt to explain fixated behaviour.

---

[35] A list which is sufficiently wide as to be almost valueless! (In a later section of the paper, Maier and Ellen add sex, body structure, and personality to the list.)
[36] Notice that Maier in this paper lists each of these *separately* as frustrating, whereas originally all three had to be present simultaneously before the total situation could be called frustrating.

# Chapter 3

# FRUSTRATION AND AGGRESSION

The frustration-aggression hypothesis (Dollard *et al.*, 1944) was the end-product of many observations, stemming from the work particularly of McDougall (1923) and Freud (1920).[1] The systematic presentation of the thesis in 1939 by Dollard and his associates, however, has stimulated a large amount of research, which it is the purpose of this chapter to survey. In doing so, we shall first put forward (together with the relevant evidence) the main propositions of the Yale school; then consider briefly one important extrapolation from the theory; and finally consider some of the main criticisms which have been put forward against the theory.

## I. THE FRUSTRATION-AGGRESSION HYPOTHESIS

In its original form, the frustration-aggression hypothesis involved two basic assumptions which were stated in an extreme form. These were:

1. 'Aggression is always a consequence of frustration' (Dollard *et al.*, 1944, p. 1).[2]

2. '. . . the occurrence of aggressive behaviour always presupposes the existence of frustration . . .' (ibid., p. 1).

A number of definitions are of crucial importance in the Yale system. The most important of these are:

### 1. Instigator

An instigator is defined as 'some antecedent condition of which the predicted response is the consequence' (ibid., p. 3). Two points should be noted about instigators. In the first place, they may be either internal or external – the existence of the first kind being inferred

---

[1] Dollard *et al.* (1944, pp. 14–19) give a brief historical background to their theory.

[2] References to this volume are to the English edition, published in 1944.

from behavioural signs such as facial expression, verbal comments, etc. Secondly, it is considered that the term instigator has a reference much wider than that of the term 'stimulus'.[3]

## 2. Strength of instigation

This is indicated 'by the degree to which the instigated response competes successfully with simultaneously instigated incompatible responses' (ibid., pp. 3–4).

## 3. Goal-response

A goal-response is an 'act which terminates a predicted sequence' (ibid., p. 4).

## 4. Frustration

This term is defined in two separate ways. The *dependent* definition asserts that frustration is 'an interference with the occurrence of an instigated goal-response at its proper time in the behaviour sequence' (ibid., p. 5), the result of which is an act of aggression.[4] The *independent* definition states frustration is 'that condition which exists when a goal-response suffers interference' (ibid., p. 8).

## 5. Aggression

This term is also defined in two separate ways. The *dependent* definition asserts that aggression is 'that response which follows frustration, reduces only the secondary, frustration-produced instigation, and leaves the strength of the original instigation unaffected' (ibid., p. 8). The *independent* definition states that aggression is 'an act whose goal-response is injury to an organism (or organism-surrogate)' (ibid., p. 8).

Armed with these definitions and assumptions, the authors proceeded to outline as systematically as possible the factors affecting the appearance, non-appearance, or transformation of aggressive behaviour consequent upon frustration.[5] Four aspects of the general

[3] This is curious, since it would seem to be more logical to think of 'instigators' as being a sub-class of stimuli.

[4] A dependent definition of frustration is not actually given in the monograph and the one given here has been constructed from the quotation given, together with the additional phrase. The reader will note that Dollard *et al.* appear to be confusing here the *frustrating situation* (dependent definition) and the *frustrated organism* (independent definition).

[5] The whole scheme is a remarkable *tour de force*, since little or no experimental evidence to substantiate the hypotheses was available at the time. Subsequent research has, in fact, modified very little the general scheme as here presented.

frustration-aggression hypothesis may be considered and the general line of approach of Dollard *et al.* will be followed fairly closely.

## 1. The strength of instigation to aggression

This does not, of course, refer to the overt behaviour of the individual, but to an inferred state, or drive, which may, or may not (according to principles to be outlined later), result in an aggressive act. Four factors which may affect the strength of instigation to aggression have been suggested:

a) THE STRENGTH OF INSTIGATION TO AGGRESSION WILL VARY DIRECTLY WITH THE STRENGTH OF INSTIGATION TO THE FRUSTRATED RESPONSE

That is, an individual strongly motivated to reach a goal will be more strongly instigated to aggression than an individual weakly motivated to reach the same goal, if the goal is unattainable, and the strength of the barrier to the goal is held constant in each case.

Three experiments have been reported which support the general hypothesis. Sears and Sears (1940) produced frustration in infants by withdrawing the bottle before hunger was satisfied. The strength of instigation to the goal-response of feeding was varied by withdrawing the bottle after varying amounts ($\frac{1}{2}$, $2\frac{1}{2}$ or $4\frac{1}{2}$ oz.) of milk had been consumed. The strength of instigation to aggression was measured by the latency (in seconds) to crying. Table 3.1 shows that the hypo-

TABLE 3.1

LATENCY OF CRYING AS A FUNCTION OF
TIME OF WITHDRAWAL OF BOTTLE

| Oz. milk taken before withdrawal | Latency of crying |
|:---:|:---:|
| 0·5 | 5·0 |
| 2·5 | 9·9 |
| 4·5 | 11·5 |

Source: Sears, R. R., and Sears, P. S. 'Minor studies of aggression: V. Strength of frustration-reaction as a function of strength of drive'. *J. Psychol.*, 1940, **9**, 297–300

thesis was supported. Haner and Brown (1955) gave children the task of placing marbles in holes. With an unspecified time limit urging the children on, Haner and Brown induced frustration by terminating the trial arbitrarily before the task was completed. The strength of instigation to the goal-response was varied by terminating the trial after the child had placed 9, 18, 27, 32, or 36 marbles (the goal being 36 marbles). The strength of instigation to aggression was measured by having the subject press a lever after each trial, the pressure being secretly recorded. The results were in agreement with prediction, pressure increasing as the child was failed closer to the goal.[6]

Positive results were also obtained by Finch (1942) who found that 'frustration-response incidence' (including aggression) increased as a direct function of number of hours of food deprivation when the animal was then placed in a frustrating situation (in this case being unable to obtain food).

b) THE STRENGTH OF INSTIGATION TO AGGRESSION WILL VARY DIRECTLY WITH THE DEGREE OF INTERFERENCE WITH THE FRUSTRATED RESPONSE

That is to say, if two individuals have an equal instigation to a goal-response, the individual whose instigation is the more strongly prevented from reaching satisfaction will manifest a stronger instigation to aggression. A number of studies are relevant to this hypothesis. Thus Hovland and Sears (1940) argued that aggression would be expected to increase during years of depression since universal goal responses would be frustrated more than during years of prosperity. They attempted to show that there was a positive correlation between the number of lynchings per year and changes in economic indices based on the farm value of cotton crops and per acre value of cotton in 14 Southern States.[7] Mintz (1946), however, effectively criticized this study on statistical grounds, principally the non-linearity of the trends of the curves examined and the use of tetrachoric coefficients, resulting in spuriously elevated correlations, and the evidence of Hovland and Sears must therefore be disregarded.[8] A more important source of confirmation was the study of Graham et al. (1951). They investigated the influence of aggression

[6] Haner and Brown make the important criticism of the experiment of Sears and Sears (1940) in particular, and of the Yale school in general, of failing to distinguish in their experiments between drive strength and habit strength. This problem will be considered later.

[7] Lynchings, of course, represent a very indirect measure of instigation to aggression, and are in fact an example of *displacement* of aggressive responses since 'by no conceivable stretch of the imagination could the victims of lynchings, either Negro or White, be considered responsible for the value of cotton or the general level of business activity' (Hovland and Sears, 1940, p. 307).

[8] No reply to Mintz's criticisms has been forthcoming from Hovland and Sears.

itself as a frustrating situation. Fifty incomplete sentences were scaled for frustration value (e.g. 'he hit me, so I . . .' was given a high rating) and ordered into five catergories of decreasing strength of frustration. Adolescent subjects were required to complete the sentences, and their completions were then rated for aggressiveness. The hypothesis tested was that there would be a positive relationship between degree of frustration (indicated by the aggression-ratings of the incomplete sentences) and the amount of aggression shown in the responses.

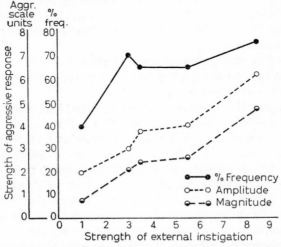

Fig. 3.1. Strength of aggressive response as a function of strength of frustration. (Source: Graham, F. K., Charwat, W. A., Honig, A. S., and Weltz, P. C. 'Aggression as a function of the attack and the attacker'. *J. abnorm. soc. Psychol.*, 1951, **46**, 512–20.)

Using three measures of response strength (per cent frequency, amplitude, and magnitude) the results shown in Fig. 3.1 were obtained. It is clear that the hypothesis was confirmed and a linear trend obtained.[9] Supporting evidence for the general hypothesis is also to be found in the study by McClelland and Apicella (1945), using derogatory verbal comments and induced failure in a card-sorting test, as sources of frustration. As the experimenter's hostility increased, the proportion of verbal responses of the subjects (classified into a number of different categories) shifted reliably towards

[9] Graham *et al.* use the term 'strength of external instigation' in their paper to refer to the external frustrating stimulus situation. This should not be confused with the term 'strength of instigation to aggression', as used by Dollard *et al.*, which refers to an internal state of the subject following upon frustration.

aggressiveness (provided responses indicating anger may be classified as aggressive).[10]

c) THE STRENGTH OF INSTIGATION TO AGGRESSION WILL VARY DIRECTLY WITH THE NUMBER OF FRUSTRATED RESPONSE SEQUENCES

Finch (1942) showed that 'frustration-response' incidence increased with repetition of the frustrating situation. More dramatically, Palmer (1960) found that convicted murderers had been subjected to significantly more physiological and psychological frustrations during childhood than had their control brothers. The murderers also showed fewer socially acceptable forms of aggression release.

d) THE STRENGTH OF INSTIGATION TO AGGRESSION WILL VARY DIRECTLY WITH THE NUMBER OF RESPONSES (OTHER THAN AGGRESSIVE RESPONSES) WHICH ARE EXTINGUISHED THROUGH NON-REINFORCEMENT AS FRUSTRATION PERSISTS

In other words, if frustration calls out a number of mutually incompatible responses, the instigation to these responses will lessen as frustration persists. The extinction of these alternative responses will itself constitute an additional frustration, and hence the instigation to aggression will be increased. This proposition was first explicitly formulated by Miller (1941).[11] Otis and McCandless (1955), using pre-school children, showed a significant decrease, under conditions of repeated frustration, in non-aggressive activities; and a reliable increase in aggressive behaviour, thus supporting the hypothesis.

## 2. The inhibition of acts of aggression

Given that the subject is in a frustrating situation, and is strongly instigated to aggression, whether or not a direct aggressive response occurs is a function of the balance of excitatory forces (which we have just discussed) and inhibitory forces, to which we now turn. Two main propositions have been put forward by the Yale school.

a) 'THE STRENGTH OF INHIBITION OF ANY ACT OF AGGRESSION VARIES POSITIVELY WITH THE AMOUNT OF PUNISHMENT ANTICIPATED TO BE A CONSEQUENCE OF THAT ACT'

---

[10] The studies of both Graham et al. and McClelland and Apicella are open to serious objection, in that it is arguable that the situations invoked by them were not meaningfully frustrating at all. The subject who responds to verbal aggression by the experimenter with counter verbal aggression may not be frustrated at all, but merely be responding directly, i.e. his verbal aggression may be a direct and successful goal-response. Graham et al. indicate awareness of this criticism.

[11] The reader will notice that an important modification of the original extreme form of the theory is implied here. This will be discussed later.

F

(provided the strength of instigation to aggression is held constant) (Dollard *et al.*, 1944, p. 24). By punishment, the authors intend anything which is the equivalent of pain to the recipient. Thus, punishment may include the actual infliction of pain, injury to a loved object or person, and the anticipation of failure, as well as the more obvious instances of failure to reach a goal-object. A great deal of evidence is available with respect to this hypothesis.

Thus, Doob and Sears (1939) constructed sentences which described various kinds of social situations involving frustration.[12] A number of sentences indicating aggressive, non-aggressive, or substitute responses to this situation were given and the subject was required to choose between the items on the basis of various criteria. The two criteria important for our present purpose were: that item which would have been most satisfying to do; and that item which would have resulted in most trouble (i.e. punishment) if done. Doob and Sears found that: the most satisfying response checked tended to be aggression; the response from which most punishment was anticipated was the aggressive response; and the overtness of aggression indicated varied inversely with the amount of punishment anticipated as a consequence of such behaviour.[13]

A direct demonstration that aggressive behaviour may give rise to aggression-anxiety has recently been provided by Hokanson (1961). He compared groups of high-hostility and low-hostility subjects with respect to changes in physiological indices of anxiety from a resting state to a situation involving frustration. He found that, although there was no difference between the groups initially, the high-hostility group showed a significantly greater change in the physiological indices used (towards a higher level of anxiety) when frustration was induced than did the low-hostility group. It seems reasonable to assume that the high-hostility group has in the past expressed its hostility very readily, has been punished frequently for that expression, and hence now tends to develop anxiety-responses in situations likely to lead to an outburst of aggressive behaviour.

A number of specific predictions arising from this general hypothesis have been confirmed.

i) *Permissiveness with respect to aggression will reduce the antici-*

---

[12] For example: 'You saw an item in the paper which described a case of conspicuous and unnecessary brutality and cruelty on the part of the police.'

[13] Similarly, in an actual experimental (doll-play) situation, Chasdi and Lawrence (1955) found that punishment (verbal reprimand) for aggressive doll-play led to a reduction in such aggression in subsequent sessions.

*pation of punishment and/or increase the anticipation of reward for aggression.* In either case, an increase in aggression should follow. For both frequency and intensity of aggression, Chasdi and Lawrence (1955) found that this was the case in doll-play sessions.

ii) *The instigation to aggression will be inhibited to a greater extent when the frustrators are of high status in the eyes of the frustrated subject than when they are of low status.* This follows from the increased anticipation of punishment for aggression towards high-status figures. Thus, Graham *et al.* (1951), in the study already described, in addition to varying the strength of external frustration, utilized five types of instigator, i.e. parent, sibling, friend or classmate, authority (policeman or teacher), and inferior. They found that inferiors, siblings, and friends evoked significantly more aggression than either parents or authority, and concluded that '. . . the greater the punishment-threatening value of an instigator, the *fewer* and the *less intense* will be the aggressive-responses evoked by him' (Graham *et al.*, 1951, p. 518).[14] Essentially similar results were obtained by Cohen (1955) and by McKellar (1950). It may be noted that both of these experiments involved the use of hypothetical, not actual, frustrations. In a more dramatic 'real-life situation' (Thibaut and Riecken, 1955) the subjects were realistically frustrated by high-status (HSI) or low-status (LSI) instigators[15] and their hostility measured by analysing the content of assessments of the instigator before and after the frustrating experience. On a 7-point scale of aggression, the mean scale score of communications addressed to the HSI was 3·33 and to the LSI 4·67 (p = ·03), that is, assuming the instigation to aggression was equal in both groups, the subjects facing a HSI inhibited some of their hostility.

Similarly, Worchel (1957) found that subjects frustrated on intellectual tasks were able to express their hostility more freely to an assistant in the absence of the experimenter, than when the experimenter remained.

iii) *The instigation to aggression will be greater when group organization is high, than when it is low.* It would be predicted from the

[14] In this study there was a significant interaction effect between the type of instigator and the strength of instigation, e.g. the amount of aggression increased significantly with increased degree of instigation when the instigator was a sibling, friend, or inferior; but did not increase for any level when the instigator was a parent.
[15] The subjects were Army personnel who were frustrated by a confederate of the experimenter wearing the uniform of an officer superior to the subject in rank (HSI) or lower (LSI).

frustration-aggression hypothesis that anticipation of punishment for aggression would be less when the individual was a member of a group than when he was facing the instigator alone. It might also be predicted that *within group* aggression would be greater in an organized than an unorganized group, since punishment-expectations would be more clearly defined in the former than in the latter and would in any case be *less* since an organized group by definition is one within which the occurrence of hostility does not lead to disintegration.

Again the results are generally positive. Thus, M. E. Wright (1943) found that children frustrated in pairs more freely expressed aggression against the instigator than when frustrated on their own. Pepitone and Reichling (1955) formed highly cohesive and poorly cohesive groups and subjected them to frustration in the form of an insulting lecture. The expression of hostility within the groups when left on their own was recorded and it was found that the highly cohesive group (1) expressed significantly more hostility than the poorly cohesive group, and (2) expressed that hostility significantly more often directly against the instigator (i.e. showed less need to displace its hostility). These results are similar to those of French (1944), who found that organized groups could more freely express aggression than unorganized groups. An interesting gloss on these results is provided by Thibaut's (1950) finding that the cohesiveness of low-status teams *increases* significantly in the face of continuing frustration, when aggression cannot be expressed directly against the instigator. Both this study and that of Lanzetta (1955) suggest that intra-group aggression under frustration may actually decline when the instigator is perceived as an individual of high status.

The famous study by Lewin, Lippitt, and White (1939) combined both group activities and different kinds of leadership. Thus, three comparable groups were formed and observed under authoritarian, democratic, and *laissez-faire* leadership. It was found that overt hostility in the groups with an authoritarian leader was either very high (forty times as great as in the groups with a democratic leader) or very low. Thus, a distinction was drawn between apathetic groups and aggressive groups under authoritarian leadership. The highest level of aggression, however, was found in the *laissez-faire* group. These differences did not draw forth any very convincing explanation from Lewin and his colleagues.

An extreme form of the inhibition of aggression has been labelled as 'autistic hostility' by Newcomb (1947). Autistic hostility arises when an individual reacts to criticism or insult by withdrawing from communication with the frustrating person on that particular matter, although normal relationships may be maintained with respect to other areas of behaviour. Indirect evidence of such hostility was obtained in a study by Thibaut and Coules (1952). When subjects were frustrated by their partner but were not permitted to express their hostility, a large proportion of them wished to quit the experiment; for subjects in the group allowed to express hostility, there was a correlation of $-\cdot47$ between post-experimental residual hostility and willingness to continue. A negative correlation was also found between initial disposition towards the instigator and the number of units of communication made during the experiment, but before the frustration mentioned above (i.e. the more hostile the initial disposition, the less communication).

b) 'IF THE STRENGTH OF INSTIGATION (TOWARDS AGGRESSION) IS INCREASED, HOWEVER, IT MAY BECOME STRONG ENOUGH TO OVERCOME THE ANTICIPATION OF PUNISHMENT' (Dollard *et al.*, 1944, p. 26). This prediction is based on the general assumption that 'the strengths of antagonistic or incompatible responses summate negatively in some algebraic manner' (ibid., p. 26). The only evidence so far on this point is that of Doob and Sears (1939) in the experiment described earlier. They found a positive correlation between the strength of instigation to aggression and the amount of overt aggression manifested.

## 3. The object of acts of aggression

It is clear from everyday observation that the object of aggressive behaviour is not always identical with the frustrating object. In considering this aspect of the frustration-aggression hypothesis, we must carefully distinguish between three independent factors – response generalization, stimulus generalization, and substitution. Taken in conjunction with the factor of inhibition already discussed, these factors help to account for the direction which the aggressive behaviour may take.

a) RESPONSE GENERALIZATION

It is extremely important to notice that response generalization is defined by Dollard *et al.* (1944) in two distinct ways.

i) The *direct* act of aggression against the frustrating obstacle will generalize to other similar acts of aggression. Thus, if the most direct act of aggression is physical assault, there will be activated also by the same stimulus other acts of aggression, such as direct verbal assault, indirect verbal assault, aggressive fantasies, and so on. In accordance with the principle of generalization, as the aggressive acts decrease in similarity to the direct act, so the tendency to perform them will decrease. Such generalization will usually take place in the *absence* of the direct aggressive act. In this instance, there is no question of inhibition through anticipation of punishment.

ii) If the direct act of aggression could be carried out but is *inhibited* through anticipation of punishment, then response generalization is likely to take place also, the most probable response being that which is most similar to the inhibited one.[16] But in this case, the response is said to have been *displaced*.

b) STIMULUS GENERALIZATION

As with response generalization, two distinct meanings are attached to this term.

i) The aggressive response to the frustrating obstacle will be directed not merely to that obstacle, but also to stimuli perceived by the frustrated person to be similar to the primary frustration, and will diminish in intensity as the objects generalized to become less similar. Thus, if verbal aggression is directed towards the boss by an employee, it will tend to generalize to other superior personnel in the firm, or to the boss's family. Again, such generalization will be particularly likely to occur in the *absence* of the primary target.

ii) If, however, the direct act of aggression is inhibited because of anticipation of punishment, then that act may be *displaced* against stimuli seen to be similar to that of the boss.

The Yale school has paid little attention to the phenomenon of generalization in the first sense described above[17] and have concentrated on the phenomenon they call displacement.

c) SUBSTITUTION

A substitute response is defined as 'any action which reduces to some degree the strength of the instigation, the goal-response to which was prevented from occurring' (Dollard *et al.*, 1944, p. 6). Now, it is clear that the notion of substitute-response also involves the principle of generalization. However, substitution may be clearly dis-

---

[16] Important qualifications to this statement will be discussed later.
[17] The essential distinction drawn here is, however, recognized by Dollard *et al.* (1944, p. 29, footnote 2) when they 'distinguish between (*a*) that spread of aggression which is assumed to occur whether or not the direct aggression is inhibited, and (*b*) the displacement of aggression which . . . should occur only when the more direct form of aggression is inhibited.'

tinguished from response or stimulus generalization *by its consequences*. Any act which results from the instigation to aggression will reduce the instigation to aggression if it is successful, but *it will not reduce the instigation to the original goal-act*. A substitute-response, on the other hand, *does* reduce the instigation to the original goal-act, in that the goal is, as it were, partially attained. Substitute acts, therefore, are not at all aimed at the frustrating obstacle, but are aimed at substitute goals. The distinction is not an easy one to grasp, but is clearly valid.

It can be seen that prediction as to the behaviour of an individual in response to frustration of a goal-object has now become exceedingly complex, for account must be taken of both response and stimulus generalization of the excitatory (or aggressive) aspects, of the inhibitory aspects (which themselves will generalize), and of the possibility of substitute goals. The actual behaviour which emerges will therefore be a function of the algebraic summation of positive and negative response tendencies.[18]

There is a good deal of experimental evidence for the generalization, both of the same reponse to different stimuli, and of different responses to the same stimulus and we need not refer to it here. Instead, we turn now to the evidence for the two kinds of displacement, and for substitution.

a) DISPLACEMENT FROM ONE AGGRESSIVE RESPONSE TO ANOTHER WITH STIMULUS CONSTANT (RESPONSE GENERALIZATION

Surprisingly little empirical work has been carried out in this area of research, but two studies provide support for the proposition. French (1944) frustrated organized and unorganized groups by giving them soluble problems which, however, could not be solved in the time available. Although the organized group showed a higher degree of frustration than the unorganized group, the aggressive reaction was more directly expressed in the organized group (by physical attacks, etc.) than in the unorganized group. More directly relevant is a recent study by Dinwiddie (1955). This study is important because Dinwiddie obtained separate measures of the instigation to aggression and of the instigation to inhibition of the aggression.[19] A

[18] This problem will be taken up again in the chapter on conflict.
[19] Strength of instigation to aggression was measured by the Moldawsky Hostility Index, and strength of instigation to inhibition of aggression by the Taylor Anxiety Scale and a measure of 'social anxiety' (anxiety being assumed to be a valid indication of degree of inhibition).

continuum of response dissimilarity was constructed by utilizing the Rosenzweig Picture Frustration Test, and offering a choice of responses of varying degrees of hostility to the situation portrayed. When instigation to aggression was held constant, a correlation of +·394 was found between 'social anxiety' and amount of displacement; while, when 'social anxiety' was held constant, a correlation of —·626 was found between instigation to aggression and amount of displacement. Considering the crudeness of the methods available for measuring instigation to aggression, anxiety or instigation to inhibition, and displacement of aggression, these results are encouraging. Dinwiddie's study is also notable as one of the few in this field which attempt to hold constant one factor while varying others.

b) DISPLACEMENT FROM ONE STIMULUS TO ANOTHER WITH AGGRESSIVE RESPONSE HELD CONSTANT (STIMULUS GENERALIZATION)

Miller (1948b) investigated both the generalization which occurs in the *absence* of the frustrating stimulus, and the generalization which occurs when the aggressive response to the frustrating stimulus is *inhibited* through anticipation of punishment. Miller's theory about the way in which displacement occurs is a complicated one and consideration of it must be deferred until a later chapter. For the present, we shall simply look at the evidence to see if displacement of aggressive responses has been demonstrated. McKellar (1949) analysed both introspectively (on himself), and by means of a questionnaire (on groups) the kinds of aggression aroused by various frustrating situations. He found that non-overt aggression was much more common than overt aggression, that verbal aggression was more common than physical, and that when overt aggression did occur, it was usually directed against some object other than a human adult. Each of these three manifestations could reasonably be attributed to displacement.

An important deduction within the general displacement theory was put forward by Sears (1951), who argued that the more severely a child is punished for aggression by his mother in the home, the greater the amount of aggression he will show in doll-play. This follows from the theory that punishment leads to inhibition of the aggression in the home and hence the aggression will be displaced on to similar objects, such as dolls. In its most general form, the 'permissiveness hypothesis' states that: *parental permissiveness leads to both high direct aggression and high fantasy aggression*; *parental non-*

*permissiveness leads to low direct aggression and high fantasy aggression.* The reader will recognize this as a direct prediction from the general displacement hypothesis. Thus, Lesser (1957) found a correlation of +·47 between overt and fantasy aggression when the mother encouraged aggressive behaviour; but the correlation was —·41 when the mother discouraged aggressive behaviour.[20] Collateral support for the hypothesis is found in a number of studies which indicate that the expression of direct aggression becomes progressively more inhibited in older children (Bridges, 1931; Green, 1933; Jersild and Markey, 1935; Bender *et al.*, 1936; Bach, 1945; Ammons and Ammons, 1953; Sears *et al.*, 1957).

On the whole, therefore, the evidence is fairly compelling that aggressive behaviour is learned by children by identification with the parents and at the same time its direct expression may become progressively inhibited through punishment. The punishment in itself, of course, constitutes a further frustration and may increase the general level of aggressiveness.[21] However, a study by Hess and Handel (1956) throws a different light on the matter. They tested the hypothesis that 'the influence of the personality of the parents is sufficiently powerful to create significantly greater personality resemblances between individuals within a family than exists between members of different families' (Hess and Handel, 1956, p. 205). They made pair-comparisons between parents and their children, and between parents and children not their own, using a composite aggression score derived from 17 variables. For all pairs of related persons the median correlation was +·425; for non-related pairs it was +·370. The lack of difference indicates the general influence of culture, rather than training techniques within the family. To take a more specific example, the median correlation for father/son was +·475; and for non-related male adults/boys was +·422. The results for other comparisons were very similar. The results suggest rather convincingly that aggressive behaviour is transmitted to children through the general cultural ethos which imposes itself to a considerable extent on families and determines which child-training

---

[20] Studies by R. R. Sears (1951), Doob and Sears (1939), Mussen and Naylor (1954), Livson and Mussen (1957), and Graham *et al.* (1951) support these findings, while Bornston and Coleman (1956) and Fry (1952) additionally indicate that the inhibited aggression may be turned against the self, or outwardly displaced. Crandall (1951) has shown that frustration does produce increased punishment expectancy.

[21] Seward (1945a) has presented evidence concerning the inhibition of aggression through fear in animals.

techniques will be used. The study suggests also that child-training techniques which run counter to the general cultural demands could produce severe conflict in the child.

The influence of cultural differences in the form of social class has been investigated in a number of studies. The general expectation has been that punishment for aggression would be less severe among the lower classes and that there would, therefore, be social class differences in aggressiveness, both in its overt and fantasy aspects. Overt aggression would be more freely expressed by the children of lower-class parents, whereas the children of higher-class parents would be expected to be more inhibited in this respect. This was certainly the case in the study by McKee and Leader (1955). Similarly, Livson and Mussen (1957) found a *negative* relationship between ego control capacities and the amount of direct aggression in middle-class children; while Mussen and Naylor (1954) found a *positive* relationship between overt and fantasy aggression in lower-class children, provided the degree of anticipation of punishment was taken into account. On the other hand, both Body (1955) and Muste and Sharpe (1947) found a higher incidence of aggressive play in children from high socio-economic families. These conflicting findings may result from the use of somewhat different situations for the measurement of aggression. To be strictly comparable, measures of direct aggression within the home would have to be compared with measures of indirect aggression (in doll-play, fantasy, etc.) outside the home and in the absence of the parents.

These results illustrate nicely the complexities involved in making deductions within the framework of the frustration-aggression hypothesis. Thus, it is clear that both stimulus and response generalization are involved (since the *object* of the aggression is changed from mother to doll, and the *form* of the aggression from physical or verbal direct attack to physical or verbal fantasy attack). Furthermore, since punishment produces inhibition (or aggression-anxiety, as it is sometimes called) the expression of aggression in the doll-play situation could be a function of either displacement or a reduction in aggression-anxiety in the permissive doll-play situation, or both. Clearly we are again faced with the necessity for independently defining the various factors rather than deducing the presence or absence of one factor from the changes in another and thus arguing circularly. This difficulty was recognized by Levin and Turgeon (1957) who had further deduced that displaced aggression shown in doll-play would itself be inhibited if the original inhibition of overt aggression (the mother) were present at the session. Accordingly preschool children were given two doll-play sessions. In the first session the child was present with the experimenter; in the second, one additional person (either the mother or a stranger) was present. The

## TABLE 3.2

### AGGRESSION SCORES IN TWO DOLL-PLAY SESSIONS

| | Mother present | | | | Stranger present | | | |
|---|---|---|---|---|---|---|---|---|
| | Session I | | Session II | | Session I | | Session II | |
| | Mean | SD | Mean | SD | Mean | SD | Mean | SD |
| Boys | 16·40 | 17·62 | 41·20 | 29·39 | 29·80 | 21·34 | 23·60 | 16·69 |
| Girls | 6·40 | 10·49 | 10·60 | 14·08 | 7·40 | 2·19 | 3·80 | 5·85 |

Source: Levin, H., and Turgeon, V. F. 'The influence of mother's presence on children's doll-play aggression'. *J. abnorm. soc. Psychol.*, 1957, **55**, 304–8

results of the experiment are shown in Table 3.2. As can be seen from the table, 'aggressiveness clearly increases from the first to the second session when the mother is watching the child and decreases when a stranger is present. Every one of the ten experimental children increased in aggressiveness when the mother was present' (Levin and Turgeon, 1957, p. 306). It is clear that factors other than displacement must be considered to explain these results.[22]

Experimental verification of Miller's hypothesis was obtained in an ingenious study by Murney (1955), who, like Dinwiddie, in the study already quoted, attempted to define independently the instigation to aggression and the instigation to inhibition of aggression. In order to do this, he factor-analysed need-press variables of the TAT which on *a priori* grounds seemed relevant to aggression and to anxiety. Two factors were extracted which seemed to be reasonable measures of the variables. Displacement was measured in the following way. An aggressive figure from the MAPS test (an army

---

[22] Levin and Turgeon put forward a reasonable *ad hoc* explanation of this result, to the effect that children punished for the direct expression of aggression in the home may indulge in fantasy aggression in the home, and this form of aggression may not be punished (or may even be approved) by the mother. This explanation, if valid, would mean that the displacement theory of aggression may require considerable modification.

officer) was depicted dressing down unjustly a subordinate (a private). The subject was given a set of figures, which had previously been ranked (by other groups) in terms of an aggressive similarity dimension to the officer figure, and was asked to indicate against which of the figures (including the officer) the private would express physical aggression. Two predictions, paralleling those made by Dinwiddie in the case of response generalization, were involved. The first prediction was that, with instigation to aggression held constant, there would be a *negative* correlation between strength of instigation to inhibition of aggression and degree of similarity between the aggressive officer figure and the figure actually chosen as the recipient of the private's aggression, i.e. it was predicted that inhibited individuals would displace the private's aggression away from the original instigator on to an object less capable of retaliation. A correlation of $-.72$ supported this prediction. Similarly, it was predicted that with instigation to inhibition of aggression held constant, there would be a *positive* correlation between strength of instigation to aggression and of similarity. A correlation of $+.82$ supported this prediction. A coefficient of multiple correlation which took account of both the excitatory and inhibitory variables simultaneously (i.e. their interaction) attained a value of $+.86$.

Miller's hypothesis was not substantiated by Fredericksen (1942), who found that frustrated children *increased* in submissiveness to other children, when the prediction was that they would displace aggression felt against the source of frustration (the teacher) on to other available objects. In the absence of independent measures of instigation to aggression and instigation to inhibition of aggression, however, this result cannot be considered too seriously. We may conclude, therefore, that the most careful studies to date have provided impressive evidence (in view of the difficulties in this work indicated) for the validity of Miller's theory of displacement.[23]

Dollard *et al.* (1944) extended the theory of stimulus generalization to include displacement of aggression from the instigator to the self, i.e. the aggression, instead of being expressed outwardly, is turned inwards. It would seem that two conditions are necessary for self-aggression to occur in this way. In the first place, the frustrated individual and the frustrating individual must have some charac-

[23] Evidence for displacement of responses other than aggressive ones will be considered in the chapter on conflict; while the important application of displacement theory to the explanation of prejudice will be discussed later on in the present chapter.

teristics in common, otherwise displacement could not take place. Secondly, self-aggression would presumably take place only when inhibition of the aggressive response towards the frustrating person has generalized to all possible variants of the aggression. Dollard *et al.* made three specific predictions concerning such self-aggression.

i) '*Instigation to self-aggression should be relatively stronger when the source of frustration is perceived to be the self than when it is perceived to be some external agent*' (ibid., p. 34), because inhibition of aggression by the self constitutes a new source of frustration.

ii) '*There should be a greater tendency for inhibited direct aggression to be turned against the self when it is inhibited by the self than when it is inhibited by an external agent*' (ibid., p. 34), because inhibition of aggression by the self constitutes a new source of frustration.

iii) '*Other conditions being constant, self-aggression should be a relatively non-preferred type of expression which will not occur unless other forms of expression are even more strongly inhibited*' (ibid., pp. 34–5), because self-aggression involves punishment, which itself inhibits aggression.

Unfortunately, little experimental work of any value has been directed at these predictions, except the studies by Bornston and Coleman (1956), and Fry (1952), already referred to.

c) SUBSTITUTION

As previously indicated, a substitute response is a response directed at an alternative goal whose attainment reduces the instigation to the original goal. One of the simplest examples given by Dollard *et al.* (1944, p. 42) is the substitution of eating for sucking behaviour. From the example given, it is clear that substitute behaviour may eventually completely satisfy the instigation to the original goal, and in such instances direct or displaced aggressive responses arising out of the original frustration involved in cessation of breast-feeding will disappear. It is further clear that there will often be transition periods during which both substitute and aggressive responses are being indulged in.

The conditions under which substitute responses (rather than direct or indirect aggressive responses) would be predicted to occur in the face of frustration were not stated by Dollard *et al.* (1944) and indeed, as hypothesized by Doob and Sears (1939), in the study already quoted, would appear to be indistinguishable from conditions leading to displacement. Thus, Doob and Sears predicted that 'there should be a greater frequency of substituted responses when subjects express a greater amount of anticipation of punishment for being aggressive' (p. 295), and that frequency of substitute-responses should vary inversely with the strength of the frustrated goal-responses (because the stronger the goal-instigation, the more likely frustration is to lead to aggression). The second hypothesis of Doob and Sears was supported, i.e. as drive-instigation to the goal-object increased, the proportion of substitute-responses decreased.

Apart from the Doob and Sears paper, only Masserman and Siever (1944) have produced experimental evidence for substitute behaviour. Thus, a non-dominant cat will not approach food while a dominant cat is eating, but will try to obtain a mouse introduced beneath the grill floor. As soon as the dominant cat finishes eating, however, the non-dominant cat will approach the food.

### 4. Catharsis

The consequences of the aggressive act, whether it occurs directly or in displaced fashion, were not worked out in any detail by Dollard *et al.*, but they did formulate two propositions.

a) 'THE OCCURRENCE OF ANY ACT OF AGGRESSION IS ASSUMED TO REDUCE THE INSTIGATION TO AGGRESSION'

(ibid., p. 36). It may be noted in connection with this proposition that no mention is made of the aggressive act being successful in attaining its object. Presumably, however, it is intended by the authors to be read with the implication that the aggressive act will be 'successful' in inflicting injury on its object. In evaluating studies relating to this proposition it is important to remember that changes in aggressive behaviour may result from the interaction of several factors, and unless these factors are carefully controlled, the results are likely to be equivocal.

Three factors are of particular importance in connection with the catharsis hypothesis.

i) A careful distinction must be drawn between the strength of instigation to aggression, which is not directly measurable, and the level of overt aggressive behaviour. Thus, a subject whose overt level of aggressive behaviour is low could behave in this way either because he has only a weak instigation to aggressive behaviour or because he has a high instigation to inhibition of aggressive behaviour. Clearly, failure to make allowance for these distinctions could lead to ambiguous results.

ii) It must be clearly recognized that, unless the factor of inhibition is controlled, an *increase* in aggression following the expression of aggressive behaviour would not necessarily invalidate the catharsis hypothesis. Thus, if we place the subject in a situation where aggression may be freely expressed, a subject with high instigation to aggression and little inhibition of aggression might well show a reduction in aggressive behaviour over a number of sessions. However, a person with high instigation to aggression and high inhibition of the expression of that aggression, might very well show an *increase* in aggressive behaviour over a number of sessions because the permissiveness of the situation reduces inhibition (i.e. there is no expectation of punishment).

iii) Finally, the empirical demonstration that aggressive behaviour shows a decline if it is expressed freely does not in itself constitute proof of the catharsis hypothesis. We have already seen that the expression of aggression may arouse counter-aggression and inhibition and it is quite possible that even the expression of aggression in a permissive situation may give rise to anxiety and hence lead to inhibition. Thus, initially aggression may increase because of the lifting of inhibition, but the mere expression of aggression may lead to a re-imposition of the inhibition. Wurtz (1960) has even suggested that anxiety induced by aggressive behaviour which has been punished may, by classical conditioning, tend to evoke aggression, that is, anxiety may serve both as an inhibitor of, and stimulus to, aggression.

It is obvious, therefore, that the three factors of strength of instigation to aggression, strength of instigation to the inhibition of aggression (the resultant of these two factors being the expressed aggressive behaviour), and 'aggression-anxiety', as it has been called, must be controlled or separately evaluated and partialled out, if necessary, in any study of catharsis. It is unfortunate that most of the relevant studies on catharsis are inconclusive because of failure to control these factors.

Feshbach (1956) divided children aged 5–8 years into High Aggression and Low Aggression groups on the basis of behaviour ratings. They were then randomly assigned to one of three situations. The *Aggressive Toy Group* was given four 50-minute sessions at each of which a record was played, a story read, and free play was then allowed. A different aggressive theme (Indians, cowboys, soldiers, and pirates) was chosen for each session and the children's behaviour during free play was rated for aggressive acts. The *Neutral Toy Group* was treated in the same way, except that the four themes were trains, circus, farm, and store. The *Control Group*, of course, was given only the free play. Now, Feshbach himself points out that two opposite predictions can be made concerning changes in aggressive behaviour over the four sessions. In terms of the catharsis hypothesis, a *reduction* in the amount of aggressive behaviour would be expected over time in the permissive free play situation. On the other hand, if the child's aggressiveness *outside* the free play situation were inhibited through anticipation of punishment, then an *increase* in aggressive behaviour would be expected in the free play situation. For Feshbach's two groups, therefore, one would predict that the cathartic effect would be present in the High Aggression children to a greater extent than in the Low Aggression children, who would be expected (on the assumption that their aggression is inhibited) to show an increase in aggressive behaviour. The first effect was not found, i.e. there was no reduction in aggressive behaviour after the experimental sessions. However, the Low Aggression boys did show a significant increase in aggression in the free play situation. In the one case, the catharsis hypothesis is unsupported by the facts; in the other the difficulty of making a precise prediction is indicated. The difficulties, of course, are not insuperable and, as we have seen, both Murney (1955) and Dinwiddie (1955) were largely successful in overcoming them.[24]

Some experiments have tried to overcome the difficulties referred to earlier by the experimental induction of hostility followed by catharsis or no-catharsis opportunity. Clearly, however, such studies must control for individual differences in hostility *prior to* the experimental induction and will also be affected by aggression-anxiety. Thibaut (1950), in the experiment previously described, found that the frustrated low-status teams, which were subsequently allowed to acquire high status, initially showed an increase in aggressive behaviour following success, followed by a decline, whereas the low-status teams whose frustration was allowed to persist showed a further decline in aggression after its demand for participation was rejected. In another experiment Thibaut and Coules (1952) induced hostility in the subject by means of a series of communications between the subject and a confederate of the experimenter. One group of subjeects was allowed to reply to the final very insulting communi-

[24] Earlier studies by Bach (1945) and by Appel (1942) are similarly open to several interpretations of the results. Feshbach also failed to make the distinction urged above when choosing his High and Low Groups.

cation from the confederate; the other group was not. Before and after this experimental procedure, the subject wrote a personality sketch of the confederate. When the sketches were analysed for hostile, friendly, and neutral comments towards the confederate, the results shown in Table 3.3 were found. The differential increase in

### TABLE 3.3

CHANGES IN FREQUENCY OF THREE CONTENT
CATEGORIES FOR TWO GROUPS

| Group | Pre-experimental sketches | | Post-experimental sketches | |
|---|---|---|---|---|
| | Mean | SD | Mean | SD |
| *I (Catharsis)* | | | | |
| Hostile | 30·9 | 22·9 | 67·6 | 19·1 |
| Friendly | 46·0 | 24·0 | 16·8 | 15·0 |
| Neutral | 23·1 | 14·8 | 15·6 | 16·0 |
| *II (Catharsis)* | | | | |
| Hostile | 33·2 | 30·4 | 75·5 | 20·4 |
| Friendly | 46·4 | 25·9 | 7·5 | 11·7 |
| Neutral | 20·4 | 21·9 | 17·0 | 16·7 |

Source: Thibaut, J., and Coules, J. 'The role of communication in the reduction of interpersonal hostility'. *J. abnorm. soc. Psychol.*, 1952, **47**, 770–7

hostility for the two groups is in the predicted direction but does not attain significance. However, the differential decrease in friendliness was in accordance with expectation and was significant. A second experiment, however, indicated that the differences shown in Table 3.3 were probably due to an increase in hostility on the part of the group not allowed to communicate after frustration, rather than to a *decrease* in hostility on the part of the communicating group. If this suggestion were verified, then the evidence would be against the catharsis hypothesis. It is also noteworthy that, in any event, the evidence would suggest only a minor role for catharsis, since *both* groups show very marked increases in aggressiveness following frustration, whether permitted catharsis or not.

Support for the catharsis hypothesis was obtained in an experiment by Pepitone and Reichling (1955). Subjects were exposed to frustration in the form of an extremely insulting lecturer. Following this, the lecturer left the room and the subjects were observed

G

through a one-way screen, various categories of behaviour being recorded (verbal hostility, neutral talk, and silent behaviour). It was found that the subjects expressing most hostility during the free period expressed greater *liking* for the instigator on his return than did subjects expressing least hostility. Again, however, the results are ambiguous, because of failure to control for aggression-anxiety and because of the assumption that there were no differences in prior instigation to aggression among the subjects.

Rosenbaum and de Charms (1960) exposed their subjects individually to verbal attack by a person unknown to them. One group was then forced to sit in silence, a second group was allowed to respond directly verbally, and a third group was allowed to hear another person attack the attacker. Each subject then wrote a sketch of the attacker from which a residual hostility score was calculated. Within each group sub-groups high and low in self-esteem were formed. No differences between the three groups high in self-esteem were found but reduced residual hostility following direct or vicarious communication was found for the groups low in self-esteem. The results are rendered equivocal, however, by the usual failure to obtain a pre-experimental measure of hostility level. Thus the very large difference in residual hostility score between the high and low self-esteem groups allowed no communication following attack may be regarded as indicating level of hostility in the absence of any means to reduce it. But if this is so then the high and low self-esteem groups *either* differed in amount of induced hostility (thus rendering the differences between the three groups high in self-esteem quite equivocal) *or* the groups high in self-esteem repressed hostility to an equal degree under all conditions. The results do, however, provide partial support for the catharsis hypothesis.

Finally, an experiment by Feshbach (1955) also supported the catharsis hypothesis. His hypothesis was that the 'fantasy expression of hostility will partially reduce situationally induced aggression' (p. 3). He used three groups, in two of which aggressive attitudes were induced by the experimenter's insulting behaviour. The *Insult Fantasy Group* was then given the opportunity of expressing its induced hostility indirectly through TAT stories, while the *Insult Control Group* was given neutral tasks. Both groups were then given the Rotter Sentence Completion Test and an attitude questionnaire and compared for amount of aggressive behaviour. A *Non-Insult Fantasy Group* was given only the TAT, followed by the Rotter and the questionnaire as a control for the effects of fantasy *per se*. Feshbach was able to show that the Insult Control Group showed significantly *less* aggression on the TAT, and significantly *more* aggression in the questionnaire than the Insult Fantasy Group, thus supporting the hypothesis. Feshbach considers that fantasy aggression may be drive-reducing either through response generalization from direct, overt aggression or through a gradient of reward: 'if in the past covert aggressive thoughts and wishes preceded and/or accompanied overt aggressive responses which were reinforced, then preceding covert verbal responses may acquire secondary reinforcing properties' (Feshbach, 1955, p. 10). A serious flaw in Feshbach's experimental design is his failure to equate his groups for attitude towards the instigator before frustration began.

On the other hand, a very carefully controlled experiment by A. E. Siegel (1956) failed to find any reduction in aggressive play activity following film-mediated fantasy aggression. However, it should be noted that aggression was directly induced in Siegel's subjects by showing a film with high aggressive content, rather than by inducing frustration.

This brings us to the end of our survey of the literature pertaining to the frustration-aggression hypothesis and we shall now turn briefly to some applications which have been made of the theory.

## II. APPLICATIONS OF FRUSTRATION-AGGRESSION THEORY

In the remainder of their book, Dollard *et al.* (1944) attempt to show that the frustration-aggression hypothesis may be fruitfully applied to a wide variety of phenomena. Thus, they discuss in turn the socialization process, adolescence, criminality, politics, and primitive culture patterns, adducing a wealth of evidence from a wide variety of sources. Here, we shall concern ourselves with one application only, for which experimental evidence is available, namely, the scapegoat theory of prejudice.

The most comprehensive statement of the scapegoat theory of prejudice has been made by Zawadski (1948). According to him, four stages are involved.[25] The first stage is the occurrence (presumably

[25] Zawadski himself does not regard these four stages as constituting an adequate conceptualization of a comprehensive account of a scapegoat theory or prejudice.

on repeated occasions) of the frustration-aggression sequence. The second stage involves the failure of the aggressive response to frustration, either through inhibition resulting from punishment of the aggression, or through running up against immovable inanimate circumstances. The third stage involves the consequent displacement of the aggressive response on to minority groups. The final stage involves the rationalization of the displaced hostility, which is usually unconscious and, therefore, not recognized as a prejudice, and may be justified in one or more of three ways. The prejudiced individual may blame the minority group for his own failures; may project his own feelings of guilt or anxiety on to the minority group; and may indulge in stereotyping, that is, he will tend to ignore individual differences within the minority group and treat all its members as alike. The minority group is chosen as the preferred displaced object because its members have some characteristics in common with the prejudiced individual (stimulus generalization) and also because, being a minority group, it is less likely than other groups or individuals to be able to retaliate, i.e. the anticipation of punishment for aggression is small.

Put in this way, the hypothesis not only sounds reasonable but would seem to be relatively easy to test. Thus it would be predicted that if a group of individuals is frustrated and given the opportunity of displacing its aggression on to a minority group, it will do so. Again, it would be predicted that prejudiced individuals would show greater general aggressiveness than non-prejudiced individuals. Thirdly, it would seem to follow that prejudiced individuals would have a history of greater frustration than non-prejudiced individuals and that the formers' aggressive response to frustration would have been more often denied direct expression. However, the experimental investigation of the scapegoat theory of prejudice has proved unexpectedly difficult. Let us take as an example the prediction that the prejudiced subject, if frustrated, will show more aggressive behaviour than the unprejudiced individual. Two difficulties arise in testing this proposition. In the first place, the prejudiced individual may, as a result of many experiences, have learned to inhibit the direct expression of aggression, and may therefore show as little direct aggression under frustration as the unprejudiced person. Secondly, the prejudiced person may, by the displacement of aggression on to minority groups, actually discharge his aggressive responses in this way, and appear as a non-aggressive person in situations other than those involving prejudice. With these problems in mind we will now briefly survey the main experimental results.

Three studies have concerned themselves with the question whether frustrated aggressive feelings will be directed towards minority groups, if these groups are available. Miller and Bugelski (1948) frustrated individuals in camp by giving them long tests on a day during which they would usually go to the cinema and were particularly strongly motivated to go on this occasion. Attitudes towards Japanese and Mexicans before and after the frustration were measured by a rating scale on which the subject checks ten desirable and ten undesirable traits as being present or absent in the average Japanese and Mexican. Table 3.4 shows the results obtained, which

TABLE 3.4

MEAN CHANGE IN FAVOURABLE AND
UNFAVOURABLE TRAITS AFTER FRUSTRATION

|  | Favourable traits | | Unfavourable traits | |
| --- | --- | --- | --- | --- |
|  | Before | After | Before | After |
| Mean | 5·71<br>3·03 | 4·11<br>3·06 | 2·93<br>2·70 | 3·26<br>2·76 |
| C.R. | 2·05 | | 0·47 | |

Source: Miller, N. E., and Bugelski, R. 'Minor studies of aggression: II. The influence of frustrations imposed by the in-group on attitudes expressed towards out-groups'. *J. Psychol.*, 1948, **25**, 437–42

indicate a decline in the number of *favourable* traits checked after frustration, but no change in the number of unfavourable traits. Stagner and Congdon (1955), however, were unable to repeat these results, but point out several important differences between their experiment and the earlier one.[26] Cowen *et al.* (1959), however, allowed for these differences in their recent study, and were able to demonstrate a significant increase in anti-Negro prejudice following frustration on an insoluble problem. They, in turn, point out the

[26] The principal differences in the later study were: the level of frustration was probably less; the frustrating situation may have been perceived as non-arbitrary (i.e. justified) rather than arbitrary by the subjects; aggression may have been directed against the self instead of outwardly; and the high level of intelligence of the group may have led to their interpreting the frustration in a rational way.

possible operation of certain factors which might account for these differences.[27]

A group of studies has been concerned with what might be termed the correlates of prejudiced attitudes. All of these really refer, in one way or another, to personality characteristics of prejudiced persons. Thus, Mussen (1950) correlated amount of aggression shown in TAT stories with prejudice revealed towards Negro boys on two attitude tests before and after white and Negro boys had spent some time together in camp. He found that aggression and prejudice correlated together $+\cdot39$ before the camp, and $+\cdot59$ after the camp. Furthermore, boys high in prejudice *before* contact with Negroes 'had more aggressive and dominance needs, more hostility towards their parents, and more feelings of aggressive press from the environment than boys who were low in prejudice' (Mussen, 1950, p. 440). These findings are equivocal, of course, since they may demonstrate merely that there are individual differences in a trait of general aggressiveness.

This difficulty was recognized by Lindzey (1950) who attempted to test three propositions: high-prejudice subjects will displace aggression more readily than low-prejudice subjects; will show more outwardly directed aggression; and will have a lower frustration threshold. As with Mussen, aggression was measured by analysis of TAT stories, but also by several other methods. Lindzey could find no differences between the groups in degree of outwardly expressed aggression, and no difference in tendency towards displacement, though he was able to show that aggression will be displaced if its direct expression is denied. He did, however, find that the prejudiced person has a lower frustration threshold. Lindzey suggests that prejudiced persons may have already displaced their aggression upon minority group members and hence in unrelated situations do not appear in general more aggressive nor displace aggression more than low-prejudice persons.[28]

With such factors generally uncontrolled, it is not surprising that conflicting results have been obtained by different investigators.

---

[27] Most important of these was the influence of the social desirability variable, discussed below. Thus, Stagner and Congdon used strong evaluative terms (e.g. kind-cruel), forcing their subjects to choose between two extreme characterizations.

[28] Although Lindzey expresses dissatisfaction with this *ad hoc* hypothesis, it is by no means an unreasonable one, and not without parallels in other fields. Thus, the paranoid person may appear perfectly reasonable and normal until the 'complex' relating to his delusions is touched upon.

Thus, Lesser (1958b), using a sociometric procedure to measure anti-Semitism, obtained a correlation of +·60 between extrapunitiveness on the Rosenzweig P–F Scale and anti-Semitism score for non-Jewish boys. Gough (1951), on the other hand, could find no difference in extrapunitiveness between high and low scorers on the Levinson–Sanford Scale of anti-Semitism. In a more extensive study, Morse and Allport (1952) used three scales of anti-Semitism (hostility, i.e. tendency to exclude Jews from own group; anti-locution, i.e. making unfavourable statements about Jews; and aversion, i.e. tendency to avoid Jews) and attempted to relate the three kinds of prejudice to seven criterion factors logically independent of anti-Semitism. Three of the hypothesized causal variables are relevant here:

i) *Anti-Semitism varies directly with feelings of self-frustration*, where by 'self-frustration' is meant 'the generalized and characteristic feeling of *self*-blocking, which results probably from inhibitions, fears, and the like' (p. 209).

ii) *Anti-Semitism varies directly with feelings of frustration whose explanation of source is unwarrantedly assigned to some external agent or condition (projected frustration).*

iii) *Anti-Semitism varies directly with circumstance frustration*, where 'circumstances' frustration is defined as 'the extent to which the individual is actually blocked by other individuals and by other circumstances' (p. 210).

The results of this study are indicated in Table 3.5. Taken with other results not presented here, Morse and Allport concluded that:

> If frustration is taken to mean circumstance frustration and anti-Semitism is taken to mean discrimination, we find that the association of circumstance frustration and hostility (discrimination) requires an accompaniment of either national involvement or of personality insecurity[29] to be significant. . . . If those who use the frustration-aggression theory to explain anti-Semitism mean frustration through conscious inner difficulties and conflicts, i.e. frustration feelings as a characteristic of personality, they are using a theory which has no support at all from our results. . . .
> The 'scape-goat' theory, which attempts to explain anti-Semitism by *unconscious* mechanisms such as projected and displaced blame

[29] Morse and Allport showed in their paper that the most significant factors in producing anti-Semitism are (1) national involvement; (2) differential loyalty to Americans; and (3) personality insecurity.

## TABLE 3.5

COVARIATION OF ANTI-SEMITISM WITH THREE
HYPOTHESIZED CAUSAL FACTORS

| Causal factors | Self-frustration | Projected frustration | Circumstance frustration |
|---|---|---|---|
| Hostility | 0·00 | 0·07 | 0·27** |
| Anti-Locution | 0·02 | 0·03 | −0·19* |
| Aversion | 0·19* | 0·18* | 0·08 |

\* Significant at ·05 level
\*\* Significant at ·01 level

Source: Morse, N. C., and Allport, F. H. 'The causation of anti-Semitism: an investigation of seven hypotheses'. *J. Psychol.*, 1952, **34**, 197–233

for inner frustration, guilt feelings, and the like, received only slightly more support (Morse and Allport, 1952, p. 226).

Much in line with these findings, Gough (1951) could find no significant correlation between anti-Semitism and intro-punitiveness, impunitiveness, obstacle-dominance, ego-defensiveness, or need-persistence.

The victims of prejudice, of course, are themselves being frustrated continuously and it would follow from this that members of minority groups who perceive themselves as the victims of prejudice should in turn manifest prejudiced attitudes towards other minority groups, since the victim of prejudice is usually in no position to indulge his aggressive feelings directly against his tormentor. Allport and Kramer (1946) related reported degree of victimization with degree of prejudice against other minority groups. The results for more and less victimized Catholics with respect to their anti-Negro

## TABLE 3.6

PERCENTAGES OF MORE VICTIMIZED AND LESS VICTIMIZED
CATHOLIC SUBJECTS WHO FALL INTO THE LESS PREJUDICED
AND MORE PREJUDICED HALF OF THE ANTI-NEGRO SCALE

| Group | N | Less anti-Negro | More anti-Negro |
|---|---|---|---|
| More victimized | 54 (52) | 22 (34·6) | 78 (65·4) |
| Less victimized | 53 (84) | 38 (45·2) | 62 (54·8) |

Sources: Allport, G. W., and Kramer, B. M. 'Some roots of prejudice'. *J. Psychol.*, 1946, **22**, 9–39; and (in brackets) Rosenblith, J. F. 'A replication of "some roots of prejudice"'. *J. abnorm. soc. Psychol.*, 1949, **44**, 470–89

prejudices are shown in Table 3.6, with the results of Rosenblith's (1949) repetition of the study in brackets. It is clear that the hypothesis is supported (similar results were found for the anti-Semitic scale). Allport and Kramer did not find wholly unequivocal results, however. Thus, the more victimized Jewish subjects tended to turn their aggression against their own group, i.e. to be more anti-Semitic than less victimized Jews, but at the same time might be *more*, or *less*, prejudiced against Negroes. Frustrated members of minority groups, in other words, may develop more sympathy towards other minority groups, rather than displace their aggression on to them. Lesser (1958b) found a correlation of $+\cdot48$ between extrapunitiveness and anti-Semitism *for Jewish boys*, which may help to account for these results of Allport and Kramer.

A study by Feshbach and Singer (1957) suggests that an important neglected variable in the study of the scapegoat theory of prejudice lies in the nature of the frustrating situation and whether it involves personal or shared threats. They measured attitudes towards Negroes following a discussion of topics involving varying degrees of personal as opposed to shared threats. 'Personal threat' topics included (1) difficulties of adjustment in marriage; (2) possibility of the subject becoming mentally ill; and (3) possibility of severe personal injuries in a fire. 'Shared threat' topics included (1) effects of floods and hurricanes; (2) possibility of atomic war and its aftermath. Although their results were not entirely unequivocal, in general the hypothesis that communications arousing personal threats would result in an increase in social prejudice was supported.

Finally recent studies by Berkowitz (1959) and by Berkowitz and Holmes (1959) suggest that 'the tendency to displace aggression against an available target . . . may vary with (*a*) the personality characteristics of the frustrated individual, and (*b*) the individual's prior level of dislike for the potential target ' (Berkowitz and Holmes, 1959, p. 565). With regard to personality factors, Berkowitz (1959) holds that the highly prejudiced person will displace aggression more than the non-prejudiced person, *when both are in a frustrating situation which arouses an equal degree of hostility*. In other words, whether or not displacement occurs will be a function, not merely of the objective fact of frustration, nor of the availability of objects on which to displace, but also of the personality of the individual.[30]

---

[30] Berkowitz (1959) makes it quite clear that he is *adding* a factor to those postulated by the Yale school and discussed earlier, not denying their validity.

Berkowitz and Holmes (1959) investigated the influence of 'prior level of dislike for the potential target' on the generalization of hostility. The design of the experiment is shown in Table 3.7. Individuals

TABLE 3.7

DESIGN OF EXPERIMENT BY BERKOWITZ AND HOLMES

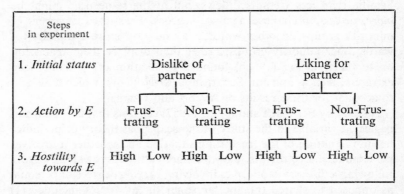

| Steps in experiment | | | | | | | | |
|---|---|---|---|---|---|---|---|---|
| 1. *Initial status* | Dislike of partner | | | | Liking for partner | | | |
| 2. *Action by E* | Frus-trating | | Non-Frus-trating | | Frus-trating | | Non-Frus-trating | |
| 3. *Hostility towards E* | High | Low | High | Low | High | Low | High | Low |

Source: Berkowitz, L., and Holmes, D. S. 'The generalization of hostility to disliked objects'. *J. Person.*, 1959, **27**, 565–77

were paired initially into two groups. In one group initial dislike of partner was induced by the subject receiving unjustified electric shocks, apparently from the partner. A questionnaire (Q1) given after the shocks was used as the basis for initial liking or disliking. Then each group was subdivided in terms of whether or not the subject was frustrated directly by the experimenter (who accused the subject of cheating). At this point a second questionnaire (Q2) was completed, and the four sub-groups further divided on the basis of degree of hostility shown towards the experimenter. In the final phase, the pairs of subjects worked together on a difficult practical problem and a final questionnaire (Q3) was then given. Berkowitz and Holme's hypothesis was that whether or not the aggression resulting from frustration by the experimenter would be displaced on to the subject's partner would be a function of initial induced liking or disliking, that is, that the displacement would not solely be a function of frustration. Using Q1 as a baseline for hostility towards partner, significant changes in the predicted direction were found for the comparison of Q1 with Q3, but not of Q1 with Q2. Berkowitz and Holmes were able to show also that the initial dislike for partner generalized to the experimenter and that the final contact with partner increased liking for him if he was previously liked; but increased dislike for him if he was previously disliked. Similar findings were reported in a later study by Berkowitz and Holmes (1960).

The recent studies by Berkowitz and his colleagues have given a new lease of life to the study of the relationship between aggression and prejudice. It is worth remembering, however, that the scapegoat theory of prejudice was never intended as a *sole* explanation of prejudice-formation and that as a partial explanation, with suitable modifications, the general evidence would appear to support its validity.

## III. CRITIQUE OF THE FRUSTRATION-AGGRESSION HYPOTHESIS

Since the frustration-aggression hypothesis with its ramifications employs the constructs of modern learning (especially Hullian) theory, any basic criticisms of it are coterminous with fundamental criticisms of such theories (e.g. Koch, 1954). We need not, therefore, go into them at this point. Instead, we shall look at the more specialized criticisms of the frustration-aggression theory which have been made since 1940. For the sake of convenience, we shall consider the criticisms under a number of rather loose headings.

a) THE MEASUREMENT OF AGGRESSIVE BEHAVIOUR

It is an extraordinary fact that very little direct experimental work has been carried out on this basic problem. Broadly speaking, three principal techniques have been used.

i) *Questionnaire measurement.* Buss and Durkee (1957) constructed scales for each of the following possible independent areas of hostile behaviour: assault; indirect hostility; irritability; negativism; resentment; suspicion; verbal hostility. By means of item-analysis they constructed a 75-item questionnaire, including 60 true and 15 false items.

Zaks and Walters (1959a) constructed a 12-item scale from an original pool of 33 items. These items discriminated between various criterion groups which would be expected, on *a priori* grounds, to differ in aggressiveness. Thus, the scale distinguished normal adults from prisoners convicted of crimes of violence and normal from delinquent adolescents. Its test-retest reliability was shown to be satisfactory. A later validation study (Walters and Zaks, 1959) showed that the scale discriminated successfully between situationally frustrated and non-frustrated groups; and between individuals rated by their peers as aggressive and individuals rated as non-aggressive.

It is interesting to note that the 12 items of the scale included none of the items from the original pool which were obviously indicative of aggressive tendencies, such as 'I often feel like smashing things'. The reasons for this are not difficult to imagine.[31]

ii) *Time sampling of behaviour.* Sears *et al.* (1940) used this technique in a study of subjects who underwent 24 hours of sleep deprivation. In some instances the observations were made through a one-way screen, at other times in the subjects' presence.

iii) *Analysis of fantasy.* Here the person's aggressive behaviour may be recorded directly or indirectly. Thus, in child-study, in particular, the child's aggressive responses in a doll-play situation may be recorded (Phillips, 1945; Pintler, 1945) and related to his behaviour in real life situations. In more indirect situations the child's fantasy productions may be recorded and analysed for aggressive content, e.g. by the use of the TAT (Lindzey, 1950; Child, Frank, and Storm, 1956; Gluck, 1955b; Lindzey and Tejesy, 1956); the Rorschach (Elizur, 1949; Gluck, 1955a; Towbin, 1959; Smith and Coleman, 1956); the Rosenzweig Picture Frustration Test (Gough, 1951); or cartoons (Patterson, 1960); and then related to his overt aggressive behaviour in various situations.

Miller (1941) has offered a valuable hint as to how the instigation to aggression may be determined if neither an overt nor a covert aggressive response is manifested. In the first place, the factors inhibiting aggression (e.g. fear of punishment) may be reduced, when the aggressive response will appear if present. Secondly, it may be possible to add to the present frustration, frustrating circumstances which have previously been shown *not* to elicit aggression because of their weakness. Summation of the two sets of stimuli may now produce an overt aggressive response, where neither separately was capable of doing so. These two methods are, of course, straight deductions from learning theory. While the second technique has

[31] Buss and Durkee also show quite clearly that in measuring hostility by questionnaire methods, the variable of social desirability (Edwards, 1953, 1957) must be considered carefully. If the alternative responses (e.g. hostile, non-hostile) are put to the subject in too crude a form, then he will almost invariably choose what is obviously the socially desirable or approved response. Allison and Hunt (1957) also note that subjects obtaining high scores on the Social Desirability Scale express aggressive tendencies to frustration only when to do so is regarded as socially acceptable.

received little attention, the first, as we have seen, has been employed widely.

b) IS THERE A GENERAL FACTOR OF AGGRESSIVENESS ?

Since so little systematic attention has been paid to the measurement of aggressive behaviour, it is not surprising that there have been few studies concerned with the generality of aggressiveness. Three strands of evidence may be mentioned.

i) *Questionnaire measurement*. Two different aspects of hostility have been measured by means of questionnaires.

(1) *General attitudes*. Buss and Durkee (1957) factor-analysed the eight scales previously referred to and rotated to simple structure.

TABLE 3.8

ROTATED FACTOR LOADINGS FOR MEN AND WOMEN

| Variable | Men | | | Women | | |
|---|---|---|---|---|---|---|
|  | I | II | $h^2$ | I | II | $h^2$ |
| Assault |  |  |  |  |  |  |
| Indirect hostility | ·17 | ·54 | ·27 | ·19 | ·61 | ·38 |
| Irritability | ·11 | ·40 | ·37 | ·00 | ·48 | ·38 |
| Negativism | ·23 | ·22 | ·25 | −·03 | ·48 | ·34 |
| Resentment | ·59 | ·12 | ·55 | ·57 | ·04 | ·45 |
| Suspicion | ·66 | −·02 | ·60 | ·54 | ·02 | ·45 |
| Verbal hostility | ·05 | ·63 | ·64 | ·04 | ·49 | ·44 |
| Guilt | ·29 | ·03 | ·14 | ·50 | ·28 | ·33 |

Source: Buss, A. H., and Durkee, A. 'An inventory for assessing different kinds of hostility'. *J. consult. Psychol.*, 1957, **21**, 343–99

The results for men and women separately are shown in Table 3.8. Factor I appears to define hostility in terms of its 'emotional' or attitudinal component; while Factor II appears to define hostility in terms of its 'motor' component.

More recent studies by Bendig (1961a, 1961b) and Sarason (1961) have confirmed (with minor reservations) the two factors isolated by Buss and Durkee, and have additionally shown them to be independent of emotionality or neuroticism, anxiety, and social desirability. The outlook is thus extremely promising as far as the measurement of hostile attitudes and behaviour is concerned.

(2) *Social attitudes*. The early work of Ferguson (1939), Stagner (1944a, 1944b, 1944c), and Eysenck (1944, 1947a) has been reviewed at some length by Eysenck (1950, 1954) and need not be detailed here. Briefly, Eysenck concludes from his surveys that there is a

general factor of 'aggressive attitudes' and that this general factor is derived from a combination of two 'primary social attitudes, namely, conservatism and tough-mindedness. The general factor is derived from the correlation of attitudes towards war, force, nationalism, fascism, intolerance, and capital punishment.' [32]

ii) *Fantasy measurement*. It will be remembered that Graham *et al*. (1951), using the sentence completion technique, measured the aggressiveness of response to five strengths of external instigation to aggression paired with five types of instigator-parent, sibling, friend or classmate, authority figure, and inferior. They obtained evidence for a general factor of aggressiveness by demonstrating high correlations between the aggressive scores towards the five types of instigator. Using a special set of ten TAT pictures designed to elicit fantasy aggression, Lesser (1958a) utilized Guttman's (1950) scalogram analysis and obtained a coefficient of reproducibility of ·91, indicating approximation to a perfect scale, and implying that the scale was measuring a unitary variable, which was presumably one of fantasy aggression. A much more extensive study of the TAT was reported by Murney (1955), who picked out all the needs and press indicating explicitly or implicitly aggression. The frequency of occurrence of each of these needs and press in five TAT stories was tabulated for the sample taking the test, tetrachoric correlations calculated and Thurstone's complete centroid method with rotation to simple structure carried out. One factor was interpreted as indicating 'hostile withdrawal' and a second factor as indicating 'aggressive responses'. These factors would seem to be essentially similar to those of Buss and Durkee (1957). [33]

Two important questions concerning fantasy aggression have not yet received the attention which they merit. Firstly, what is the relationship between 'behavioural' (or overt) aggression of various kinds, and fantasy aggression? Secondly, does the expression of fantasy aggression indicate enduring dispositions, or is it more often simply a temporary experimentally induced manifestation?

With regard to the first question, it will be clear from what has already been said that the relationship between fantasy and overt

---

[32] The interested reader is referred to Eysenck (1954) for a detailed review of the literature on social attitudes.

[33] Animal studies are not mentioned here, because the results seem unclear (see, for example, Hall and Klein (1942), Fredericson (1952), for opposing conclusions. Hall (1941) and more recently Scott (1958) have reviewed the animal literature.).

aggression will be a complex one, depending on at least three variables. Thus, we have already seen that in children the correlation will be (1) positive when parental permissiveness is high for the direct expression of aggression; but (2) negative when parental permissiveness is low (Lesser, 1957; R. R. Sears, 1951). In line with this result, Kagan (1956) found a positive relationship between fantasy and overt aggression in boys rated by the teacher as manifesting extreme overt aggression (this involves the assumption, of course, that high overt aggression involves low anticipation of, or at least fear of, punishment). On the assumption, already discussed, that lower-class parents are more tolerant of direct aggression, Mussen and Naylor (1954) predicted and found a significant positive correlation between overt and fantasy aggression in the children of such parents. Smith and Coleman (1956) reported a curvilinear correlation between hostile content in Rorschach protocols and indices of overt hostility, high and low amounts of hostility being correlated with a *low* incidence of overt hostility while average amounts of fantasy hostility were associated with a *high* incidence of overt hostile behaviour.

An important study by Patterson (1960), using cartoons as stimuli for aggression fantasy responses, attempted to obtain independent measures of aggressive fantasy (indicated by the occurrence of uncontrolled or controlled counter-aggression, or displaced aggression) and the inhibition of aggressive fantasy (indicated by the occurrence of reaction formation, passivity, dependency, and expectation of punishment). Patterson was able to show that an index which included measures of both these variables was able to predict the tendency to indulge in overt (behavioural aggression) better than either measure taken singly.

The interpretation of these results, however, is complicated by the operation of the third factor, namely, catharsis following the expression of aggression. Thus, the positive relationship between fantasy and overt aggression when permissiveness is high would be complicated by the fact that the overt expression of aggression would reduce the instigation to aggression of all other kinds, *including fantasy aggression*. The final correlation would, of course, also be a function of many other variables, especially the interaction of both stimulus and response generalization of aggressive tendencies. These difficulties may account for the conflicting results obtained by A. E. Siegel (1956) and Feshbach (1955). They both predicted that the expression of hostility in fantasy would reduce the expression of overt aggression. As we have already seen, Feshbach obtained positive results, but Siegel did not obtain comparable results in her study.

Finally, an important study by Jensen (1957) throws light on the second question posed above and offers further qualifications to those listed above. He used three groups of boys, designated by their teachers as respectively *bad aggressive, good aggressive,* or *passive.* The TAT stories of these groups were scored for aggressive themes; punishment of aggression; defence against aggression; and the direct expression of aggression (in the form of tabooed sex, violence, and language, content). Jensen found that the three groups did not differ either in the amount of fantasy aggression shown, or in the 'modifiers' of aggression (punishment themes, etc.). However, on every one of the ten TAT cards used, there was a direct relationship between the social expression of aggression (as rated by teachers) and the behaviour sample variables of the TAT (tabooed sex, violence, and language, content). Jensen's study is important for two reasons. Firstly, because it throws serious doubt on the general dynamic hypotheses that the non-aggressive, passive individual has inhibited his aggressive impulses and will therefore displace them in fantasy. Rather, it tends to support the notion of natural differences which reflect themselves *both* in ordinary social contact and in the TAT. Secondly, because Jensen points out that many of the studies previously discussed here have *induced temporary states of aggression in the subject experimentally* and therefore have failed to investigate the relationship between *habitual* behavioural aggression and fantasy aggression. As Jensen points out, the socially aggressive subject expresses his aggression on the TAT, but not through fantasy. Rather, his aggression is displayed directly through the occurrence of overt sexual content, words of violence, etc. The passive, non-aggressive subject, on the other hand, really is passive in general and therefore will not show fantasy aggression on the TAT *unless* he is temporarily frustrated *by the experimenter.*

Jensen's experiment throws some doubt, therefore, on the displacement hypothesis as a characteristic reaction following the inhibition of direct aggression, and stresses rather the influence on both direct and fantasy aggression of more enduring modes of reaction. It seems likely that many of the problems associated with this area of investigation of the frustration-aggression hypothesis would best be solved by a combination of careful experimental design, adequate *independent* measurement of all of the variables involved, and the application of factorial methods of analysis.

The evidence for a general factor of aggressiveness in humans, it is clear, is not as yet particularly compelling, except perhaps in the field of social attitudes, but the results obtained show a fair amount of agreement. There is an urgent need for studies comparing aggressiveness in different modalities.

c) 'UNLEARNED' AGGRESSIVE BEHAVIOUR

Whether or not a general trait of aggressiveness exists, the fact is that individuals are from time to time more or less aggressive in a variety of ways and in a variety of situations. Even if we assume the general validity of the frustration-aggression hypothesis, it still remains a problem as to how the aggressive behaviour is acquired. There is no unequivocal evidence supporting the occurrence of spontaneous ('unlearned') aggressive behaviour in animals and humans. In the animal field, for example, Fredericson (1950) found evidence of spontaneous fighting in male mice in the apparent absence of frustrating situations, but it was rare in female mice (Fredericson, 1952). Similarly, using rats, Hall and Klein (1942, p. 382) concluded that there was clear evidence 'that aggressiveness is a basic inborn temperamental trait or disposition', and this conclusion was supported by Seward (1945b).

Studies with young children indicate that there is a good deal of 'natural' aggression which manifests itself at a very early age (Bach, 1945; Baruch, 1941; Fite, 1940; Levy, 1937; Weiss-Frankl, 1941). Thus, in a recent study, Ammons and Ammons (1953) used a very simple doll-interview technique (in which the child is placed before a miniature playground but, instead of indulging in fantasy play, answers questions about hypothetical situations) and found a very high level of counter-aggression on the part of the child as early as age two and reaching a peak at age three. The important point, of course, concerns the relative lack of individual differences in aggressiveness at this early age. These results would be in line with the expectations of Bender *et al.* (1936), who studied individual case histories, answers to questionnaires about aggressiveness, and responses to toy situations and pictures. Their main conclusion was that initially aggression arises out of natural exploratory behaviour, and is therefore merely the obverse of constructiveness. In other words, the 'aggressive' young child may merely be trying to find out how a clock works when he takes it to pieces. According to this thesis, trouble

H

starts because the child's explorations are naturally in part suppressed (usually with punishment) by the parents. The child's exploratory aggressiveness then becomes displaced in aggressive verbalizations which in turn (being punished) are displaced into fantasy. (There is, of course, no quarrel here with the Yale school.)

Closely related to the question of 'unlearned' aggression are age and sex differences in aggressiveness. The investigation of these variables rather neatly illustrates the difficulties of drawing clear-cut conclusions from the available evidence. Perhaps the most extensive study in this area is that by P. S. Sears (1951), who exhaustively analysed the doll-play of normal pre-school children aged 3–5 years. She recorded the frequency, direction, content, and latency of doll-play aggression and related these dependent variables to the independent variables of sex, age, sibling status, and father's absence. Like almost all investigators in this field she found that boys are significantly more aggressive than girls at each age level. This fact in itself tells us nothing about the causation of aggressiveness. However, Sears also found that the mean difference in aggressiveness between boys and girls *increased* with age, boys, of course, gaining the more rapidly. Now Sears explains this change in terms of differential learning conditions. While this is most probably the correct explanation, the operation of constitutional factors cannot be ruled out. Thus boys might well be gaining more rapidly than girls in physical stature and strength at these ages. The issue could, in fact, be determined only by special experiments. This sex difference in aggressiveness has been confirmed by many other workers for fantasy aggression (e.g. Hartup and Himeno, 1959; Levin and Sears, 1956); but the results for behavioural aggression are not so clear (McKee and Leader, 1955).

With respect to age, the results are often contradictory for reasons which will be clear from our discussion of the influence of child-training and cultural practices on aggression. Thus, Walters *et al.* (1957), using direct observation of behaviour, found that aggressive responses (both physical and verbal) increased steadily for boys from 2 to 5 years, but this was only the case for verbal aggression in girls. MeKee and Leader (1955), however, found no such differences in behavioural aggressiveness over the same age range. Lebo and Lebo (1957) found that six-year-old children made the majority of aggressive verbalizations while twelve-year-olds made the least. In doll-play, P. S. Sears found little change in aggressive play from 3 to 5 years.

The picture is complicated by the facts that the *form* of aggression has been shown to change with age (Bridges, 1931; Green, 1933; Jersild and Markey, 1935; Fite, 1940; Ammons and Ammons, 1953), socio-economic status (McKee and Leader, 1955; Muste and Sharpe, 1947), sibling status and absence of father (P. S. Sears, 1951), and many other variables, which cannot be discussed here.

d) THE LEARNING OF AGGRESSION BY IDENTIFICATION

As Eysenck (1950) pointed out, aggressive attitudes and behaviour, whether individually generalized or not, could arise in a number of different ways. They could be the result of previously experienced frustrations and learned ways of responding to these frustrations; or they could be learned habits which are not necessarily the result of frustration, but of other processes such as identification or imitation; or, as we have seen, they could be learned contents based on innate predispositions. With regard to the second possibility unquestionably the most significant study is that of Levin and Sears (1956). The chain of reasoning presented by Levin and Sears is a complex one, but is well worth careful consideration. Six assumptions seem to be involved in their reasoning: (1) In the doll-play situation, the child can and does assume various roles, including those of his parents; (2) the child identifies with those people who reward and/or punish him, especially the parents; (3) in doll-play, he can act out his identifications and reveal his conception of the parent's roles; (4) since he will recognize parental aggression[34] and discriminate much from little aggression he should approximate in his doll-play the level of aggression he perceives to be characteristic of that parent; (5) the strongest identification will be with the like-sex parent by about the age of five (but this will be more difficult of achievement for boys, since both sexes initially identify with the mother); (6) the father's level of aggression will determine the frequency of aggression in the doll-play situation for boys, and the mother's level for girls. Further, perception of the father's level of aggression will be a function of the child's general perception of the male sex role as aggressive, and of personal experience of parental aggression.

Thus, for boys, the child-rearing antecedents of aggression should be: (1) degree of identification with parents, because the male role is the aggressive one; (2) severity of punishment, because this adds information in the form of perception of his father's level of aggression;

[34] Morgan and Gaier (1956) have presented direct evidence that children do recognize parental aggression.

(3) the father as chief disciplinarian, because this increases the distinctiveness of cues indicating that males are aggressive. For girls, on the other hand, the antecedents should be: (1) degree of identification with the parents, but only if the mother is aggressive, because the female role is not ordinarily seen as aggressive; (2) severity of punishment, because this provides an aggressive role model; (3) the mother as chief disciplinarian.

### TABLE 3.9

MEAN PERCENTAGE AGGRESSION IN TWO DOLL-PLAY
SESSIONS ACCORDING TO DEGREE OF IDENTIFICATION
AND AGENT OF PUNISHMENT (BOYS)

|  | High identification | | Low identification | |
|---|---|---|---|---|
|  | Father punishes | Mother punishes | Father punishes | Mother punishes |
| Session I | 20·8 | 13·8 | 8·0 | 12 |
| Session II | 27·3 | 23·7 | 15·6 | 23·6 |
| N | 36 | 24 | 28 | 38 |

Source: Levin, H., and Sears, R. R. 'Identification with parents as a determinant of doll-play aggression'. *Child Develpmt.*, 1956, **27**, 135–53

To test this general model, Levin and Sears gave 379 five-year-old children two sessions of doll-play and recorded the frequency of aggressive acts and neutral positive acts. They then related the aggression scores to ratings on three variables obtained during interviews with the mothers. These variables were: (1) degree of identification of child with parent; (2) severity of punishment for aggression towards parents; (3) which parent was the usual punisher. The results for aggression in the case of boys are shown in Table 3.9. High identification with father does correlate with high aggressiveness in doll-play, but severity of punishment did not influence aggression in this study. The results for girls were less clear cut, but there appeared to be an interaction between severity of punishment and mother-as-agent, i.e. girls are aggressive only if the mother is aggressive also. Thus, it is clear that the child can learn to be aggressive by identifying with the parent and in the absence of frustration.

  e) COGNITIVE FACTORS AND AGGRESSION

The frustration-aggression hypothesis has been criticized on the grounds that it fails to take account of cognitive factors. Thus, Pastore (1950) argued that the factor of reasonableness or unreasonableness of the situation, *from the point of view of the subject*, is involved as a necessary condition in determining whether or not a frustrating situation leads to aggression. A frustrating situation may well be tolerated if the subject understands the reason for it. He goes on to criticize the studies of Sears, Hovland, and Miller (1940) and of Miller and Bugelski (1948) on the grounds that the procedures must have seemed arbitrary and irrational to the subjects. He also points out that, in the sleep deprivation experiment, although the subjects of the experiment became aggressive, the experimenters, who also were deprived of sleep, did not! In a subsequent paper, Pastore (1952) repeated the work of Doob and Sears (1939), but included questions referring to both arbitrary and non-arbitrary situations. Thus, in the arbitrary situation, the statement might be: 'Your date phones at the last minute and breaks the appointment without an adequate explanation'; in the non-arbitrary: 'Your date phones at the last minute and breaks the appointment because he (or she) had suddenly become ill.' In the arbitrary situation, and using 10 items, the subjects chose the aggressive response an average of 6·34 times; whereas the corresponding figure for the non-arbitrary one was only 3·65. Very similar results were reported by Cohen (1955), and by Rothaus and Worchel (1960). Similar criticisms of the frustration-aggression theory have been made by Kaplan and Goodrich (1957), who stressed the importance of cognitive misinterpretation of what objectively might be a quite innocuous situation and by Ichheiser (1950), who pointed out that a response labelled 'aggressive' by the experimenter, might to the subject simply be a defence against attack. Specifically, Ichheiser argued that the frustration-aggression hypothesis ignored (1) the difference between the perspective of the acting individual and the perspective of other people to whom this action refers; and (2) the role of misperceptions in the area of self-perception and social perception.

These objections can be overcome quite easily by stressing once again the distinction between a frustrating situation, and a frustrated individual. It is clear that, provided we have separate measures of these two variables, we can predict what situations are likely to frustrate one individual rather than another. In other words, whether or not a particular situation is reacted to as frustrating or not by a particular individual, will be a function *both* of the external situation and the past experiences and probably constitutional make-up of the individual. Whether individual differences in 'frustration threshold' are the product of constitutional factors, or learning, or both is a question which will be dealt with in a later chapter. It would, however, be quite unfair to the Yale school to accuse them of being unaware of this particular aspect of the problem.[35]

Two recent studies by Berkowitz (1960a, 1960b) have attacked cognitive factors rather more directly. Berkowitz suggests that the effect of repeated frustrations on hostility will depend on whether or not the frustration is expected. In his experiments, either hostility or friendliness was set up between two subjects by note-writing. The attitudes thus induced were then either *confirmed* or *contradicted* by further notes. Berkowitz hypothesized that if frustrating behaviour is expected on the basis of previous experience, hostility to the second act will be less than if such behaviour is 'out of character'. In accordance with the hypothesis, Berkowitz found appropriate change or lack of it. In terms of Berkowitz's judgemental theory (Berkowitz, 1960c) 'when a person makes a judgement, he essentially compares the stimulus with some standard, and a contrast effect occurs in this process to the extent that the stimulus differs from the standard' (Berkowitz, 1960b, p. 428). Thus, an unexpected frustration will, by contrast with the preceding friendliness, be perceived as more severe than would be the case if the frustration followed previous events of a similar kind.

Shapiro (1957) has tested the general hypothesis that 'aggressive and withdrawn children would differ in the degree to which they perceive the world to be threatening and in their perceptions of their resources for dealing with this threat' (p. 381). Specifically, he predicted that behaviourally aggressive children would: (1) 'estimate the size, strength, and ability of child figures to be greater than do withdrawn children and, similarly, estimate the size, strength, and ability of child figures to be greater in relation to those of the parental figures than do withdrawn children'; (2) 'expect punishment for various acts to be less severe than do withdrawn children'; (3) 'describe the immediate outcome of situations as more favourable than do withdrawn children' (p. 381). Using groups of aggressive, withdrawn, and well-adjusted normal boys, Shapiro was able to verify

---

[35] It should be noted that there is no inconsistency in talking about a frustrating situation which does not frustrate a particular individual any more than there is in talking about a learning situation in which no learning is taking place.

clearly only the third hypothesis, and to show that aggressive boys do perceive the child figure as significantly stronger than do withdrawn boys, as measured by the size of their figures. Thus there is some evidence that the cognitive expectations of aggressive children are different from those of withdrawn children and normal children.[36, 37]

f) INFLUENCE OF DIRECT TRAINING IN AGGRESSIVENESS

Davitz (1952) measured aggressiveness and constructiveness of play in a pre-frustration situation in two groups. He then trained one group in aggressiveness, the other in constructiveness. Both groups were then frustrated rather realistically, for fifteen minutes, and then given a period of free play again. The change in aggressiveness and constructiveness from the first to the second free-play situation was measured. It was found that the group trained in aggressiveness showed 14 gains, 5 losses, and 1 tie in ranking on constructiveness. The comparable figures for the group trained in constructiveness were 6 gains, 11 losses, and 3 ties in ranking on aggression; and 12 gains, 8 losses in ranking on constructiveness. Thus, it is clear that training can significantly influence behaviour following frustration.

A recent study by Simkins (1961) showed that aggressive verbal behaviour could be rather easily induced by operant conditioning techniques. Subjects were required to make up sentences using a given pronoun and one of two given verbs (one hostile, one neutral). Sentences which utilized the hostile verbs were reinforced either verbally or materially. Simkins found that, not only did the use of hostile verbs in preference to neutral verbs increase steadily during the training sessions, but the tendency generalized to test sentences *without further reinforcement*. It is hardly surprising therefore that, as we have seen, aggressive behaviour may be learned by the child within the family circle, if the parents consistently approve of the child's aggressive behaviour. Lövaas (1961) has shown that exposure to symbolic aggression produced a significant increase in the rate of responding to aggressive reinforcing stimuli.

g) METHODOLOGICAL CRITICISMS

Finally, we may consider briefly some of the criticisms on more

[36] Goldstein and Rawn (1957) did not find any change, following frustration, in line pressure or figure size in drawings but did find a significant increase in frequency of specific drawing details indicating aggression, such as threatening gestures.

[37] The importance of cognitive factors in the frustration-aggression theory of prejudice was stressed by Zawadski (1948) and worked out in some detail by Krech and Crutchfield (1948).

general grounds which have been urged against the frustration-aggression hpothesis.

i) The hypothesis was immediately criticized on the grounds that it suggested that the only consequence of frustration was aggression. This part of the hypothesis was quickly rephrased by Miller (1941) to read 'frustration produces instigations to a number of different types of response, one of which is an instigation to some form of aggression' (p. 338). Furthermore, 'if the instigations to other responses incompatible with aggression are stronger than the instigation to aggression, then these other responses will occur at first and prevent, at least temporarily, the occurrence of acts of aggression' (ibid., p. 339). If these first responses do not lead to a reduction of the original instigation (to a goal-response) they will extinguish and aggression becomes more likely (i.e. its rank in the hierarchy of responses becomes higher). This reformulation of the general hypothesis was, of course, essential, since the theory itself was couched in terms of Hullian learning constructs. Since the whole of this book is concerned with various kinds of reaction to frustration, we need not elaborate upon Miller's point further here.[38]

The important question does arise, however, as to what kinds of situations are most likely to call forth aggressive behaviour, either learned or innate. Perhaps the most important distinction here is that made between *privation* and *frustration*. As Mowrer (1949) has put it: 'it is doubtful if any primary drive is ordinarily strong enough alone to lead, when blocked or denied, to anger and aggression. It is only when there is appetitive involvement, and what may be called the *intent* to gratify the primary drive, that frustration can be experienced in full force' (p. 178).[39] Clearly this qualification is very similar to the distinction discussed earlier between arbitrary and non-arbitrary situations, and the cognitive element. Levy's (1941) distinction between physiological and social frustration stresses much the same point. Levy insists that physiological deprivation (e.g. the frustration of the sucking need in puppies and children) is only rarely followed by aggression. Frustration produces aggressive responses only where personal relationships are concerned. All of

---

[38] Sears (1941) has discussed briefly some of the non-aggressive reactions to frustration.

[39] Mowrer equates frustration with *deprivation*, i.e. 'a taking away or withholding of something that has been accepted as a desired objective, with full appetitive arousal' (Mowrer, 1949, p. 178). Notice carefully that the distinction between privation and deprivation (frustration) is identical with that made by other authors between deprivation (privation) and frustration.

these authors are in fact urging that aggression is primarily produced by the frustration of *secondary* drives, not primary drives, and particularly by the frustration of social relationships (Maslow, 1941) and it is interesting to notice that Hartup and Himeno (1959), in the study previously noted, showed that aggression could be produced by the simple technique of social isolation.

ii) The catharsis hypothesis has come in for a good deal of criticism and was particularly attacked by Morlan (1949). He pointed out a number of logically absurd predictions which followed from it, e.g. that hostility towards minority groups should be allowed expression, since this would lead to a general reduction of hostility on the part of the persecutors; whereas repression would simply constitute a further frustration, leading to a more explosive outbreak of hostility eventually. He also points out that Dollard himself originally maintained exactly the opposite theory, namely that the expression of aggression often leads to its strengthening, rather than the opposite. Morlan's arguments, however, can scarcely be accepted as a valid criticism of the frustration-aggression hypothesis. For one thing, the general catharsis hypothesis which he criticizes is obviously intended by the authors to apply, *other things being equal*, and it is well known that in psychology other things never are equal. Furthermore, it is important to distinguish here between the learning of aggression (which Morlan maintains could never occur if the catharsis hypothesis were true) and the performance of aggression. While the catharsis hypothesis will apply in both cases, in the former it may well be overcome by the increment of aggressive habit resulting from reinforced learning. The catharsis hypothesis is not logically absurd. It is difficult to test in an unequivocal manner.

iii) Finally, mention should be made of what is perhaps the most important criticism which can be made of the Yale school. It was first raised by Haner and Brown (1955), but is much more general than as stated by them. They point out that the term 'instigation to aggression', as used by Dollard *et al.*, refers to reaction potential (to use Hull's terms), but that all their *examples* of instigation to aggression refer only to the *drive* part of the equation and not to the habit part. Thus, instigation to Aggression $(_sE_r)$ is a function of aggressive drive (D) times strength of aggressive habit $(_sH_r)$ and clearly the reaction potential could vary widely both between persons (according to differences in strength of D and $_sH_r$) and *within one person*, depending in the latter case both upon the strength of aggressive drive (D) and the particular aggressive response or responses (habits, $_sH_r$) activated by the particular situation. Clearly independent measures of these variables are required. Equally clearly, however, the *effective* reaction potential ($_s\bar{E}_r$) in this system will be a function, not only of the two variables making up the reaction potential, but also of the two inhibitory variables forming part of the general Hullian equation. Thus, the drive to inhibit aggression ($I_r$) and the specific inhibiting habits (responses) already learned ($_sI_r$) will have to be separately measured, if individual differences in the face of the same situation are to be accounted for. Unless these variables are measured independently experimental results become very difficult to interpret, particularly where divergent results are obtained by different experiments. One example will suffice. Feshbach (1955) measured differences in aggressiveness following insult when groups were either allowed to express their hostility in fantasy following frustration, or were not allowed to express it. Significant differences were found. But Feshbach did not attempt to equate his subjects for initial level of aggression before frustration, i.e. he assumed his subjects were equated for *general* level of aggressive drive and strength of aggressive *habits*. Furthermore, he did not control for differences in the inhibitory variables, i.e. general level of drive to inhibit aggression and strength and kind of inhibitory habits. This catalogue could unfortunately be repeated for many of the studies previously mentioned. Although the problems involved are very considerable, serious efforts to solve them have been made, notably by Dinwiddie (1955) and Murney (1955), and the work of these authors showed certainly serve as a paradigm for the future.

One conclusion is certain, however. It is clear, on the basis of this review, that the charge of over-simplicity against the Yale school can no longer be maintained and in fairness to them it should be pointed out that there is not a hypothesis which has been tested since in this area of investigation which has not been directly deducible from their conceptual schema. We can see, therefore, that the propositions put forward by the Yale school have proved extremely profitable by the only valid test of the adequacy of a theory, that is, that it should mediate a large amount of significant experimental work. By this test the frustration-aggression theory passes with flying colours.[40]

[40] The author's indebtedness to the brilliant earlier reviews of this topic (Himmelweit, 1950, and Berkowitz, 1958) will be apparent to those who have studied these papers. The present survey, however, can claim to cover a wider field than either of the earlier reviews.

# Chapter 4

# FRUSTRATION AND REGRESSION

As Sears (1943) pointed out, the term 'regression' has been used to refer to a number of different phenomena. Sears himself distinguishes four fundamental forms of regression. The first of these he calls *object regression*, which may be defined as the return to an earlier fixation if a later form of the fixation is frustrated. Thus, if a man has a strong attachment to his mother, which he later transfers to his wife: then, if the attachment to the wife is frustrated, the man may regress to the earlier attachment. Sears translates this phenomenon into terms of secondary reward learning, i.e. 'those persons or objects that are associated with gratification become loved for themselves alone' (Sears, 1943, p. 78). Thus, the child originally fixates on the mother because of primary gratification; later, the mother alone becomes the object of fixation, even in the absence of primary rewards.[1]

The second form of regression Sears calls *drive regression*. This involves a change both of the object of fixation and of the erotogenic zone which served as the source of stimulation. Thus, the sexually frustrated husband may regress not only to the earlier mother fixation as object, but also to one of the earlier stages of development (anal, oral) postulated by Freud as involving fixation stages during development.

Both of the above forms of regression are derived directly from the writings of Freud. A third kind of regression, which may or may not be related to these two forms, has been extensively investigated by experimental psychologists, and is called *instrumental act regression*.[2] It would certainly be true to say that these experimental psychologists *hoped* that instrumental act regression would serve as an experimental paradigm of object regression as defined by Freud.

---

[1] Sears does not explain how the fixation persists in the absence of primary reward.

[2] Instrumental act regression has also been called *retrogression* by Lewin (Barker, Dembo, and Lewin, 1941), and *habit regression* by Mowrer (1940).

113

The fourth form of regression Sears prefers to call *primitivation* because it refers to a non-specific form of regression, the meaning of which will become clear shortly.

In this chapter, we shall deal firstly with the experiments of Lewin and his colleagues on 'primitivation' and then with the work on instrumental act regression and hypnotic age regression.

## I. REGRESSION AS A FORM
## OF PRIMITIVATION OF BEHAVIOUR

The most important study in this area is that by Barker, Dembo, and Lewin (1941),[3] which is concerned with the effects of frustration on the behaviour of young children in a controlled play situation.

It is important to notice first the meaning attached to the term 'regression' by BDL. They define regression as 'a primitivation of behaviour, a "going back" to a less mature state which the individual has already outgrown' (BDL, 1941, p. 1), which is clearly linked to (and is the reverse of) Lewin's theory of stages of development in young children. In particular, regression as defined by BDL does not refer to the reactivation of any *specific* response which has been previously acquired and then superseded by a later, more mature response. Such a situation is referred to by BDL as 'retrogression', a term used by Lewin more generally to indicate a return to a type of behaviour characteristic of a previous stage in the life history of *an individual*. In regression, however, the behaviour observed need not be identical, nor even similar to, any particular kind of behaviour shown by *the individual* at an earlier stage of development.

Regression, therefore, may be measured by reference to the behaviour characteristic of children *as a group* at a particular stage of development. Thus, a five-year-old child may be said to have regressed if his behaviour under frustration is similar to that of the average three-year-old child. Now development is characterized by a number of features:

1. Behaviour increases in the *variety* which it shows;
2. At the same time, this increasing variety of behaviour does not result in chaos, since it also becomes increasingly *organized*;

---

[3] For the sake of brevity, we shall refer to this study as that of BDL. A shortened version of the study may be found in Barker, Dembo, and Lewin (1943). The present discussion, however, is based entirely on the original monograph.

3. There is an *extension* of the Life Space, i.e. of the area of activities and interests which occupy the child's attention;
4. There is an increase in the interdependence in behaviour, i.e. in the extent to which different activities are brought together as a unit (whereas increased organization refers to *single* units of behaviour);
5. There is an increase in the realism of the child's behaviour. [4]

Thus, regression would be implied if a child under frustration showed such characteristics as a simplification of behaviour (less variety); a decrease in organization of the behavioural unit of action; a decrease in the areas of interest and activity; dedifferentiation [5] and decrease in the organization of the person; and a decrease in realism. [6]

BDL considered that the characteristics of development outlined above would manifest themselves particularly clearly in a situation which involved imaginative play; and that conversely, regression would also be apparent (under suitably controlled conditions) in such a situation. If constructiveness of play could be shown to be a function of increasing development (as indicated for instance by increase in chronological and mental age), then regression would be indicated in any situation where there was a decline in constructiveness of play. Furthermore, the use of the play situation has many other advantages – it lends itself to a reasonable degree of quantification of behaviour while at the same time preserving a situation which is a natural one as far as the child is concerned.

BDL's argument thus far may be summarized briefly: a frustration situation [7] may lead to an individual in that situation becoming frustrated. If this happens, then regression in behaviour will occur (1) towards the original goal of the person and/or (2) in regard to other forms of activity. Whether or not regression has occurred may be determined by an examination of the constructiveness of play in a controlled situation.

The experiment actually carried out by BDL is so well known that

[4] BDL admit that these five categories may not be independent of each other. For example, the extension of the life space could be a necessary consequence of the increasing variety and organization of behaviour.

[5] Differentiation refers to an increase in the number of units within the organism; dedifferentiation is the opposite process.

[6] A decrease in realism would be indicated, for example, by a failure in realistic perceptions, e.g. by the presence of misinterpretations, or even hallucinations.

[7] Like Maier, BDL distinguish quite clearly between a frustrating situation and a frustrated organism.

a brief description of the procedure will suffice. The subjects were 30 children with the characteristics shown in Table 4.1.

## TABLE 4.1

CHARACTERISTICS OF SAMPLE IN EXPERIMENT OF
BARKER, DEMBO, AND LEWIN (1941)

| G.A. (months) | | M.A. (months) | | I.Q. | |
|---|---|---|---|---|---|
| Mean | Range | Mean | Range | Mean | Range |
| 45·2 | 28·61 | 55·4 | 30–82 | 121·9 | 100–157 |

(n = 30)

Source: Barker, R. G., Dembo, T., and Lewin, K. 'Frustration and regression: an experiment with young children'. *Studies in Topological and Vector Psychology II*. State University of Iowa: *Studies in Child Welfare*, Vol. 18, No. 1, 1941

The experiment fell into two main parts:

### 1. Free play

The children were given 30 minutes of unrestricted play with a set of toys (set A).

### 2. Frustration

a) PRE-FRUSTRATION PERIOD

On the day following free play the children were again given set A, but these toys were now presented together with a much more attractive set of toys (set B). As soon as the child had become involved in play in this situation (about 5–15 minutes was allowed) the next step began.

b) FRUSTRATION PERIOD

The less attractive toys were removed to another part of the room, a wire mesh barrier was drawn down and ostentatiously padlocked so that the more attractive toys were not available for play, but were clearly visible behind the barrier. The child was now allowed to play with the toys of set A for 30 minutes.

c) POST-FRUSTRATION PERIOD

This period followed, being simply a situation in which the child was given a further opportunity to play with the more attractive toys, in order to nullify any severe effects of the frustration period.

The child's play and other behaviour was recorded independently by two observers, one seated in the room, one observing through a one-way screen from outside. The two records were combined into a single record for purposes of analysis. The records were then divided into 'psychologically significant units of activity' (ibid., p. 61) or units of action. Several units of action combined together constituted an 'episode of behaviour'. The units of action of several children were rated for 'constructivity' on a 7-point scale and the remaining records were then scored, using this rating scale. A mean constructivity score was thus derived for each child, by weighting in the duration of each play unit, according to the formula:

$$\text{Mean Cr.} = \frac{\Sigma\,[\text{Cr.(u)} \times \text{Dur.(u)}]}{\Sigma\,[\text{Dur.(u)}]}$$

where     Cr.(u) = constructiveness rating of a play unit;
         Dur.(u) = duration of a play unit;
and $\Sigma\,[\text{Dur.(u)}]$ = total duration of play.

The reliability of the scale was assessed in two ways: (*a*) by the correlation between constructiveness at different stages of free play, i.e.

for 1st and 2nd thirds, r = ·72
for 1st and 3rd thirds, r = ·39
for 2nd and 3rd thirds, r = ·48,

and (*b*) by correlating the constructiveness of play units of 'odd', with play units of 'even', length (i.e. play units of length 1–15 minutes were correlated with units of length 16–30 minutes, etc.). This correlation was ·79.

The validity of the scale was assessed by the correlation of constructiveness with mental age (r = ·73) and chronological age (r = ·79) in the free-play situation.

BDL distinguished two major kinds of activity which they proposed to analyse, and two major kinds of play. The two types of activity were (1) free activity, i.e. play with the accessible toys, or occupation with non-toy objects (diversions); and (2) barrier or escape behaviour, i.e. attempts to reach the inaccessible toys or attempts to 'leave the field' altogether. The two types of play they distinguished were 'primary' (where the child's whole attention is directed towards the toys), and 'secondary' (where the child both plays with the toys and simultaneously indulges in some other form of behaviour, such as talking to the experimenter).

BDL were able to show that there was a significant change in the frequency of occurrence of the various kinds of activity from the free-play to the frustration situation. These changes are shown in Table 4.2.

TABLE 4.2

FREQUENCY OF VARIOUS ACTIVITIES IN FREE
PLAY AND IN FRUSTRATION

| Activity | Mean time (seconds)[8] | | C.R. |
|---|---|---|---|
| | Free play | Frustration | |
| Barrier behaviour | 19·50 | 510·50 | 11·47 |
| Primary play | 1144·17 | 569·83 | 8·88 |
| Escape behaviour | 49·67 | 112·67 | 2·68 |
| Activities with E | 76·83 | 95·50 | 0·56 |
| Island behaviour | 36·17 | 52·00 | 0·77 |
| Activities at window | 36·67 | 38·50 | 0·04 |
| Looking and wandering | 26·50 | 18·17 | 0·71 |

Source: Barker, Dembo, and Lewin: op. cit.

It is clear that there is a significant increase in barrier and escape behaviour and a significant decrease in primary play in the frustration situation.

It was also shown that primary play was more constructive than secondary play (the mean constructiveness of primary play was 4·54; of secondary play 2·71).

Next, the authors showed that primary play showed a significant decline in constructiveness under frustrating conditions, as shown in Table 4.3.

Since primary play only is considered here, the lowered constructiveness cannot be accounted for solely by the increase in secondary play (which as we have seen is lower in constructiveness than primary play) under frustration, though the latter does seem to account for part of the decline. It was also shown that, although the length of the play unit declined in frustration, this did not account for the decrease in constructiveness.

So far BDL have concerned themselves with overall group changes

[8] The statistical treatment of the data is unsatisfactory throughout the monograph. Thus, although time scores usually require transformation to reduce skewness, no measures of dispersion are given in the above table, and significance estimates are frequently omitted.

### TABLE 4.3

CONSTRUCTIVENESS OF PRIMARY PLAY

|  | Free play | Frustration |
|---|---|---|
| Mean Cr. | 5·11 | 4·35 |
| SD | 0·28 | 0·31 |

Source: Barker, Dembo, and Lewin: op. cit.

from free play to frustration. As we pointed out before, however, they maintain also that the same objectively frustrating situation may frustrate individuals to a greater or lesser degree. For some children, the inaccessibility of the more attractive toys will be very frustrating indeed; for others, scarcely at all. We turn now, therefore, to a consideration of groups of 'strongly' frustrated children as compared with 'weakly' frustrated children. Two groups were formed and objectively defined by the amount of time spent in barrier and escape behaviour. A child showing a large change in such behaviour in the frustration situation as compared to the free-play situation was designated a 'strong frustration' individual and vice versa.[9]

Table 4.4 shows the change in activities from free play to frustration for the strong and weak groups.

It is clear from Table 4.4 that primary play relative to other 'free' activities diminishes in the frustration situation for the strong group, but not for the weak groups. Table 4.5 indicates that when the constructiveness of primary play alone is considered, there is a significant decline for the strong group, but not for the weak group.

It is also interesting to note that the strong frustration group showed higher constructiveness of play in the free-play situation than did the weak frustration group. Once again, the significant decline in constructiveness of play was not accountable for in terms of an

[9] This procedure is not very satisfactory in that a child with a large amount of escape behaviour (indicating intense frustration) in the free-play situation might show little increase in the frustration situation and hence be designated 'weakly' frustrated. It would probably have been simpler to choose the groups on the basis of barrier behaviour in the frustration situation alone. Secondly, it should be noted that only escape behaviour could be shown in the free-play situation since at that stage there was no barrier. However, it may be noted that in terms of *absolute* amount of barrier and escape behaviour *in the frustration situation* there is no overlap between the groups.

I

## TABLE 4.4

PERCENTAGE OF TOTAL EXPERIMENTAL TIME SPENT IN
VARIOUS ACTIVITIES FOR
STRONG AND WEAK FRUSTRATION GROUPS

|  | Strong | | Weak | |
|---|---|---|---|---|
|  | Free play | Frustration | Free play | Frustration |
| Barrier behaviour | 1·2 | 44·2 | 1·9 | 22·9 |
| Escape behaviour | 3·9 | 10·4 | 3·1 | 3·8 |
| Primary play | 86·1 | 62·7 | 86·2 | 87·4 |
| Play with E | 5·6 | 18·5 | 7·7 | 4·6 |
| Island behaviour | 2·9 | 9·7 | 2·4 | 2·9 |
| Window activity | 3·5 | 5·9 | 1·5 | 3·8 |
| Looking and wandering | 1·9 | 3·2 | 2·2 | 1·3 |

Source: Barker, Dembo, and Lewin: op. cit.

increase in secondary play nor a decrease in the length of the play units.

The data were further analysed in terms of *Episodes of Behaviour*. Here interest lay in the analysis of *changes* in the sequence of play over time. Thus a period of play in which barrier and escape behaviour predominated and only secondary play occurred was allocated to the lowest Episode category (I); the highest kind of Episode (V) indicated a period in which play predominated and practically no barrier or escape behaviour occurred. Mean constructiveness scores for each episode-level were calculated and showed a clear increase from the lowest to the highest episode, as shown in Table 4.6.

These results confirmed the previous analyses.

Finally, BDL investigated the relationship between emotional

## TABLE 4.5

CONSTRUCTIVENESS OF PRIMARY PLAY FOR STRONG
AND WEAK FRUSTRATION GROUPS

| Mean constructiveness | Free play | Frustration | C.R. |
|---|---|---|---|
| Weak frustration | 4·66 | 4·54 | 0·25 |
| Strong frustration | 5·36 | 4·25 | 4·97 |

Source: Barker, Dembo, and Lewin: op. cit.

## TABLE 4.6

### MEAN CONSTRUCTIVENESS OF EPISODES

| | Episode category | | | | |
|---|---|---|---|---|---|
| | I | II | III | IV | V |
| Mean Cr. | 1·81 | 3·31 | 4·19 | 4·43 | 5·63 |

Source: Barker, Dembo, and Lewin: op. cit.

behaviour and the occurrence of regression. Eighteen different kinds of behaviour (crying, whimpering, sighing, singing, laughing, etc.) were recorded and divided into two categories, those indicating satisfaction on the one hand, and dissatisfaction on the other. Each 'satisfying' item was given a value of $+1$; and each 'non-satisfying' action a value of $-1$, and this score weighted for length of unit as before. The total score for an individual represented his 'Mood Index'. Table 4.7 shows the main results.

It is clear that frustration leads to an alteration in emotional behaviour (from satisfaction to comparative dissatisfaction) and that the change is greater for the strong compared with the weak frustration group (again it is interesting to note that the strong frustration group shows a higher degree of satisfaction in the free-play situation than the weak frustration group, just as it showed a higher constructiveness).

## TABLE 4.7

### MEAN MOOD INDEX

| | Free play | Frustration | Difference |
|---|---|---|---|
| Mean mood index (MMI) | 259·17 | 44·83 | −214·33 |
| MMI – strong frustration group | 310·75 | 27·25 | −283·50 |
| MMI – weak frustration group | 156·00 | 80·00 | −76·00 |

Source: Barker, Dembo, and Lewin: op. cit.

The authors reserve judgement on the interpretation to be placed on these results in relation to their main problem. From the point of view of subsequent discussion, however, two things should be carefully noted. Firstly, there are two possible interpretations: (1)

that emotional behaviour is itself a form of regressed behaviour;[10] (2) that emotion can be considered to be a cause of regression.[11] BDL tentatively conclude that 'it seems to be possible to consider both the emotional behaviour and the lower constructiveness as behavioural symptoms of a regression of the person, brought about by some factors of the frustration situation' (ibid., p. 204) – in other words, they lean towards the first interpretation of negative emotional behaviour as a form of regression, not as a cause of regression. Secondly, it should be noted particularly that when constructing their episode categories, the authors found it necessary to include two special categories of behaviour, namely, real substitutes ($S_1$) and irreal substitutes ($S_2$). A real substitute includes 'episodes in which play with the available toys is either a substitute for, or a means of approach to, the inaccessible toys' (ibid., p. 163), e.g. 'fishing' through the barrier with the available fishing pole, pretending to catch the obstructed toys. An irreal substitute on the other hand involves 'episodes in which conversation about the toys occurs' but not including social attempts to obtain them. Now it was found that where real substitute activities took place in the frustration situation, the duration of happy actions increased markedly; where irreal substitute activities occurred, happy actions were less frequent.

The results for categories $S_1$ and $S_2$ suggest that in those cases where real substitutes occurred, emotional expressiveness became similar to that which would have occurred had the obstructed toys been obtained . . . in the cases of irreal substitutes . . . the occurrence of happy actions was much less frequent than in a completely satisfying situation. These findings suggest that irreal substitutes reduce the pain and tension of frustration, but do not supply the satisfactions of reality (ibid., p. 200).

The experiment carried out by BDL is justly famous.[12] Before passing on to a detailed criticism of it, however, two serious weaknesses should be pointed out, which, all other considerations apart, would indicate the utmost caution in accepting the results at their

[10] The wording is that of the monograph, but it would be more accurate to say that emotional behaviour may show regression or lowered constructiveness.

[11] Again, the form of expression is unfortunate. It would be better to say that certain kinds of emotional response can cause regression – clearly, the large *positive* score for the Mood Index in free play indicates that some emotional responses may facilitate play and other kinds impede it.

[12] Despite its fame, little attempt has been made to repeat the findings of BDL. A study by M. E. Wright (1942) did, however, replicate many of the findings reported above.

face value without independent replication. A basic proposition in the whole argument is that which accepts constructiveness of play as an index of developmental maturity. This presupposes a valid and reliable measure of constructiveness and its standardization for the appropriate age levels. It is, however, in just this respect that the study is weakest. The total number of children tested was only 30 and the numbers became small indeed when divided into age-groups (10 aged 2–3 years; 12 aged 3–4 years; 8 aged 4–5 years). Any mean changes in constructiveness based on such small numbers would have to be regarded very tentatively. Additionally, the group was a very highly selected one, all the children having an I.Q. of 100 or more (average I.Q. = 122). Secondly, the construction and use of the scale of constructiveness was not carried out in any very rigorous fashion and contamination could easily have occurred, since the scorers were the examiners who would have known which records referred to free play and which to frustration. The application of statistical tests of significance was not consistent and there was at least one instance of a difference being interpreted as a 'true' difference where a statistical test would have shown this not to be the case.[13] Finally there is lacking in their study an essential control group. It is possible that the decline in constructiveness could have been a function of practice effects leading to satiation, i.e. that during the second period of play with the original toys, constructiveness declines, not because of frustration, but simply because these toys have lost interest for the child as a result of his having played with them for so long. To control for this possibility, a control group would be required which would not be put in a frustration situation but would simply be given two periods of free play.

We turn now from these general defects to more specific criticisms of the study which argue that the results of the study lend themselves to interpretations other than that accepted by B.D.L. Two major alternative interpretations will be considered here.

Child and Waterhouse (1952) accept as reliable the finding that a frustration situation will lead on average to a decline in the constructiveness of play. The alternative explanation they put forward to account for the decline is that 'frustration of one activity will produce lowered quality of performance[14] in the second activity to the extent

---

[13] This is pointed out by Child and Waterhouse (1952).
[14] Child and Waterhouse use this term in preference to 'regression' since behaviour may vary in degree of organization both positively and negatively.

that it leads to the making of responses that are incompatible with or interfere with the responses of the second activity' (ibid., p. 353). With a good many of the arguments which Child and Waterhouse put forward in favour of their explanation of the findings we need not concern ourselves since they seem to be largely irrelevant to the main issue. Furthermore, some of their arguments are quite misleading. They argue, for example, that in an earlier paper Barker put forward 'essentially this interpretation . . . and it is the sole interpretation offered there for the lowered constructiveness found in the experiment' (ibid., p. 353). What Barker (1938) actually wrote, however, was that where there is 'a division of the perceptual-cognitive-motor functions between two simultaneous actions . . . the individual may day-dream or talk about his lost love while at the same time responding to the exigencies of the immediate reality' (p. 148), and hence this may lead to impaired efficiency or complete dominance of one mode of activity. Now it seems clear that here Barker is simply referring to what he later called secondary play, which by definition involves competing activities, e.g. the child plays with the toys but at the same time indulges in other behaviour. Since BDL are at some pains to stress that secondary play is less constructive than primary play it is obvious that they would not deny (1) that interfering or competing responses do occur as a result of frustration, or (2) that these responses result in a decrease in primary play and an increase in secondary play under frustration. Further it is clear that they accept barrier and escape behaviour as forms of competing or interfering responses. The point at issue therefore is not whether such responses occur but whether the constructiveness of primary play is lowered under frustration *solely* because of an increase in the number of interfering responses or for other reasons additionally. Child and Waterhouse spend a good deal of time showing that it is 'extremely likely that the children's play in the frustration period would be subjected to a great deal of interference' (ibid., p. 357) and that 'play with the toys of set A was in fact interfered with by other overt behaviour, more during the frustration period than during the free-play period' (ibid., p. 358). Both of these assertions and the accompanying evidence would be willingly admitted by BDL, but the evidence presented thus far by Child and Waterhouse in no way demonstrates that interfering responses actually did cause the lowered constructiveness of primary play in the frustration situation but only that they reduced the amount of primary play which took place by comparison with the free-play situation. Child and Water-house can only argue by analogy that since overt behaviour gave clear indications of interfering responses, it is reasonable to assume that such interference taking place covertly must have been responsible for the decline in constructiveness of play as well. This, of course, in no way follows – it could equally plausibly be argued that the competing responses manifest themselves only by an increase in secondary play (which by definition, as we have seen, involves competing responses) in frustration and that the decline in construc-tiveness in primary play is due to other causes entirely.

However, Child and Waterhouse do present further arguments which must be taken more seriously. They argue first that within the frustration situation itself 'variations in quality of performance are correlated with variations in the extent to which interfering re-sponses are being made' (ibid., p. 359). And they are able to show that 'the correlation between constructiveness of play and time spent in barrier and escape behaviour, during the frustration period is . . . —0·72' (ibid., p. 360).[15] Clearly, in terms of BDL's theory there should be no consistent relationship between these two variables. Similar findings apply to an analysis of episodes of behaviour under conditions of frustration.

Most importantly, Child and Waterhouse believe that their theory of competing responses mediates certain predictions relating to the behaviour of the children in the free-play situation (whereas the theory of BDL is more restricted in that it applies only to the conse-quences of frustration). More specifically, it follows from the inter-ference theory that primary play should be more constructive than secondary play in the free-play situation; and the difference is indeed highly significant in the predicted direction. Secondly, they predict, and find, that constructiveness of play is negatively correlated with time spent in other activities (r = —·83 with C.A. and M.A. par-tialled out).[16] The particular point of interest here is that the corre-lation is found in a non-frustration situation.

The importance of the alternative theory proposed by Child and Waterhouse is twofold. In the first place it seems to be a more in-clusive theory than that of Barker, Dembo, and Lewin in that it can account for important findings both in the free-play situation and in

[15] But only when the effects of chronological age and mental age are par-tialled out.

[16] 'Other activities' here refers to 'island' behaviour, etc., *not* to barrier be-haviour, since clearly the latter could not occur in the free-play situation.

the frustration situation. Secondly, and more importantly, it lies within the main body of learning theory and therefore enables us to relate these findings to many others. However, one very serious difficulty in the theory of Child and Waterhouse may be mentioned here. They make no mention whatever in their first paper of the fact that in the frustration situation, barrier and escape behaviour does not decline from beginning to end.[17] On the basis of orthodox learning theory we should expect the barrier and escape behaviour to extinguish rapidly *since it is never reinforced* in the frustration situation.

A study by Davis (1958), which purports to support the criticisms of Child and Waterhouse, may be mentioned here. According to Davis differential predictions concerning correlations between content categories can be made, following either BDL or Child and Waterhouse.

According to the BDL interpretation, those categories which are related to the strength of frustration would be negatively related to constructiveness. The BDL interpretation would therefore predict that the categories of mood satisfaction-unsatisfaction index and escape behaviour would correlate negatively with constructiveness. The CW[18] interpretation would predict that those categories which imply the strongest interference states would correlate negatively with constructiveness, specifically, that the category of barrier behaviour would correlate negatively with constructiveness (Davis, 1958, p. 505).

Making use of data provided in BDL's monograph, and calculating the appropriate correlations, Davis found a significant negative correlation between constructiveness and barrier behaviour, but nonsignificant correlations between Mood Index and constructiveness, and between Mood Index and escape behaviour. It is difficult to follow Davis's reasoning, or to accept his differential predictions. In the first place, BDL themselves report a significant increase in barrier behaviour following frustration (see Table 4.2). Secondly, as we have already seen, BDL formed their 'strong' and 'weak' frustration groups by calculating the difference in time spent in barrier and escape behaviour in free play and frustration, i.e. they actually

---

[17] This may be deduced indirectly from (1) BDL's demonstration that constructiveness of play does not decline within the frustration period; and (2) Child and Waterhouse's demonstration of a correlation of −·72 between constructiveness of play and amount of barrier and escape behaviour within the frustration situation.

[18] CW = Child and Waterhouse.

used barrier behaviour as a criterion of the amount of frustration. Since amount of frustration correlates negatively with degree of constructiveness it follows that *both* the CW and the BDL models would *predict* a negative correlation between constructiveness and amount of barrier behaviour. Hence Davis's prediction is not a crucial test.[19]

The second alternative explanation of the results of BDL's experiment derives from the fact that the study lacked a control group to partial out the possible effects of continued play activity *per se*. In other words, it has been argued that as play activity continues, and particularly if new toys are not made available, the constructiveness of play may decline, at first gradually, then more rapidly. In such circumstances, it would not be surprising if both the quality of the play declined and alternative activities replaced play with the toys.[20] Now it would be a mistake to suppose (as Child and Waterhouse (1952) appear to in their footnote reference to satiation as an alternative explanation) that BDL were unaware of the phenomenon of satiation and its possible relevance to their results. As is well known, the widespread used of the term 'satiation' derives primarily from its constant use by Lewin, whose students carried out a long series of experiments on the phenomenon long before the frustration experiment. Furthermore, in at least one instance, Lewin (1954, p. 932) explicitly asserted that 'if continued long enough, repetition may have the opposite effect, namely, a breaking-up of the larger units of actions, a dedifferentiation, unlearning, and disorganization similar to that of primitivation or degeneration. These processes are typical of psychological satiation and over-satiation'.

We need not here consider the literature on satiation in any detail[21] which has mainly concerned itself with non-play situations. Such evidence as there is is somewhat equivocal. Thus, using a simple peg-board task to a criterion of rejection and non-resumption of the task for at least 10 minutes, Burton (1941, 1942), using pre-school children, found a mean satiation time of about 35 minutes. The introduction of another child following satiation produced resumption

[19] This criticism of Davis is valid in terms of his own argument as stated above since barrier behaviour has been shown to be related to strength of frustration. It is true, however, that BDL also assert that barrier behaviour has no direct relation to strength of constructiveness (BDL, 1941, pp. 149–50). This assertion, however, is logically invalid, as shown above; and Davis's correlations support this conclusion.

[20] In this case, however, the causal sequence would be the *reverse* of the first alternative explanation.

[21] See Lewin (1935, pp. 254–7) or Lewin (1954, pp. 952–5) for brief accounts of the principal German literature on the subject.

of activity by the satiated child, the mean resumption value[22] being 34%. Now, although Burton did find that satiation took place, his results could quite easily be taken to favour a *rejection* of the hypothesis that BDL's results were due to satiation. In Burton's experiment satiation took on average 35 minutes to develop *on a simple repetitive task, without any social stimulation.*[23] BDL's children, on the other hand, were presented with many toys in a social atmosphere and their total play periods consisted of two separated sessions totalling less than an hour's play. Furthermore, Hayes (1958), also using simple single games, found that the occurrence of satiation was a direct function of the number of responses available to the child, a finding which again would indicate that satiation as such would be unlikely to account for BDL's findings. A study by Yarrow (1948), however, does suggest that the sheer repetition of play may produce a change in various categories. Two sessions of doll-play were given to three groups of pre-school children. For group A, two sessions of non-frustrating solitary play were given. For group B, a frustrating (failure) task was interpolated between the first and second free-play situations, while for group C, a 'satiation task' (placing pegs in a board) was inserted. Yarrow concluded that 'many types of behaviour changed simply as a result of the previous session of play' (Yarrow, 1948, p. 37).

The evidence, therefore, with respect to the satiation hypothesis is not conclusive. The results of Yarrow, however, and the fact that Lewin has on other occasions stated that satiation can lead to primitivation of behaviour, suggests the need for a repetition of the BDL study with the appropriate control group.

## II. INSTRUMENTAL ACT REGRESSION

The earliest direct experimentation on instrumental act regression appears to be that of Hamilton and Krechevsky (1933), who defined regression 'as a reversion to an earlier, well-established mode of behaviour, and persistence in that mode despite the relative inefficiency of that behaviour in solving the problem confronting the organism' (p. 238). They further assumed that for regressive behaviour to appear the subject must be placed in a strong emotional situation. In an attempt to demonstrate regression, they trained rats

---

[22] As measured by a comparison of the number of pegs inserted during the first 15 minutes of satiation and resumption periods.
[23] The experimenter having left the room after instructing the child.

to take a right turn in a T-maze. This initial habit was then replaced by a left turn in the same maze.[24] One group of rats was then shocked in the alley just before the choice-point; a control group continued to exercise the second habit. As would be expected, the control rats showed no change in response; but 11/18 experimental rats reverted immediately to the former response.[25] As a further control, a group of rats which had been taught only one response in the maze was similarly shocked in the alley just before the choice-point. All 19 of these rats fixated the *ongoing* response.

The experiment of Hamilton and Krechevsky clearly demonstrates what they call fixation, but it does not necessarily demonstrate regression, a fact of which the authors themselves were aware. It is equally plausible to argue that the rats merely fixated whatever response they were *about to make* at the moment of shock. Since the second habit at the point at which shock was introduced was not perfectly learned, it is possible that some rats in the experimental group were about to make a 'false' turn. This hypothesis would also account for the fact that more than one-third of the experimental animals fixated the *new* response.[26] Thus we arrive at the first important requirement in any experiment purporting to demonstrate regression: *the habit to which regression is expected must be so much less in strength than the ongoing habit that the probability of its evocation in the experimental situation (prior to the introduction of shock) is effectively nil.*

Sanders (1937) used the apparatus shown in Fig. 4.1, where the space between G1 and G2 represents a delay chamber. Sanders

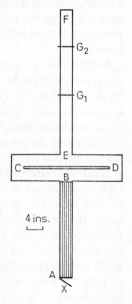

4 ins.

Fig. 4.1. Apparatus used in the experiment by Sanders. (Source: Sanders, M. J. 'An experimental demonstration of regression in the rat'. *J. exp. Psychol.*, 1937, **21**, 493–510.)

---

[24] The correct response in each case was taking the shorter arm of the maze, which was reversed for the learning of the second habit.

[25] There was no evidence of a tendency to *random* responses on the part of the experimental animals, i.e. the behaviour was not simply disorganized by the shock. Results similar to those of Hamilton and Krechevsky were found by O'Kelly (1940a) using the open-field situation, and by Duncan (1948).

[26] Precisely the same objections apply to O'Kelly's study.

strengthened the initially *preferred* (innate or natural) response of the animal to turn left or right at choice-point B, by differential delay in the chamber G1-G2. By a simple reversal of the differential delay, Sanders was then able to induce the animals to adopt a new habit opposite to their natural preference. In her attempt to demonstrate regression various procedures were used. Shock just before the choice-point led to reversion to the first habit in four out of five rats; however, shock *outside* the apparatus did not lead to regression. Both these results are in line with those of Hamilton and Krechevsky. A loud noise just before the choice-point produced equivocal results. Injections of caffeine and adrenalin did not produce regression. The fact that regression took place even when the second habit was overlearned by comparison with the first appears to meet the basic requirement laid down above. Finally, if after the animal had regressed it was shocked just before it made the regressive response, it did not revert to the second habit, but fixated the ongoing response. Sanders concluded from this that regression takes place to a type of behaviour ontogenetically lower than that regressed from.

Martin (1940) correctly criticized Sanders on the grounds that all her results except the initial one involving shock were contaminated by the fact that she used the same groups of rats in each experiment, a procedure which is quite inadmissible in this particular problem. He also made a notable advance in distinguishing between the natural preference of the rat and an old habit. Thus he first of all allowed the rat to manifest its natural preference (habit 1); then overtrained it on a habit opposite to its natural preference (habit 2); then trained it on a new habit *while it was being shocked in the starting alley* (habit 3). In this situation, the rats could either (1) regress to habit 1; (2) fixate the current habit 2; or (3) adopt the new habit 3. Martin found that the rats did not regress to habit 1, but tended to fixate on habit 2, as manifested by the longer time it took the rats to move from habit 2 to habit 3, compared with moving from habit 1 to habit 2. This fixation on habit 2 took place in spite of the similarity between habits 1 and 3. Martin interpreted these results to mean that 'untrained preferences and trained responses have the same kind of weight in determining the relative strength of responses under shock, and that whichever is greater in amount, will dominate' (Martin, 1940, p. 7). In a further experiment, he was able to demonstrate a direct correlation between the tendency to regression and the relative amounts of training on the preferred and trained responses.

The second important requirement of any regression experiment therefore is that *a clear distinction be made between natural preferences and learned preferences* (Aebli, 1952).

The importance of motivational determinants on regressive behaviour was further investigated in a series of experiments by O'Kelly (1940b). Habit 1 was learned under normal or reduced motivation, and in one instance was followed by shock. Similarly habit 2 was learned under normal or reduced motivation. After the criterion

TABLE 4.8

PATTERNS OF MOTIVATION, SHOCK, AND SATIATION IN
FIVE EXPERIMENTS BY O'KELLY (1940b)

| Experiment | Habit 1 | | Habit 2 | |
|---|---|---|---|---|
| | Motivation | Conditions after criterion is reached | Motivation | Conditions after criterion is reached |
| Control | Normal | — | Normal | Shock |
| 1 | Normal | Shock | Normal | Shock |
| 2 | Normal | — | Normal | Satiated |
| 3 | Reduced | — | Normal | Shock |
| 4 | Normal | — | Reduced | Shock |
| 5 | Reduced | — | Reduced | Shock |

Source: O'Kelly, L. I. 'An experimental study of regression: II. Some motivational determinants of regression and perseveration'. *J. comp. Psychol.*, 1940b, **30**, 55–95

of learning for habit 2 was reached, the usual shock in the approach alley was introduced, with one exception where the second habit was overlearned to satiation point. The various combinations used in O'Kelly's five experiments and a control experiment are shown in Table 4.8. The drive used was thirst, where reduced motivation indicates that 75% of the total daily intake was given half an hour before the experiment. In the control experiment, regression was expected and found in the usual way. In experiment 1 regression should be less than in the control experiment. In experiments 2, 4, and 5, regression should predominate, being most prominent in experiment 4. In experiment 3 perseveration should predominate.

All of these predictions were verified, except that in experiment 4, regression could not be demonstrated because all of the rats fixated the *initial* habit. Four points may be noted about O'Kelly's experiment. Firstly, he was able to demonstrate regression without the use of shock (experiment 2). Secondly, he was able to show that fixation and regression apparently varied according to the laws of learning, thus verifying Martin's contention. Thirdly, he maintained that the animal's behaviour was always an attempt at *rational* adjustment to the situation, i.e. that regression does not imply primitivation of behaviour but rather represents the most competent way of dealing with a problem situation. Fourthly, O'Kelly confirmed earlier findings that regression is by no means a universal response to shock under these experimental conditions. Both in this study, and a later one by O'Kelly and Biel (1940), perseveration responses (i.e. fixation of the ongoing response) were found to be more common than regression.

Mowrer (1940) also stressed the positive nature of regression in so far as behavioural changes are always progressive in the dynamic sense. In his experiment, a control group of rats learned to press a pedal to turn off a gradually increasing shock. The experimental group learned to sit up on their hind legs to avoid the shock and were then transferred to the habit of pressing the pedal. When pressing the pedal resulted in a slight shock Mowrer found that the control group continued to press the pedal, whereas the experimental group returned to the original habit of sitting up on their hind legs. Mowrer's results stressed the importance of previous learning in producing regression, since the control group showed no tendency to emulate the experimental group.

Now a common criticism of all of the experiments so far discussed is that they do not unequivocally demonstrate regression since the experimental situation seriously restricts the freedom of response of the animal. For example, in the experiment of Sanders (1937) and Martin (1940) the maze situation allows for only two responses to be made in the face of shock, i.e. a left turn or a right turn. If the animal reverts from the new to the old habit, therefore, it may simply be avoiding the response which has been shocked. We thus arrive at the third major requirement of any experiment on regression: *when the ongoing habit is frustrated (by shock, or satiation, etc.), provision must be made for habit progression as well as habit regression.*[27] The

[27] The term 'habit progression' is taken from Mowrer (1940).

only experiment to incorporate this requirement clearly[28] is that of Whiting and Mowrer (1943). They used the apparatus shown in Fig. 4.2. Nine groups of five rats each were used. In the first part of

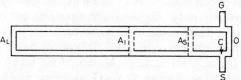

Fig. 4.2. Diagram of the elevated maze employed in the experiment by Whiting and Mowrer (the removable barriers are represented by dotted lines). (Source: Whiting, J. W. M., and Mowrer, O. H. 'Habit progression and regression – a laboratory study of some factors relevant to human socialization'. *J. comp. Psychol.*, 1943, **36**, 229–53.)

the experiment, each group was allowed to explore that part of the maze on which they were later to be trained (under conditions of non-reward). They were then trained to take the path S–G in preference to the short ($A_S$), intermediate ($A_I$), or long ($A_L$) paths. The second part of the experiment involved training the rats to abandon S–G and adopt S–$A_S$–G; S–$A_I$–G; or S–$A_L$–G instead. Nine groups were formed by using three methods of extinguishing S–G. For three groups S–G was not rewarded (groups SN, IN, and LN); for three groups S–G was blocked by a physical barrier at the point shown in Fig. 4.2 (groups SB, IB, and LB); and for three groups shock was provided midway between S–G (groups SP, IP, and LP).[29] In this way, each group *progressed* from S–G to one of the other alternative routes. In the third part of the experiment, all pathways were thrown open for 75 trials.

Whiting and Mowrer made six specific predictions:

1) Pathway S–G would be learned during initial training in preference to the other three pathways because (*a*) it was more quickly reinforced, and (*b*) it required less effort to reach the goal. This prediction was clearly verified.

2) When pathway S–G was no longer reinforced (through non-reward, shock, or blocking) the pathway S–$A_S$–G would be progressed to more readily than either of the other two; and pathway

[28] It would be unfair to the earlier experimenters to condemn them outright for failing to meet this requirement. Thus, in Sanders' experiment, the fact that the regressed response was not itself abandoned when shocked is presumptive evidence for the genuine occurrence of regression; as is the fact that the ongoing response was not actually prevented from occurring.

[29] During this part of the experiment, rats being trained to take an alternative route to S–G would find the other parts of the maze blocked off. Thus, groups SN, SB, and SP could take *only* S–G *or* S–As–G, but not the other alternatives.

S-$A_I$-G more readily than pathway S-$A_L$-G, for the same reasons as in the first case. This prediction was also verified.

3) Animals *shocked* for making an incorrect response would abandon S-G more readily than animals *non-rewarded*, because non-reward involves only fatigue, whereas punishment involves both fatigue and pain. This prediction was verified.

4) Under free choice conditions, following habit progression, regression to the original habit (S-G) would be most rapid in the group which had progressed to S-$A_L$-G, and least rapid in the group which had progressed to S-$A_S$-G, because the 'long' habit, having being acquired (as already demonstrated) with the greatest difficulty, would be the least stable. This crucial prediction was verified – the group shifted to S-$A_L$-G showed the greatest number of S-G runs under free choice and this difference persisted over all 75 trials. Furthermore it will be clear that the S-$A_L$-G group, during the free trials, *had available to them both the alternative pathways* (S-$A_S$-G, and S-$A_I$-G) and thus was not merely presented with only two possibilities of action.

5) The groups progressing to the new habit under shock conditions should show least regression under free choice conditions, because the new habit was reinforced by food, escape from shock, and escape from fear of shock, whereas the other groups were reinforced only by food. This prediction was verified.[30]

This brilliant experiment provides strong evidence for the occurrence of instrumental act regression in a situation in which all the factors previously shown to be important are carefully controlled. It is unfortunate that little attempt has been made to demonstrate whether or not instrumental act regression can take place in more general situations in animals, or whether it occurs in humans (as contrasted with the more general primitivation postulated by Lewin). Antonitis and Sher (1952), however, did demonstrate a phenomenon they called 'social regression' in rats. The animals were allowed to explore an area in one corner of which another rat was present in a cage. They were then repeatedly shocked in the centre of this area without being allowed to explore in the other rat's corner, but were able to escape the shock by running to other corners of the area. When they were replaced in the original situation (i.e. without shock and with all areas available), they showed a significant increase in

[30] The sixth prediction was related to the effects of 'forced' trials and is not relevant to this discussion.

tendency to spend time in the vicinity of the stimulus rat as compared with a simple test-retest control group, and a second control group which was retested after shock, but with the stimulus rat still absent. In a second experiment, Antonitis and Sher showed that whether this social regression occurred or not depended upon whether the shocked rats had had social experiences in early life.

In humans, instrumental act regression appears to have been demonstrated only by Barthol and Ku (1959). They taught two groups of subjects to utilize two different methods of tying a bowline knot to a criterion of five perfect trials in four seconds or less. The groups were then severely frustrated by being given a very difficult and prolonged intelligence test under very trying conditions and, following this, simply required to 'tie a knot'. Of the 18 subjects, 16 reverted to the first learned method.[31] It should be noted carefully that this demonstration of regression does not involve the actual prevention of one of the responses and is, in a sense, similar to the experiments of Sanders, and others, where the shock was given *before* the choice-point.[32]

There seems little reason to doubt that the phenomenon of instrumental act regression may occur in animals and humans and the simple demonstration of Barthol and Ku should lead to an increased interest in this aspect of regression in human beings.

## III. HYPNOTIC AGE REGRESSION

The alleged phenomenon of hypnotic age regression has been reviewed recently by the writer (Yates, 1961) and need not be considered in detail here. The phenomenon consists of the apparent reactivation of earlier forms of behaviour under hypnosis, when it is suggested to the subject that he is now, for example, four years old. The regression has been demonstrated in a variety of ways. A few direct comparisons have been made (Sarbin, 1950; Orne, 1951; True, 1949) in which the subject's performance under hypnosis in the regressed state has been compared with his known performance at the earlier age. More commonly, the comparison has been indirect, in

---

[31] It is interesting to note that no subject 'regressed' to simpler methods of tying a knot than the bowline method although the post-frustration instruction was deliberately left in a non-directive form.

[32] It is impossible to agree with the contention of Barthol and Ku that their demonstration refutes Lewin's notion of primitivation. Clearly the two phenomena could occur independently of each other.

K

that the subject's performance has been compared with that of the average child in the normal state at the age in question. Many measures of performance have been used, which the present author, in his review, divided into 'simulable' and 'non-simulable'. That is, it is clear that on some of the tests used the subject would be able to simulate[33] with a considerable degree of accuracy the performance of a young child, whereas on other tests simulation would be very much more difficult. Among the simulable tests which have been used are the Binet (Platonow, 1933); the Wechsler–Bellevue Intelligence Scale (Kline, 1951); the Otis Performance tests (Kline, 1950); and various kinds of motor tasks, such as drawing-a-man, etc. (Orne, 1951). In addition, the behaviour of the subject in the regressed state has been carefully observed (McCranie et al., 1955). Among the comparatively non-simulable measures used have been the Bender Gestalt (Crasilneck and Michael, 1957); the Rorschach test (Bergman et al., 1947); and physiological measures, such as the presence or absence of the plantar response (Gidro-Frank and Bowersbuch, 1948), the Babinski reflex and the EEG (McCranie et al., 1955).

The major controversy has centred around the question as to whether the change in behaviour which indubitably occurs under hypnosis represents a genuine regression to earlier forms of behaviour, or whether the subject is indulging in role-playing and attempting to 'play out' the hypnotist's suggestion that he is four years old to the best of his ability, making use of his own memories, general knowledge of how children in general behave at the age of four, and so on. In general, those psychologists who have investigated the phenomenon clinically (usually only on a single case) have supported the theory that genuine regression takes place; whereas those psychologists who have investigated the phenomenon experimentally have concluded that the crucial variable involved is that of role-playing.[34] As a result of the controversy, at least six conditions of testing have been utilized at one time or another. In addition to the extremes of performance in the waking state versus performance under hypnosis with regression to an earlier age directly suggested, subjects have been tested in the normal waking state with deliberate attempted

[33] It is not, of course, suggested that the subject is deliberately cheating.
[34] A notable exception is found in the experimental work of Kline (1953, 1954), who distinguishes between genuine regression (which he considers a well-established phenomenon) and spurious regression (i.e. that due to the subject playing a role), and the more recent studies of Reiff and Scheerer (1959).

recall of earlier events; in the normal waking state with instructions to simulate regression; in the standard hypnotic state without regression; and in the hypnotic state with instructions to simulate regression.

The principal results obtained can be stated very briefly. There can be no doubt that regression can be produced under hypnosis, the extent and accuracy of the regressed behaviour apparently being a function of the complexity of the responses reactivated. Regression has never been shown to be complete in the case of complex mental tests (Sarbin, 1950) but has been shown in the case of physiological functions in particular. Further, in a particularly impressive experiment, True (1949) regressed his subjects to ages 10, 7, and 4 years, and asked them on what day of the week their birthday and Christmas Day fell in that year. The results, as summarized in Table 4.9, show a remarkable degree of accuracy.

TABLE 4.9

PERCENTAGE OF SUBJECTS CORRECTLY IDENTIFYING
DAY OF BIRTHDAY AND CHRISTMAS DAY

| Age regressed to | Birthday | Christmas Day |
|---|---|---|
| 10 years | 92 | 94 |
| 7 years | 84 | 86 |
| 4 years | 62 | 76 |

Source: True, R. M. 'Experimental control in hypnotic age regression states'. Reprinted from *Science*, 1949, **110**, 583–4

Secondly, there is equally no doubt that regression can be produced in the waking state by asking the subject to simulate the suggested age. Thirdly, regression can be produced in the hypnotic state by asking the subject to simulate the suggested age level. Fourthly, when proper controls are applied, hypnosis appears to facilitate simulation, as compared with simulation in the waking state. Fifthly, there is no difference between the amount of regression obtained in the hypnotic state as between simulation and direct suggestion. The data of Crasilneck and Michael (1957), as shown in Table 4.10, summarize results for the Bender Gestalt test in these four conditions. All differences were significant, except that between the hypnotic states.

Various theories have been put forward to account for these results,

### TABLE 4.10

MEAN MATURATIONAL LEVEL ON BENDER GESTALT TEST
UNDER FOUR CONDITIONS OF REGRESSION

(Subjects regressed to 4 years under all conditions)

| Condition | Maturational level |
|-----------|--------------------|
| Normal waking state | 11·2 years |
| Waking state/simulated regression | 9·9 years |
| Hypnotic state/simulated regression | 7·8 years |
| Hypnotic state/suggested regression | 7·3 years |

Source: Crasilneck, H. B., and Michael, C. M. 'Performance on the Bender under hypnotic age regression'. *J. abnorm. soc. Psychol.*, 1957, **54**, 319–22

including neurological (Platonow, 1933; Kline, 1953), habit reactivation (Yates, 1961), and role-playing (Orne, 1951; Sarbin, 1950; Sarbin and Farberow, 1952) theories. So far, no convincing evidence in favour of any of these theories has been brought forward. As pointed out in the review article, a good deal more careful work is necessary in this field. It is curious, however, that little or no attempt has been made to link hypnotic age regression with instrumental act regression, on the one hand, and Lewin's theory of regression on the other. As has already been pointed out above, little experimental work on instrumental act regression has been carried out with humans, and it would seem obvious that the use of hypnosis could be combined with the instrumental act regression experimental situation to provide important evidence with respect to the reactivation of earlier habits when current habits are frustrated or (as in the case of hypnotic age regression) simply 'suggested out' of the individual. Since the phenomenon of hypnotic age regression is also potentially a powerful tool for throwing light on the more general issue in learning as to whether old habits are genuinely lost or destroyed, or simply inhibited (i.e. replaced by new habits but still available under special circumstances), the combination of the three areas of investigation discussed in this chapter would appear to offer rich rewards.

# Chapter 5
# CONFLICT

Investigations into the behaviour of organisms in conflict are virtually coterminous with the history of experimental psychology. Since an individual may be regarded as being in a state of conflict whenever alternative modes of reaction are simultaneously open to him, practically any experimental situation other than the most simple may be regarded as involving conflict. In this chapter, we shall, however, confine our attention to the most important systematic treatments of conflict, commencing briefly with the work of Luria (1932), then passing on to the important investigations of Lewin (1935) and Miller (1944, 1951, 1959) and his co-workers, with finally a brief glance at Hull's (1952) account of approach and avoidance behaviour, and some recent work from the laboratory of Cattell (Williams, 1959).

## I. LURIA'S ANALYSIS OF CONFLICT

Luria's work is important for two reasons. In the first place, he extended Jung's original method of word-association as an indicator of conflict by devising a novel technique for measuring the motor disturbances accompanying conflict. In the second place, he carried out his work entirely on humans, devising many novel and important experimental situations.

Luria rejected the view that behaviour is simply the result of the interaction of excitatory and inhibitory tendencies and took generally an organismic viewpoint that the organization of behaviour must be viewed as a function of interacting regulating systems, the disturbance of any single regulating system changing the balance of forces of the total organism. He further rejected the viewpoint that emotional disturbance could be measured by means of the physiological changes which took place, since these were peripheral in nature. He argued against this view that the central changes involved in conflict situations can be measured only by the assessment of behavioural changes occurring. 'The effect appears when something happens with the organized phenomena of activity; therefore, it should be reasonable to hope to obtain a more adequate structure of the affective process by the investigation of the fate of the active functions connected with this process' (Luria, 1932, p. 17). To this end, he devised what he called the 'combined motor method' which involved the simultaneous recording of speech reactions to verbal stimuli of a neutral or non-neutral nature, together with records of the left- and right-hand motor movements. This method has come to be called the Luria technique and has been used fairly extensively in the original and modified forms since.[1] These records reflect what goes on in the 'latent period' between the stimulus and response words, and indicate whether the central transmission is smooth or disturbed.

To investigate the latent period Luria devised many ingenious experimental techniques. Under completely natural conditions, for example, he investigated the affective disturbances[2] in students undergoing political 'cleansing' examinations and ordinary school examinations; in criminals after arrest and before their guilt or innocence was established, and in abnormal subjects. In the laboratory, he investigated the motor concomitants of complexes produced by hypnotic suggestion, involving what he claimed were experimental neuroses. Thus, under hypnosis he would tell the subject he would have a strong desire to think of the names of animals. The subject being restored to the normal state, he would then be given the usual word-association test. Conflict would arise from the clash between the subject's tendency to give his usual responses to the stimulus words and the induced tendency to give names of animals. In the same vein, under hypnosis, the subject would be told he will think of certain words but be unable to say them. In the waking state, a chain associative series will be given (e.g. to think of the names of colours) such that the prohibited word is certain to arise. The conflict will then consist of opposed tendencies both to say and not to say the prohibited word.[3]

[1] A review of work with the Luria technique in abnormals will be found in Yates (1960).
[2] It should be noted that Luria tends not to distinguish between a conflict involving incompatible response tendencies (though many of his experiments clearly involve this) and a general affective disturbance.
[3] Some of Luria's most interesting findings occur in experiments such as these. If the prohibited word is 'red', for instance, the subject may say 'carmine'. Such central resolutions produce less disturbance than attempts to solve the problem directly through the motor apparatus.

On the intellectual side, Luria distinguished between conflicts of the setting, and conflicts of defection. In the former case, the main experiment involved the sudden introduction of a foreign word into a word-association series (with instructions to give a foreign word as a response).[4] In the latter case, the subject was required to produce a 'part' association to a 'whole' stimulus. After a number of such stimuli, an impossible word was introduced, thus:

1. house – (e.g. room)
2. forest – (e.g. tree)
3. moon – ?

In all of the situations described, conflict was induced in the subject, and was reflected in various kinds of motor disturbances, both of voluntary and involuntary motor responses. Luria considered that the disturbance of the motor system was not invariably present in affective disturbance.

The expressiveness of the motor system is greater, the more it is included in a conflicting system . . . it becomes less, with the diminution of its functional connection with the conflict . . . the affective *disorganization* of behaviour begins where the problem of cortical control by the direct diffusion of excitation arises (motor impulsiveness); it disappears where the action permits the direct motor discharge of impulses; the *affect* arises in the place where the conflict begins to be connected with activity (Luria, 1932, pp. 173–4).

We need not here discuss Luria's theory of conflict in any detail. According to him, '. . . the disorganization of behaviour arises only in the case where some fairly strong system of activity is subjected to inhibition' (ibid., p. 267). He distinguishes three major kinds of conflict:

1. That which arises when the excitation is prevented at the last moment from issuing into action (as in conflicts of the setting);
2. that which arises when the subject is unprepared for reacting (as in conflicts of defection);
3. that which arises when the suppressed activity is diverted into central processes.

[4] The disturbance here was not due to the foreign quality of the word *per se*, since it occurred also in the reverse case.

The most important concept formulated by Luria is that of the 'functional barrier'. In the early stages of development, the initial cortical excitation resulting from stimulation tends to diffuse through the entire cortex, and into the sub-cortex. In terms of motor behaviour, this is revealed by a deterioration of regular pressures into irregular pressures over a very short period of time. '. . . the whole development of the neurodynamics consists in the creation of a "functional barrier" separating the excitation from direct transfer to the motor system . . .' (ibid., 1932, p. 342). In other words, the functional barrier may be equated with the general growth of cortical regulatory processes. Under extreme stress, this functional barrier breaks down and the excitation resulting from the stimulus passes directly into the motor system.

This account of Luria's work, which is of great importance, has been brief because there can be little doubt that Luria's views on the nature of conflict have changed considerably over the years, though unfortunately his later investigations are not yet available in English.

## II. LEWIN'S ANALYSIS OF CONFLICT

Working within his own frame of reference, Lewin defined conflict in 'psychological' terms as 'the opposition of approximately equally strong field forces' (1935, p. 88) or, more fully, as 'a situation in which oppositely directed, simultaneously acting forces of approximately equal strength work upon the individual' (ibid., p. 122).

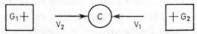

Fig. 5.1. Representation of an approach-approach conflict. (Source: Lewin, K. *A Dynamic Theory of Personality*. New York: McGraw-Hill, 1935.)

Lewin delineated three basic cases in which a conflict could be said to exist.

1) The person stands between two positive valences and is required to choose between them. It is represented in Fig. 5.1, where $G_1$ and $G_2$ are objects with positive valence and $V_1$ and $V_2$ represent the resulting forces acting on the person (C). In this type of conflict situation a decision is relatively easy, since the situation usually involves a condition of labile equilibrium. Hence, as soon as the person moves towards $G_1$ even a small distance, its valence increases further

compared with that of $G_2$ and there will be no tendency to turn back (type 1 conflict).[5]

2) The person is faced with an object which has both positive and negative valence and is required to choose between them. This situation is represented in Fig. 5.2. Thus the person is both attracted

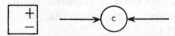

Fig. 5.2. Representation of an approach-avoidance conflict. (Source: Lewin, K. *A Dynamic Theory of Personality*. New York: McGraw-Hill, 1935.)

towards, and repelled by, the same object – a child, for instance, might want to stroke a dog, of which he is at the same time afraid (type 2 conflict).[6]

3) The person stands between two negative valences, and is required to choose between them. This situation is represented in Fig. 5.3. For example, a child might be required to carry out a task under threat of punishment (type 3 conflict).[7]

We should next note some important characteristics of such conflict situations. According to Lewin 'the strength of the field forces

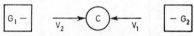

Fig. 5.3. Representation of an avoidance-avoidance conflict. (Source: Lewin, K. *A Dynamic Theory of Personality*. New York: McGraw-Hill, 1935.)

which correspond to the negative valence diminishes much more rapidly with increasing spatial distance than do the field forces corresponding to the positive valence' (1935, p. 52). Secondly, 'from the direction and strength of the field forces at the various points of the field it can be deduced that the child must move to the point P where equilibrium occurs (at all other points there exists a resultant which finally leads to P)' (ibid., p. 92). Thirdly, 'corresponding to the momentary oscillations of the situations, above all to the more or less threatening aspects [of the negative stimulus] this point of equilibrium approaches and retreats from [the stimulus with positive and negative valence]' (ibid., p. 92). Fourthly, 'the opposition of the two field forces in a conflict situation leads directly . . . to an increase in the total state of tension of the child' (ibid., p. 94).

[5] This type of conflict is now known as 'approach-approach' conflict.
[6] This type of conflict is now known as 'approach-avoidance' conflict.
[7] This type of conflict is now known as 'avoidance-avoidance' conflict.

Lewin has schematically applied these concepts in a number of ways, most importantly perhaps to a discussion of the psychological situations of reward and punishment. He contrasts reward and punishment on the one hand with behaviour determined by an original or derived interest in the goal itself. Reward and punishment are similar in that 'the child is required to perform an action, to behave in a certain way, other than that which at the moment he prefers' (ibid., p. 114).

Four possible situations are considered by Lewin:

a) COMMAND WITH THREAT OF PUNISHMENT

This situation may best be represented by Fig. 5.4.

In the situation represented, the child (C) is required to perform task (T) (having negative valence $V_T$) under threat of punishment

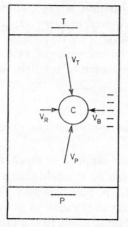

Fig. 5.4. Representation of a situation involving command with threat of punishment. (Source: Lewin, K. *A Dynamic Theory of Personality*. New York: McGraw-Hill, 1935.)

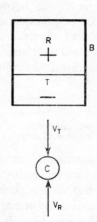

Fig. 5.5. Representation of a situation involving command with the prospect of reward. (Source: Lewin, K. *A Dynamic Theory of Personality*. New York: McGraw-Hill, 1935.)

(P), (the latter having negative valence $V_P$). The situation therefore clearly represents a conflict of type 3 (avoidance-avoidance). Lewin, however, goes much further than this. Placed between two strong negative valences, the child will naturally attempt to avoid both and hence to move out of the field. In order to force a decision, it is therefore necessary to erect a barrier around the total field situation.

This barrier may be physical (confinement in a room until the task is finished), psychological (parental threats), or ideological (appeal to the child's own values or goals). The attempt of the child to move out of the field ($V_R$) will result in its clashing with the barrier, which will therefore acquire a negative valence and hence set up a second conflict. Generally, 'the more intense the negative valence [of the task], the firmer must be the barrier' (ibid., p. 128). These opposed vectors are not isolated forces, but lead to an increase in the state of tension within the total situation.

Placed in a conflict situation of this kind, the child may react in one of a number of ways. He may execute the distasteful command (once this happens, the child has moved into a new field of forces in which, for example, the distasteful task may be seen as less distasteful). He may accept the punishment, he may act against the barrier, he may encyst (i.e. withdraw into) himself, indulge in unreal fantasy or suffer an emotional outburst.

b) COMMAND WITH PROSPECT OF REWARD

This situation may be represented as in Fig. 5.5.

In this situation, the child is faced with the prospect of reward, if he performs some distasteful act. Notice that in order to reach the object with positive valence the child must first pass through the region of negative valence – a barrier is therefore necessary, in order to prevent the child from attaining the object with positive valence by an indirect route. This situation corresponds to a conflict of type 2 (approach-avoidance). The reward vector ($V_R$) must be stronger than the unpleasant task vector ($V_T$) and its strength must vary with the unpleasantness of the task.

These two command situations are similar in that they both involve a conflict situation, increase of tension, a tendency to deviate from the unpleasant task (i.e. the need for barriers), and a lack of natural interest in performing the task. The most important difference lies in the fact that in the command/punishment situation the barrier surrounds the child as well as the task; whereas, in the command/reward situation the barrier surrounds only the reward. Thus, in the latter case the child's freedom of movement is much less restricted.

In the command/reward situation, the child's behaviour may vary from carrying out the task to the minimum extent compatible with obtaining the reward to abandoning the reward or trying to break through the barrier.

c) PROHIBITION WITH THREAT OF PUNISHMENT

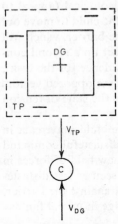

Fig. 5.6. Representation of a situation involving prohibition with a threat of punishment. (Source: Lewin, K. *A Dynamic Theory of Personality.* New York: McGraw-Hill, 1935.)

This situation is represented in Fig. 5.6. The important point to note in this example is that the punishment here does not stand before the reward (as in command/reward situations). Nor, on the other hand, does it stand behind the goal. Rather punishment is a hypothetical possibility (indicated by dotted lines in Fig. 5.6) until the child moves into the region of the desired goal. At this point, the situation changes and the child finds himself surrounded by a region of punishment, without actually first obtaining the goal. Thus, this situation is a conflict of type 2 (approach-avoidance), in which the task has both positive valence and negative valence.

d) PROHIBITION WITH PROSPECT OF REWARD

This situation is primarily a conflict of type 1 (approach-approach). A reward (positive valence) is offered for avoidance of some attractive object or activity (positive valence). However, as Lewin points out, there is also an element of punishment here, if the forbidden activity is indulged in. Thus, the situation is basically one later adumbrated by Miller, namely, a double approach-avoidance situation.

Thus, each of the four reward/punishment situations described by Lewin can be subsumed under one of the three basic types of conflict. That there are factors other than the mere existence of conflicting, approximately equal vectors at work in these situations is, of course, recognized by Lewin and indeed is a necessary deduction from the fact that four situations have to be accounted for by three types of conflict. However, Lewin's brilliant pictorial descriptions of reward/punishment situations can scarcely be said to have advanced the explanation of the effects of reward and punishment very far. We must now turn to later extensions of, and reformulations of, Lewin's initial description.

# III. MILLER'S ANALYSIS OF CONFLICT

Miller's theory of conflict bears many resemblances to that of Lewin but it is cast in behaviouristic language. In view of this it is reasonable to ask at the start whether the language of approach and avoidance is appropriate to an analysis of what is in effect discrimination learning. Nissen (1950) has argued affirmatively. Suppose an animal is presented with a two-choice situation, does he learn to make a particular *response* (e.g. left or right; up or down); or does he learn to *approach* or *avoid* a particular *stimulus*? If the former is the case, Nissen argues, then simple reversal of the stimuli should produce disorientation in the animal; if the latter, the animal should still be able to 'respond' correctly. Nissen reports an experiment with chimpanzees which shows clearly that the usual paradigm will be

$$S_{black} \longrightarrow R_{approach} \qquad S_{white} \longrightarrow R_{avoidance}$$

and not

$$S_{black\text{-}white} \longrightarrow R_{left} \qquad S_{white\text{-}black} \longrightarrow R_{right}$$

In other words, 'left-going' and 'right-going' do not have any goal-reference, whereas 'approach' and 'avoidance' have meaning only in terms of a goal-object. 'Any description of response which makes essential references to the environment (to a goal) is a description of an act to which the approach-avoidance formulation must apply' (Nissen, 1950, p. 128).

We shall begin our discussion of Miller's system at the very simple level of approach and avoidance gradients, proceeding from there to the more complex derivations.

## 1. The gradient of approach

This assumption has been well put by Brown (1948). 'When a motivated organism is suitably reinforced for approaching a given region in space, a gradient in the strength of its excitatory tendency to approach that region will be established, the strength of the tendency increasing with nearness to the goal' (p. 450).

Evidence supporting this assumption was obtained by Brown (1948). He trained rats under strong hunger drive to approach a light to obtain food in a straight alley. After training, he measured the strength of pull at points close to, and distant from, the goal.[8] He

[8] In all of these early experiments excitatory tendency was measured by attaching a special harness to the animal and directly recording the strength of pull in grams.

found that at the near point the mean pull was 56·5 gm. ($\sigma$ 33·7) while at the far point it was 40·9 ($\sigma$ 26·3). It will be noticed that the 'gradient' is very flat (i.e. generalization is considerable). This result is consonant with earlier results obtained by Hull (1934b), Lambert and Solomon (1952), and others.

## 2. The gradient of stimulus generalization of approach

The distinction between gradients of approach and gradients of stimulus generalization of approach is so important that it is necessary to introduce it at this point, although it will be dealt with in more detail later. The present concept is identical with that simply called 'stimulus generalization' to which we have already referred. We may illustrate the difference by reference to another experiment by Brown (1942a). Again he trained rats to approach a light to obtain food in a straight alley. In this experiment, however, Brown was interested in observing whether or not the strength of approach diminished as the light was changed from bright to dull, or vice versa. In this case he measured strength of pull and mean starting time to the original stimulus light and two brighter or duller lights after training on the original one. As in the previous experiment, he found a relatively flat approach gradient, that is, the rats responded almost as strongly to the dimmer or brighter lights as to the original.

Now, it should be clear that in the latter experiment, both types of gradient are involved. In learning to run to the original light, the rat establishes a simple approach gradient; in transferring this response to similar lights it is manifesting stimulus generalization of the original approach response. Furthermore, it should be noted that the *generalized* approach responses will themselves manifest a simple approach gradient.

We may mention briefly here the problem as to the interpretation of the approach gradient. There are two possible ways of accounting for the existence of an approach gradient. One of these, which appears to be favoured by Miller, treats it as simply a different kind of stimulus generalization from that involved in the gradient of stimulus generalization of approach. Since the various sections of a straight alley are usually similar it could be argued that *spatial* generalization takes place, with cues from parts of the alley other than the goal area tending to evoke partially the original response of approach. An alternative explanation would be Hull's goal-gradient hypothesis (Hull, 1934b). According to this hypothesis 'responses occurring at all points in the alley are directly conditioned to their attendant stimuli, but the habit strength of the more remote responses is weaker because of their unfavourable temporal relation to reinforcement' (Brown, 1948, p. 461).

More recently Andreas (1954) has provided evidence for a gradient of stimulus generalization of approach responses. He used an apparatus consisting of a semicircular battery of seven lights. A control group was presented with 21 pairs of stimuli with instructions to respond to only one of the pair (this was to control for any natural preferences). Two experimental groups were given training in approaching one light in preference to any other paired with it, and were then given all 21 pairs with instructions as for the control group. Andreas found that there was a decreasing tendency to choose the light on which the person was trained as the paired light became spatially closer to it, i.e. the approach tendency generalized to all the other lights in proportion to their spatial distance from the training light.

### 3. The gradient of avoidance

Brown (1948) has also provided a concise statement of this assumption. 'When an organism has escaped from a noxious stimulus located at a given region in space, a gradient in the strength of its excitatory tendency to avoid that region will be set up, the strength of the tendency decreasing with distance from that region' (p. 450).

Bugelski and Miller (1938) provided evidence for this assumption. They trained rats to avoid the lighted end of a straight alley by shock. After training the animals were divided into three groups, each of which was given test trials without shock. Group I was placed in the original part of the alley where shock was given; group II was placed 12 inches from the shock-point; and group III 36 inches. Bugelski and Miller measured the starting time and running speed of the animals when placed in the alley on the test trials. A gradient of avoidance was found for both starting time (which was slower for group II compared with group I, and for group III compared with group II) and running speed (which decreased as the rat's distance from the shock-point increased).[9] Similarly, using both strong shock and weak shock groups, Brown (1948) found a gradient of avoidance.

---

[9] As would be expected running speed in the avoidance situation showed a warm-up effect, i.e. the animal had to attain maximum speed before he could begin to show the gradient.

Thus, for strong shock, the mean pull for rats placed near the shock-point on test trials was 198·4 gm. ($\sigma$ 109·7); whereas for those placed at a distance from the shock-point it was only 2·1 ($\sigma$ 0).

## 4. Gradient of stimulus generalization of avoidance

No work on this assumption was reported until a late stage of systematization, so consideration of the experimental evidence will be deferred until later.[10]

## 5. Factors producing changes in the gradients of approach and avoidance[11]

A number of factors have been shown to influence the height of the gradients of approach and avoidance.

a) EFFECTS OF CHANGE IN DRIVE

As Brown (1948) has put it, 'the heights of the approach and avoidance gradients vary directly with strength of drive and intensity of the noxious stimulus, respectively' (Brown, 1948, p. 450). That is, in the case of an approach-response to food, increasing the animal's hunger will raise the entire approach gradient, while decreasing hunger will lower it. In the case of an avoidance-response to electric shock, an increase in the level of shock will raise the entire avoidance gradient, while a decrease in the level of shock will lower it.

With regard to the *approach* gradient, Brown (1942a) found that decreasing the hunger drive from 46 hours to 1 hour led to a decrease in average pull to the same stimulus from 65·4 gm. to 27·5 gm., and to an increase in mean starting time from 0·89 seconds to 6·67 seconds; and similar results were found in a later study (Brown, 1948).[12]

With regard to the *avoidance* gradient, Bugelski and Miller (1938) found that running speed *in the initial stages* was faster for animals started near the shock-point than for animals started at a distance. Similarly, Brown (1948) found that when placed close to the shock-point, rats which had been subjected to strong shock showed a mean pull of 198·4 gm. ($\sigma$ 109·7), whereas those subjected to weak shock

---

[10] There is of course a good deal of evidence from the general literature supporting this assumption.

[11] Although we shall consider here for the most part the approach and avoidance gradients, exactly the same considerations would apply to gradients of stimulus generalization of approach and avoidance.

[12] In all of these early studies, *different* groups of animals were used for the different drive conditions.

showed a mean pull of 141·2 gm. (σ not given); and a similar difference was found for animals started at a far point.

It would seem, therefore, that there is cogent evidence for the
assumption that increased drive raises the entire gradient of approach
or avoidance, whereas decreased drive lowers it.

b) NUMBER OF REINFORCEMENTS

Kaufman and Miller (1949) trained five groups of rats to approach
one end of a straight alley. The approach-response was differentially
reinforced for each of the five groups, to the extent of 3, 9, 27, and
81 rewarded trials for each of four groups respectively, while the
fifth group was given one reinforced trial only. Thus the groups
differed only in the amount of reinforcement, motivation being held
constant at 22 hours food deprivation. In terms of running time,
proportion of animals reaching the goal after shock, and distance of
nearest approach to the goal, Kaufman and Miller were able to
show that there was a direct positive relationship between number of
reinforcements and persistence in approach tendency under shock
conditions. The effect of increased reinforcement of approach tendency therefore is similar to the effect of increasing drive, i.e. it
raises the entire approach gradient.

c) DISTINCTIVE CUES

Bugelski and Woodward (1951) shocked rats in a starting box and
then allowed them to escape into a straight alley. For one group the
floor of the starting box and the alley was a uniform grid. For a
second group, the alley was of cardboard; while for a third group,
the alley was of cardboard and in addition the animals were required
to climb over an obstacle to get from the starting box to the alley.
Bugelski and Woodward found that the avoidance-response extinguished most rapidly in the order: starting box vs. obstacle plus
different grid; starting box vs. different grid; starting box vs. same
grid. In other words, the gradient of stimulus generalization of
avoidance will be steeper the less similar the original (goal-box) and
subsequent (alley) stimuli are.

d) INTENSITY OF STIMULUS

Little work has been reported on this factor, but Brown (1942a) considered that intensity *per se* could act as a drive and therefore raise
the entire approach or avoidance gradient.[13]

---

[13] This, of course, is in line with Miller's general position which regards strong
stimuli as drives. Presumably, whether a strong stimulus motivates approach or
avoidance would be a matter of empirical determination.

L

## 6. Intersection of approach and avoidance gradients

Fig. 5.7 summarizes many of the results mentioned so far and indicates the relationship between approach and avoidance gradients and the effects of increasing or decreasing drive.[14] We must now consider the implications of the empirical fact that the approach and

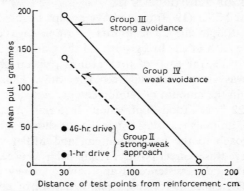

Fig. 5.7. Approach and avoidance gradients under conditions of strong and weak drive. (Source: Brown, J. S. 'Gradients of approach and avoidance-responses and their relation to level of motivation'. *J. comp. Psychol.*, 1948, **41**, 450–65.)

avoidance gradients intersect.[15] The theoretical analysis of Brown (1942b) is extremely important in this connection. He argues that at and near the point of intersection the strength of approach and avoidance tendencies will be approximately equal. Consequently, if two stimuli intermediate between the positive (approach) and negative (avoidance) stimuli are presented, a state of conflict will ensue in the animal. The limiting case will be the presentation of *identical* stimuli at different points along the continuum. In this ingenious manner, Brown is able to derive the various kinds of conflict situations already postulated by Lewin. Thus, an *approach-approach* conflict will occur when the identical stimuli are both positive. In this situation an indiscriminate approach would be predicted. A *double approach-avoidance* conflict will occur when the identical stimuli are midway between the positive and negative stimuli. In this situation, discrimination will break down. An *avoidance-avoidance* conflict will occur when the identical stimuli are both negative. Unless prevented,

[14] For the present, only approach and avoidance gradients are considered.
[15] This is not, of course, a necessary finding. It is quite conceivable that under certain circumstances the gradients would be parallel. It should also be noted that the linear relationships shown could be curvilinear. See the discussion below.

CONFLICT 153

the animal faced with this situation will leave the field. In general, Brown concludes that *these three types of conflict behaviour may be regarded as being on a continuum of indiscriminate approach-blocking-withdrawal.*

Now Brown was able to go further and postulate that since increased approach drive would raise the entire approach gradient relative to the avoidance gradient, it followed that all responses to

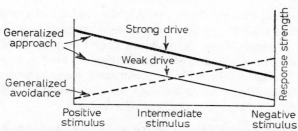

Fig. 5.8. Shift in direction of indiscriminate approach tendency as a function of increased approach drive. (Source: Brown, J. S. 'Factors determining conflict reactions in difficult discriminations'. *J. exp. Psychol.*, 1942, **31**, 272–92.)

identical stimuli would shift towards the indiscriminate *approach*. The basis of this deduction is shown in Fig. 5.8. Secondly, since increased shock will raise the entire avoidance gradient relative to the approach gradient, it follows that all responses to identical stimuli should shift towards the withdrawal type of response.[16] Finally, Brown argued that difficult discriminations should have the same properties as identical intermediate stimuli and be affected in similar ways by increased drive or shock.

To test these various deductions, Brown (1942b) trained rats to discriminate between stimulus patches of 0·02 and 5,000 foot-candles brightness (approach and avoidance tendencies). During test training, one group of rats was presented with two *positive* stimuli (both of 5,000 foot-candles brightness); one group with two *intermediate* stimuli (both of 10·8 foot-candles brightness); and one group with two *negative* stimuli (both of 0·02 foot-candles brightness).[17] Half of each group was tested under 48 hours and half under 1 hour food deprivation. Brown found that as the test stimuli shifted from approach-approach to avoidance-avoidance, the mean time to run

[16] The reader might care to construct this figure for himself.
[17] The pairs of stimuli were positive, intermediate, and negative for rats for whom 5,000 foot-candles was the original positive stimulus. The reverse relationship would hold for rats trained in the opposite discrimination.

increased for all groups (generalized withdrawal tendency). On the other hand, with an increase in approach drive from 1 hour to 48 hours, the mean time to run decreased at all stimulus values (generalized approach tendency). It will be noticed that Brown in this experiment was actually dealing with the gradients of stimulus generalization of approach and avoidance.

## 7. Greater steepness of avoidance gradient

As can clearly be seen from Fig. 5.7, the gradient of avoidance is steeper than that of approach, i.e. generalization is less. This fact follows, of course, from the previous demonstration of the intersection of approach and avoidance gradients. This phenomenon is the most crucial one in Miller's system since many important consequences flow from it, as we shall see. According to Miller and Murray (1952) the steeper gradient of avoidance

> is produced by a difference in the source of the drive motivating the behaviour. In all the experiments the approach has been motivated by the primary drive of hunger while avoidance was motivated by the learned drive of fear. According to a theory learned drive,[18] such drives are produced by internal responses which obey the same laws as overt ones. Thus, when the avoidance habit is tested in a new stimulus situation, both the fear motivating the avoidance, and the overt responses of avoidance should be weakened by generalization. On the other hand, the hunger motivating the approach is a primary drive more dependent upon physiological factors which the subject carries with him into new stimulus situations. Thus generalization will weaken *only* the responses of approach; it will *not* also weaken the drive motivating the responses. With the drive remaining more constant, the gradient of approach should be less steep than that of avoidance (Miller and Murray, 1952, p. 227).

From this general explanation Miller and Murray (1952) deduced an important consequence, namely that 'the gradient of stimulus generalization of an avoidance habit motivated by the learned drive of fear should be steeper than that of an avoidance habit motivated by the primary drive of mild pain produced by an electric shock' (ibid., p. 228). To test this hypothesis, they trained two groups of rats to escape shock by running down an alley to an 'island'. One

[18] A reference to Miller's own theory of learned fear.

group was then tested in the absence of shock ('fear' group), while the other group continued to receive shock ('pain' group). For both groups, stimulus generalization was measured by giving the test trials in a different alley. The hypothesis was confirmed. For the 'fear' group, the mean strength of pull changed from about 160 gm. to about 95 gm; whereas for the 'pain' group, the mean strength of pull remained constant at about 140 gm.[19]

These results do not, of course, in any way invalidate Miller's distinction between approach and avoidance generalization gradients, but they do widen the scope of his system to an important degree and open up new avenues of exploration.

## 8. Conflict and displacement

Much the most important aspect of Miller's theory concerns the relationship between conflict and displacement. The relationship was, as we have seen, explored to some degree by Brown (1942b) with respect to difficult discriminations. In a later paper Miller (1948b) specifically explained displacement in terms of the differential steepness of the gradients of generalization of approach and avoidance. Thus, the inhibition of an aggressive response will, as we have earlier seen, generalize to displaced responses and tend to prevent their occurrence. The aggressive response itself will also generalize. Now since the avoidance gradient (i.e. inhibition of the response) is steeper than the approach gradient (performing the response), the approach-response of aggression will be more readily elicited by stimuli remote from the original aggression-provoking stimulus than by stimuli close to it. This prediction was tested by Miller and Kraeling (1952), though not with respect to aggression. They trained rats to approach and lift a cover to obtain food at the end of a straight alley. They were then trained to avoid the food area by being shocked whenever they touched the cover. They were then given test trials (without food or shock) in one of three alleys. One group was tested in the alley used for training (wide and white); one group in an alley of intermediate similarity to the training alley (narrow and grey); and one group in an alley quite different from the training alley (very narrow and black). The predictions were that more animals would approach the goal in the narrow grey alley than the wide white alley; and more

[19] The difference between the 'fear' and 'pain' groups in initial strength of pull was due to the stronger shocks given the 'fear' group during training. This could not, however, account for the different slopes, since control groups given much stronger shocks than the 'fear' group showed no evidence of a steeper slope.

in the very narrow black alley than in the narrow grey or wide white. The prediction was verified: 28% of rats reached the goal in the wide white alley; 37% in the narrow grey; and 70% in the very narrow black. Of a control group given no preliminary approach-avoidance training and paired randomly with the three test groups, only 15% reached the goal. The results could therefore be attributed to generalization from previous training.

This study, however, suffered from two important defects. Firstly, the approach habit was the first habit acquired. Secondly, the approach habit was established by many spaced trials, and the avoidance habit by a few massed trials. Murray and Miller (1952) attempted to control these variables by reverting to the use of separate groups of rats to measure approach and avoidance. One group was trained to run along a straight alley to obtain food, while a second group was similarly trained to escape shock. Each group was given 20 training

TABLE 5.1

AVERAGE STRENGTH OF PULL IN GRAMS ON
TEST TRIALS

| Test conditions | Reinforcement | | | |
|---|---|---|---|---|
| | Continuous | | Partial | |
| | Av. 2 trials | $p$ | Av. 2 trials | $p$ |
| 1. Fear-original<br>2. Fear-different | 171·1<br>108·5 } | ·001 | 158·6<br>110·7 } | ·003 |
| 3. Hunger-original<br>4. Hunger-different | 152·3<br>145·1 } | ·30 | 117·9<br>120·8 } | ·45 |

Source: Murray, E. J., and Miller, N. E. 'Displacement: steeper gradient of generalization of avoidance than of approach with age of habit controlled'. *J. exp. Psychol.*, 1952, **43**, 222–6

trials followed by two test trials on the same alley and two test trials on a different alley. It was predicted that the shock group would show a steeper gradient of avoidance than the hunger group. The experiment was repeated using partial reinforcement during training instead of continuous reinforcement. The results are shown in Table 5.1. It is clear that for conditions involving both continuous and partial reinforcement, the gradient of stimulus generalization of avoidance motivated by fear is steeper than that of approach motivated by hunger, with the age of habit and number of training trials held constant.

The most important of this group of studies, however, was undoubtedly that of Murray and Berkun (1955). They utilized the three-dimensional model represented in Fig. 5.9, involving strength of

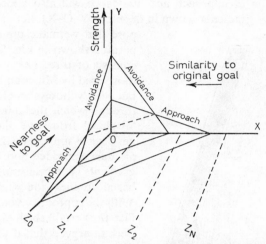

Fig. 5.9. A three-dimensional model of conflict and displacement. (Source: Murray, E. J., and Berkun, M. M. 'Displacement as a function of conflict'. *J. abnorm. soc. Psychol.*, 1955, **51**, 47–56.)

behavioural tendency, similarity between original and displaced goal, and nearness to original and displaced goal. Thus, in the figure, the Y-axis indicates the strength of the behavioural tendency, the X-axis the similarity of original and displaced goal, and the Z-axis the nearness of the animal to the goal. Now a careful study of this figure will show that the model incorporates simultaneously what we have previously referred to as the gradients of approach and avoidance (which are equivalent to the dimension of *nearness* to the goal) and the gradients of stimulus generalization of approach and avoidance (which are equivalent to *similarity* between original and displaced goal). Thus, whereas previous experiments have tended to concentrate on one or other type of gradient this model enables us to predict the effects of their simultaneous operation which, as we have already seen, will almost always be the case. The experiment carried out by Murray and Berkun will illustrate the use of the model concretely. Firstly, in the usual way they trained rats to approach a goal for food in the alley schematically represented in Fig. 5.9 by the line $Z_0$–O and then set up an avoidance-response to the same goal by shock in the usual way. Now it will be clear that approach and avoidance gradients will appear in the usual way (represented by the gradients shown in the plane Y–O–$Z_0$) and that gradients of stimulus generalization of approach and avoidance will also appear (represented by the gradients shown in the plane Y–O–X). Let us now sup-

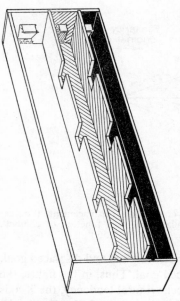

pose that we make use of the apparatus shown in Fig. 5.10 which consists of three alleys similar to those used by Miller and Kraeling but with 'windows' cut in the sides through which the animals could 'displace' from one alley to the next. Let us suppose further that the animals' approach and avoidance gradients have been initially established in the wide white alley.[20] With the approach-avoidance conflict thus established Murray and Berkun argued that if the animals are now placed in the wide white alley but with the windows available they will approach up the white alley ($Z_0$ in Fig. 5.9) until they reach the point of maximum conflict (i.e. where the gradients cross).

Fig. 5.10. The wide white, medium grey, and narrow black alleys in which the rats were trained and tested. (Source: Murray, E. J., and Berkun, M. M. 'Displacement as a function of conflict'. *J. abnorm. soc. Psychol.*, 1955, **51**, 47–56.)

At this point, they will displace into the narrow grey alley ($Z_1$ in Fig. 5.9). From Fig. 5.9 it would be predicted that they would now advance further up $Z_1$ than they had up $Z_0$ but would not actually reach the goal. When they reach the point of maximum conflict in $Z_1$, they will displace into the very narrow black alley ($Z_2$ in Fig. 5.9) and in this alley they would be expected to reach the goal since in this alley approach is always higher than avoidance. In other words, this model makes it possible to predict how far an animal will advance

[20] During this training the 'windows' were blocked off to prevent displacement.

towards the goal in a particular alley as a joint function of displaced goal to original goal and strength of approach-avoidance at any particular point in a given alley. Furthermore, when a displaced goal-response is eventually achieved, since it is not punished, the fear associated with goal-responses should diminish, this should raise the approach gradients of both kinds, and therefore an approach to the goal in the original alley should become more likely.

The experimental results obtained by Murray and Berkun verified all these expectations. Firstly they found that all 11 animals studied displaced to the nearest alley; and 8/11 displaced also to the far alley, i.e. *displacement is a resolution of conflict*. Secondly, the animals went further down the near alley then the original one; and further down the far than the near. They also displaced through openings closer to the goal in near and far alleys than in original alleys. This supports the hypothesis that *the behaviour of the animals is governed by intersecting approach and avoidance surfaces*. Thirdly, in the later test trials the animals went further down the alleys than in the earlier trials but they went proportionally further down, the more displaced the alleys were. Similarly, the animals tended to use windows closer to the goal for displacement as number of trials increased. That is, *the avoidance gradients are lowered because of the extinction of fear*. Fourthly, all 10 animals which made goal-responses in the near or far alleys eventually made goal-responses in the original alley. That is, *goal-responding in displaced situations will have a therapeutic effect on the original conflict*.

This brilliant piece of theoretical analysis and experimental verification forms a fitting climax to Miller's many years of work in this field and has well merited the attention paid to it here.

None of the experiments discussed in this section, however, have controlled for the effect of continued test trials in the *original* alley following the establishment of an approach-avoidance conflict by comparison with the effect on the resolution of the conflict of *displaced* goal-responses. This control experiment was carried out by Berkun (1957). Having set up an approach-avoidance conflict in the usual way, he ran half his rats in the far alley until they made a goal-response,[21] then ran them in the intermediate to the same criterion, and finally ran them in the original alley. The other rats continued to run in the original alley. Berkun also investigated the

[21] The alleys contained no 'windows' in this experiment.

effects of partial as opposed to continuous reinforcement of the original approach-response; and the effects of rewarding approach-responses during test trials as opposed to non-reward. He found that the average number of trials before a goal-response was made was 9·4, 3·0, and 2·6 for rats run successively in the far, intermediate, and original alleys respectively. Rats continuing to run in the original alley took on average 12·6 trials before they made their first post-shock goal-response. Furthermore, the displaced group showed faster running in the *original* alley when they reached it compared with the original group at the same stage of recovery. Berkun's results, however, were somewhat obscured by the inhibitory gradients set up in the displaced rats due to changing from the different back to the original alley. Berkun was also able to show that reinforcement of the displaced response, or partial reinforcement of the approach-response during training, increased speed of recovery from conflict. Berkun's results were confirmed in more recent work by Taylor and Maher (1959) and Maher, Noblin, and Elder (in press). In the latter study, it was noticed, however, that animals retrained under displacement did *not* tend to enter the most displaced alley closer to the goal, as found by Murray and Berkun. Coupled with the observation that Murray and Berkun always located the most dissimilar alley furthest away from the original alley, thus confounding distance with similarity, these findings led Elder, Noblin, and Maher (in press) to suggest that the rats were responding to *distance* cues, rather than to *similarity* cues.

To test this hypothesis, Elder, Noblin, and Maher (in press) used four alleys whose spatial relationship to each other could be varied. After the usual approach-avoidance training in the original alley, four rats were retrained under each of the six possible spatial arrangements of the original and three displaced alleys. The only variable which significantly affected the reinstatement of the original approach-response was that of distance of displaced alley from original alley. It is, of course, possible to argue that there is a gradient of similarity of distance which is prepotent over any gradient for colour. However, in a further study, Noblin and Maher (in press), after setting up conflict in an original white alley, extinguished the animals in either another identical white alley, or in a black alley, with distance held constant. No difference was found in extinction time for the white and black alleys.

Two other recent studies also throw some doubt on the validity of the general theory of Murray and Berkun. Thus, Smith (1960) attempted to verify the gradient of approach in more detail than was the case in Brown's (1948) study. Smith measured the strength of pull in an approach situation at five distances from the starting point. He used two kinds of rats (albino and hooded) and tested each animal at each distance, the order of testing being randomly varied and spaced at five-minute intervals. He found that, while he was able to replicate Brown's approach gradient with albino rats, hooded rats showed an *opposite* type of gradient. His results also suggested that the gradients are non-linear.

In a study by Trapold, Miller, and Coons (1960) an approach-avoidance conflict was set up in the usual runway situation. It follows from Miller's theory that if the animals are now placed in the avoidance-dominant zone of the runway (that is, between the goal and the point of maximum conflict where the gradients cross) they should retreat away from the goal up to or slightly beyond the point of maximum conflict, and then stop. In point of fact, most of the animals in these circumstances moved *towards*, not away from, the goal. (On the other hand, some of the results obtained were clearly consistent with theoretical expectations.)

Armed with these results, Maher 1961 has recently presented a particularly acute critical analysis of Miller's theory of approach-avoidance conflict. He has suggested that the empirical evidence for some of Miller's basic postulates is altogether unconvincing and that quite a number of alternative possibilities exist, particularly with respect to the relationship between gradients of approach and avoidance. As Maher points out, 'If changes in the strength of drive can change the slope of a gradient (as well as its height) then appropriate manipulation of the drive variables could produce approach and avoidance gradients which are parallel – or even steeper for approach than for avoidance.' Alternatively, one may assume that the angles of the gradients may be altered throughout ranges which overlap, in which case the postulate that the strength of avoidance increases more rapidly with nearness than does that of approach becomes merely a statement of the limiting conditions which lead to conflict. After a detailed discussion of the problem, Maher concludes that there would appear to be no *universal* slopes for gradients of approach and avoidance. The gradients which are empirically found, at least, appear to be dependent upon many factors, such as changes in motivating variables, availability of sensory cues (Smith (1960) found that the gradients disappeared altogether in dim light), species being tested, and so on.

Maher himself is inclined to favour a position which conceives of conflict as determined by gradients of approach and avoidance which

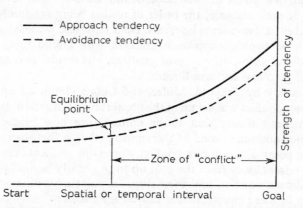

Fig. 5.11. Parallel gradients of approach and avoidance. (Source: Maher, B. A. 'Approach-avoidance conflict: an appraisal'. Mimeographed manuscript Harvard University, 1961.)

are parallel. The proposed model is illustrated in Fig. 5.11 and involves two assumptions:

1. 'The stronger of two competing response tendencies mediates behaviour only when its absolute momentary strength exceeds that of the weaker by an amount which is an increasing function of the momentary strength of the weaker.'

2. 'When competing response tendencies reach a state of equilibrium the behaviour of the organism will include responses which are not predictable from summing the strengths of the competing tendencies.'

Thus, whatever the distance of the animal from the goal, the *absolute* difference in strength of the two gradients remains the same. However, as the goal is approached the difference between the gradients relative to the strength of the weaker response tendency declines. At this point the animal should stop approaching the goal. Maher is able to show that this model mediates many of the perplexing empirical results more satisfactorily than does Miller's model, and would appear to point the way to many empirical studies. It will be realized, of course, that Maher's model is a tribute to Miller's work, since it could scarcely have been conceived without the many empirical and theoretical contributions of Miller.

The resolution of approach-avoidance conflict situations (or, indeed, their prevention) may be hastened by the experimental reduction of the fear motivating the performance of the avoidance response. That this is so has been convincingly shown by Conger (1951) in a series of experiments. Conger found that if rats with an approach-avoidance conflict were injected with alcohol they would immediately approach the goal and eat, whereas control rats injected with water did not do so. As Conger pointed out, however, these results could be due to a decrease in the strength of avoidance tendency, an increase in approach tendency, a combination of the two, or even a differential increase or decrease in the strength of both tendencies. He therefore repeated the experiment, but this time established approach and avoidance tendencies in separate groups of rats. The results indicated quite clearly that approach tendencies were unaffected by injections of alcohol (mean pull before and after injection: 154·5 and 149·7 gm.) but that avoidance tendencies were significantly reduced (mean pull before and after injection: 238·5 and 129·8 gm.).[22] Conger explains these results in terms of fear reduction in the case of avoidance-responses. This interpretation is supported by several other similar kinds of study. Thus Poschel (1957) showed that electro-convulsive shock reduced the strength of avoidance in an approach-avoidance situation, while the appropriate control experiment showing that ECS does not affect approach-responses has been carried out with confirmatory results by Siegel (1943), Brady (1951), and Hunt and Brady (1951). The latter two studies also showed that a conditioned fear-response is lost for about 30 days after ECS. Ader and Clink (1957) showed that chlorpromazine slowed up the acquisition, and speeded up the extinction of, avoidance-responses, while similar results were reported by Bailey and Miller (1952), using sodium amytal. A rather different method of manipulating fear was utilized by Taylor and Maher (1959) in the study previously mentioned. In restraining rats in the approach-avoidance conflict situation, they allowed half of them to escape from the original or displaced alley during retraining, arguing that escape would reduce the anxiety and hence retard its extinction. The result of this part of the experiment, however, was indeterminate.

[22] It will be noted that Conger did not equate his groups for strength of pull prior to injection of alcohol, which renders his results less clear.

## 9. Experimental conflict situations in humans

The scope of conflict theory has been widened by its application to relatively very simple situations in humans. Thus approach-approach, avoidance-avoidance, and approach-avoidance situations have been established, with particular attention being paid to their mode of resolution and the factors affecting the degree of conflict. The early experiment of Hovland and Sears (1938) may serve as a paradigm for the general methodology. They used a 6 × 6 inch board with

### TABLE 5.2

PERCENTAGE OF RESPONSES IN DIFFERENT CATEGORIES AS
A FUNCTION OF TYPE OF CONFLICT

| Type of conflict | Mode of resolution | | | | |
|---|---|---|---|---|---|
| | S | D | C | B | C + B |
| Approach-approach | 57·5 (71·0) | 21·25 (27·0) | 12·5 (0·0) | 8·75 (0·0) | 21·25 (0·0) |
| Avoidance-avoidance | 17·5 (44·0) | 7·5 (6·0) | 28·75 (2·0) | 46·25 (44·0) | 75·00 (46·0) |
| Approach-avoidance | 14·37 | 46·88 | 10·63 | 28·12 | 38·75 |

Sources: Hovland, C. I., and Sears, R. R. 'Experiments on motor conflict: I. Types of conflict and their modes of resolution'. *J. exp. Psychol.*, 1938, **23**, 477–93; (in brackets) Andreas, B. G. 'Motor responses as a function of type of conflict'. *Proc. Ia. Acad. Sci.*, 1950, **57**, 361–5

one or two lights of different colours in two corners diagonally opposite the starting point, which was at the mid-point of the side of the board nearest the subject. Using this simple situation, they examined four types of conflict and their mode of resolution. In the *approach-approach* conflict situation, one light only was present in each corner and the subject was instructed to move towards the light which flashed. After 20 trials (10 trials randomly interspersed) to each light, both lights flashed simultaneously on the 21st trial. The procedure was identical for the *avoidance-avoidance* conflict situation except that the subject went to the light which did not flash on the training trials. In the *approach-avoidance* situation a red and a green light in one corner only were used. If one of the pair flashed, the subject approached that corner; if the other, he avoided it by going to the opposite corner. Finally, in the *double approach-avoidance* conflict situation a red and a green light were present in both corners. The subject was to approach one colour if it flashed in either corner and avoid the other colour.

Four kinds of resolution of conflict were distinguished by Hovland and Sears on the conflict trial:

a) S – a single response only to one of the two lights.
b) D – a double reaction, i.e. a response to both signals.
c) C – a compromise reaction, i.e. going up the centre of the board instead of to either corner.
d) B – a blocking of response, i.e. no manual response at all.

The results for the first three types of conflict situation are shown in Table 5.2, together with more recent data gathered by Andreas (1950), who used a semicircular panel of lights with 13 target positions instead of the apparatus of Hovland and Sears. It will be seen that compromise and blocking responses were more common in the avoidance-avoidance than in the approach-approach situation[23] but it should be noted that the former situation precludes the usual response of simple withdrawal from the field. The approach-avoidance situation, on the other hand, mainly results in double responses, the subject first going to the positive light and then away from the negative light (situated, of course, at the same point). The double approach-avoidance situation, however, resulted mainly in blocking responses (72·5%; while blocking plus compromise responses totalled 77·5%). However, this latter result was not entirely clear since the number of *training* trials involved in the double approach-avoidance situation was four times that of the simple approach-avoidance situation (another group given 80 training trials on the simple approach-avoidance conflict situation showed twice as many blocking responses as the original comparable group).

Hovland and Sears were able to show further that familiarity with the situation did not alter the tendency to make particular types of responses. Only about 25% of subjects showed any variation in mode of resolution of the double approach-avoidance conflict, even when told that similar conflict trials could be expected after further training.

In a subsequent experiment, Sears and Hovland (1941) returned to the question of the effects of differential training on mode of

[23] Compare Brown's (1942b) contention that identical positive stimuli tend to produce generalized approach-responses.

resolution. They tested two hypotheses which have been clearly stated by Andreas (1958):

a) 'with strengths of competing response tendencies approximately equal, conflict increases as the strengths increase in absolute value';

b) 'conflict increases as the strengths of unequal tendencies approach equality' (Andreas, 1958, p. 174).

In both cases, the existence of conflict is measured by blocking responses.

Sears and Hovland (1941) attempted to test these hypotheses in an avoidance-avoidance situation by varying the amount of avoidance practice to the two lights. Four groups were given varying degrees of practice as follows:

Group D – 20 trials to one light; 1 trial to the other
Group E – 20 trials to one light; 5 trials to the other
Group F – 20 trials to one light; 20 trials to the other
Group G – 5 trials to one light; 5 trials to the other.

TABLE 5.3

PERCENTAGE OF RESPONSES IN DIFFERENT CATEGORIES
IN AVOIDANCE-AVOIDANCE CONFLICT SITUATIONS
AS A FUNCTION OF ABSOLUTE STRENGTH AND
EQUALITY OF RESPONSES

| Group | Mode of resolution | | | |
|---|---|---|---|---|
| | S | D | C | B |
| D (20 : 1) | 17·5 | 30·0 | 20·0 | 32·5 |
| E (20 : 5) | 15·0 | 17·5 | 15·0 | 52·5 |
| F (20 : 20) | 2·5 | 22·5 | 17·5 | 57·5 |
| G (5 : 5) | 5·0 | 15·0 | 30·0 | 50·0 |

Source: Sears, R. R., and Hovland, C. I. 'Experiments on motor conflict: II. Determination of mode of resolution by comparative strengths of conflicting responses'. *J. exp. Psychol.*, 1941, **28**, 280–6

The first hypothesis was tested by comparing groups F and G; the second by comparing groups D and E, and groups E and F. The results are shown in Table 5.3. The first hypothesis is not supported, though the results are in the predicted direction and a greater difference in absolute strengths might have produced significant results. The second hypothesis is supported. Andreas (1958) in a more re- fined experiment in which he varied both amount of training and level of motivation, produced results which were not entirely in agree- ment with those of Sears and Hovland. He criticized their study (rightly) on the grounds that the blocking of the subjects might simply be the result of confusion caused by the sudden introduction (without warning) of the conflict situation and the ambiguity of verbal instructions to respond. In his own experiment he studied conflict situations in which (a) the simultaneous presentation of cues was expected by the subject, instead of coming as a surprise; and (b) the avoidance tendencies were built up through trial-and-error learning. Thus, using his semicircular panel of lights, the subject was required to *avoid* lights 2 and 6, which were paired with *approach* lights 1, 3, 5, and 7. He varied the amount of training before the first conflict trial, giving 8, 16, 24, or 40 trials.[24] The subject learned that lights 2 and 6 were to be avoided because he was shocked each time he approached them. For half the subjects in each group approach- ing lights 2 or 6 resulted in moderate shock; for the other half moder- ate shock resulted followed by strong shock on the four trials imme- diately preceding the conflict trial. Andreas found that conflict was greater in groups tested under high motivation; and that conflict was greater as level of training increased prior to the conflict trial.

All of these studies have dealt with the resolution of simple motor conflicts. Arkoff (1957), however, has extended the model in an interesting manner. He created conflicts by systematically pairing with one another seven personal characteristics: adjustment, attrac- tiveness, health, intelligence, popularity, talent, and wealth. By using all possible pairings, 21 approach-approach and 21 avoidance- avoidance conflicts were created. Thus, an approach-approach con- flict was created by requiring the subject to choose between the following printed alternatives:

Which Would You Rather Be?

| More Attractive than | More Intelligent than |
|---|---|
| You Are Now | You Are Now |

An avoidance-avoidance conflict was created by substituting the

[24] Thus, in the case of the group given 8 trials prior to the conflict trial, light 2 would be paired once with lights 1, 3, 5, and 7 (4 trials); and similarly for light 6. In each case light 2 and light 6 had to be avoided. Lights 2 and 6 were never paired with each other during training trials.

M

word 'less' for 'more'. Conflict was measured by the time taken to choose. Subsequently, the subject was required to sort all 42 cards into those he found easy to resolve, and those he found hard. Arkoff found that the mean resolution time was significantly greater for avoidance-avoidance conflicts than for approach-approach; and, in terms of the sorting, that cards illustrating approach-approach conflicts were judged significantly easier to resolve than those illustrating avoidance-avoidance conflicts. Both of these results are in agreement with those of Hovland and Sears (1938) indicating that avoidance-avoidance conflicts (where withdrawal is prevented) produce most blocking.

Lanier (1941) extended conflict theory to the area of 'affective conflict'. He required his subjects to judge individually presented words as pleasant, unpleasant, neutral, or mixed (i.e. both pleasant and unpleasant). The latter category was assumed to indicate the presence of conflict (presumably of the approach-avoidance kind). Lanier found that such mixed judgements occurred for about 10% of the 50 words he used and were accompanied by an increase in judgement time and a significantly greater G.S.R.

Barker (1942) studied conflict behaviour in young boys when they were required to choose between pairs of liquids where the alternatives were (a) of similar (orange vs. pineapple) or discrepant (orange vs. vinegar) desirability; or (b) between desirable liquids (orange vs. pineapple) or undesirable liquids (vinegar and salt water). Clearly these situations represent the usual kinds of conflict situations already mentioned. Barker added a third variable in his experiment – namely, whether the situation was real or hypothetical, i.e. in the real situation the liquid chosen was actually drunk. Barker found that for both real and hypothetical situations, approach-approach conflicts were resolved more readily than avoidance-avoidance ones (where withdrawal in the latter case was prevented). He further found that blocking ('vicarious trial-and-error') and time to resolve conflict were inversely related to the 'distance' between the alternatives in a preference series.

These results with humans have not been formally incorporated into his system by Miller, but they clearly are consistent with his general theoretical position. It may be expected that the model presented by Murray and Berkun (1955) and described above will lead to a renewal of experimentation on conflict and its resolution at the human level.

## IV. HULL'S ANALYSIS OF CONFLICT

It will not be necessary to consider Hull's treatment of conflict in any great detail, since his position and that of Miller are essentially similar. In some respects, however, Hull (1952) attempted to work out the experimental implications of conflict theory in a more systematic fashion than Miller and some reference must therefore be made to both the similarities and differences in their respective treatments.

We may note firstly that Hull accepted as part of his system many of the conclusions of Miller. Thus he agreed that approach and avoidance[25] behaviour generalizes; that the generalization gradients are negatively accelerated; that the gradient of avoidance is steeper than that of approach; and that the effect of drive increase or decrease is to raise or lower the respective gradients.[26] With respect to approach conflicts, he agreed that while an organism placed exactly midway between two adient objects would choose either one on a chance basis, once a movement towards one occurred, the probability that the one would be chosen would increase rapidly;[27] and that increased drive will increase the probability of the nearer object being chosen.[28] With respect to avoidance-avoidance conflicts, he agreed that, where withdrawal is impossible (i.e. in an enclosed situation), the organism will tend to remain midway between the two objects, oscillating backwards and forwards, and that these movements will decrease in strength as the strength of the noxious abient objects increases.[29] Similarly, in an approach-avoidance conflict situation, Hull accepted Miller's theory concerning the interaction of the approach and avoidance gradients, and of the effects of increasing the strength of approach or avoidance on the point of intersection of the gradients.[30]

Hull's treatment of conflict is, however, somewhat more extensive than that of Miller and we may consider briefly a number of important additional contributions which he made to the subject. In the first place, he makes an important distinction between movement in *confined* and *free spaces* when an animal is in a state of conflict. He points out, for instance, that the generalization gradients of which

---

[25] In his chapter (Hull, 1952, Ch. 8) Hull refers to adient and abient behaviour, rather than approach and avoidance; but the terms are clearly interchangeable.
[26] Hull (1952); Theorems 53–56; 58–60.
[27] Hull (1952): Theorems 63–64. Hull is here invoking the oscillation principle.
[28] Hull (1952): Theorems 67–68.      [29] Hull (1952): Theorems 73–75.
[30] Hull (1952): Theorems 86–89.

Miller makes much use are not really linear gradients but only appear to be so because of the restriction of free movement. Thus, both adient and abient reaction potential in free space constitute plane fields of reaction potential (i.e. generalization in free space will extend 'all round' the object). Again, an organism placed midway between two abient objects in free space will move at right angles to a line connecting the two objects. The distinction between confined and free conflict situations also has implications for the effects of extraneous influences on the direction of movements of approach and avoidance. Adience in free space will always tend towards a straight line extending from the organism to the object and will return to the direct line after disturbance. In the case of abience, however, deviations from the straight line away from the object will tend not to be corrected because the deviation will usually continue to carry the organism away from the object.[31]

Secondly, Hull distinguishes clearly between conflict situations involving *homogeneous* and those involving *heterogeneous* objects. Heterogeneous objects would be involved, for instance, if one of the objects had greater incentive value than the other. In an approach-approach situation, for example, one object might involve a larger reward than the other. In such a situation that object offering the largest incentive, or of which the organism has the greatest need, will be chosen. In the case of heterogeneous abient objects, the organism will approach an equilibrium point (in a restricted situation) which will fall further and further away from the stronger abient object as an increasing function of the latter's strength. Again, if the organism is placed midway between two heterogeneous abient objects in free space, it will take a path to one side of the line connecting the abient objects, and its path will curve in the direction of the weaker object.[32]

Thirdly, by making use of his general behaviour theory Hull is able to make several novel predictions. Thus, when homogeneous adient objects are placed on a line with and in the same direction from the organism, the adient latency will be less than that for either object alone. In such a situation, however, the further away the more remote object is from the organism, the greater will be the reaction latency.[33]

The distinction which Hull made between free and confined con-

---

[31] Hull (1952): Theorems 57; 61–62; 81–82.
[32] Hull (1952): Theorems 69–70; 78; 83.    [33] Hull (1952): Theorems 71–72.

flict situations enabled him to consider detour behaviour as a special case of approach-avoidance conflict in free space. Thus, he reasoned that smooth and strictly static barriers are abient objects, possessing the special property that their reaction potential gradients normally attain early in an organism's interaction with them a practically vertical degree of steepness at the closest point of contact. Following from this, he argues that an organism which perceives an adient object (e.g. food) through the (transparent) barrier will be able to remain in the vicinity of the barrier (because of the extreme steepness of the avoidance gradient) and will discriminate between the adient object now perceived beyond the abient object, and the adient object seen in other non-barrier situations. Discrimination will take place and lead to detour behaviour.[34] Now, in terms of the theorems previously discussed, Hull is able to make quite precise predictions concerning the organism's behaviour in solving the problem. Thus, since adient behaviour, as we have seen, converges on the adient object, detour behaviour will lead immediately to resumption of the interrupted path; but the initial abient behaviour will not necessarily follow in reverse the adient path. Again the organism in making a detour will learn to prefer the one involving the shorter distance.[35] When the adient object is close to the barrier, the detour will be made with more difficulty than when the adient object is distant; and an increase in drive level or incentive value of the adient object will make the detour more difficult.[36]

It will be clear from the foregoing that Hull's account of conflict behaviour is altogether more comprehensive than that of Miller and the extension of the model to detour behaviour is especially valuable.[37] More attention has been paid to Miller's system at this stage since the empirical evidence in relation to it is much greater,[38] in spite of the wealth of experimental suggestions contained in Hull's treatment.

---

[34] Hull (1952): Theorems 90–92.        [35] Hull (1952): Theorems 93–95.
[36] Hull (1952): Theorems 100–102.
[37] In a much earlier paper, Hull (1938) had accounted for detour behaviour in much the same way.
[38] It is an extraordinary fact that, although Hull's treatments (1938, 1952) of conflict and detour behaviour contain a remarkable number of precise experimental predictions, little or no effort has since been made to test the predictions. Thus, the author counted at least 40 separate suggestions for experiments in Hull's earlier paper. Yet, practically all of them remain untested 20 years later.

## V. CATTELL'S ANALYSIS OF CONFLICT

Let us suppose that each individual possesses a number of independent attitude or sentiment structures. The strength of these structures can be measured by asking the individual whether he agrees or disagrees with appropriate attitude statements which imply a particular course of action. It has been shown empirically (Cattell, 1957) that a number of such factors do exist and may each be defined by a number of attitude statements. Although the factors are independent of each other, it is also known that the same attitude statement may have different *significant* loadings on more than one factor, and that in some instances, the factor loading will be significantly positive on one factor, and significantly negative on another factor. This means that an individual might strongly approve the course of action implied in an attitude statement if one of his attitude structures were being tapped at the time he gave his opinion of the statement; whereas he might equally strongly disapprove of it if another of his attitude structures were being tapped at the time of responding. If we make the assumption that such statements will usually tap *both* attitude structures simultaneously, then we have a basis for operationally defining a state of conflict. Now Cattell (1950, 1951) has shown that the structure of attitudes and sentiments in an individual may be assessed by the use of P-technique, which involves the repeated testing of an individual on a number of measures and the intercorrelation of these measures *for the individual*, followed by a factor analysis of the resulting correlations. Such an analysis will not only reveal the factorial structure of the individual's attitudes, but will also show the factor loadings of each measure (or attitude statement) on each factor. Using this technique, we may operationally define conflict as 'a state of competing drive and sentiment structures, as revealed by the pattern of combined positive and negative factor loadings resulting from P-technique factor analysis of test results obtained with selected, dynamic statements of attitudes' (Williams, 1959). In effect, this is a novel definition of an approach-avoidance conflict. Thus, the individual may be strongly inclined to view favourably the statement 'America should make atom bombs' because approval of this statement fits with a general attitude favouring capitalism as against communism; on the other hand, he may simultaneously be strongly inclined to view the statement unfavourably, because of an independent attitude of fear of the consequences of war. Thus, when asked to say whether he approves or disapproves of the statement, he may find it difficult to make up his mind, i.e. he will be in a state of conflict.

A recent experiment by Williams (1959), working within the framework of Cattell's system, represents an interesting attempt to measure conflict in this way. He made use of six factors isolated by Cattell and representing different motivational areas – sex, fear, parental protection, self-sentiment, self-assertion, and narcissism. The statements chosen to represent these six areas were chosen on the basis that they all had positive loadings on one of the six factors, and negative loadings on at least one other factor. Each subject was presented with all possible pairings of the fourteen statements on forty separate occasions and asked which statement of the pair he preferred. Attitude strength was measured in three ways – reaction time, number of times each attitude was chosen, and number of consequences stated for each attitude statement, the three measures being combined to give a single score. The 14 × 14 correlation matrix was factored by the complete centroid method for each individual separately and rotation to simple structure carried out. Degree of conflict for each individual was measured by summing the positive and negative loadings for each row, and adding these sub-totals.

Now this method provides, of course, an acceptable operational definition of conflict, for which Williams was able to demonstrate reasonable reliability and factorial validity. Williams, however, also tried to demonstrate its validity against various external criteria. Thus, he predicted that conflict scores derived in this way should discriminate between abnormal and normal subjects, the former showing a higher degree of conflict. He also attempted to validate the measure of conflict against psychiatric ratings, responses on other questionnaires used by Cattell, and the individuals' life history. The abnormal-normal criterion showed a significant relationship with the measure of conflict, and the other external criteria showed promising results.

This study by Williams utilized only small numbers of subjects but, in spite of the labour involved in using P-technique, the method described above would certainly appear to open up a completely new avenue of approach to the study of conflict at the human level.

# Chapter 6

# FRUSTRATION, CONFLICT, LEARNING THEORY, AND PERSONALITY

The foregoing review has covered only a part of the voluminous literature on frustration and conflict. It is not intended in this final chapter to attempt any comprehensive theory of frustration and conflict, which would at present be a task impossible of fulfilment, but rather to make some general observations concerning what appear to be the principal problems involved in this field. This will involve a number of steps, beginning with a discussion of the relationship between frustration and conflict and proceeding to a consideration of frustration as an intervening variable and the necessity for taking account of personality variables in any complete explanation of frustration and conflict.

It is a curious fact that to date little attention has been paid to the relationship between frustration and conflict. To take two striking examples, Miller and Lewin have, as we have seen, worked extensively in both areas, but have tended to ignore conflict when talking about frustration, and vice versa. Thus, the work on frustration and aggression by Miller and his colleagues (Dollard *et al.*, 1944) does not directly mention conflict;[1] while in Miller's celebrated review of conflict (Miller, 1944), there is no mention of the work on frustration and aggression. Similarly, although Lewin (1935) had a good deal to say about various kinds of conflict situations, the present author could find only two unimportant references to conflict in the monograph on frustration and regression (Barker, Dembo, and Lewin, 1941), although the frustrating situation clearly involved positive and negative valences for the child. Where frustration and conflict have been considered together, the opinions expressed have varied considerably. Thus, some authors have assumed that frus-

---

[1] As we shall see, however, the relationship is implicitly stated in that work.

174

tration leads to conflict; others that conflict produces frustration; others again that conflict and frustration are synonymous terms. In part, this confusion results from a failure to spell out the processes involved in sufficient detail; in part from an ambiguous terminology.

We shall, therefore, first proceed to a consideration of terms, then to a discussion of the relationship between frustration and conflict.

## I. TERMINOLOGY

The difficulties here result from two kinds of neglect. On the one hand it is necessary to make a clear distinction between a *frustrating situation* and a *frustrated organism*. Some authors have used the term *frustration* interchangeably, sometimes intending to refer to a frustrating situation, and at other times to a frustrated organism. In some instances, it even appears that the author assumes a perfect relationship between the two. But it should be clear that an organism placed in a frustrating situation need not necessarily be in a state of frustration any more than an organism placed in a learning situation necessarily learns. A more important source of confusion arises from the failure to distinguish clearly between *responses indicating a state of frustration in the organism* (frustration-responses) on the one hand, and *responses to that state of frustration* (responses to frustration) on the other. Again, it is clear that two organisms may, when placed in a standard frustrating situation, experience the same or different amounts of frustration, but that even if they experience the same amount of frustration, their reactions to that experience may be quite different. In this connection it may be noted that in most of the literature we have considered in previous chapters, we have been dealing with responses *to* frustration, and not with frustration-responses.[2] To summarize: *organisms placed in objectively defined frustrating situations will experience frustration to varying degrees and will manifest varying responses to this state of frustration.* We will now consider each of these variables in turn.

a) FRUSTRATING SITUATION

This term has been used very loosely and very widely. Indeed, it is possible to argue that *any* situation involving the attainment of a goal constitutes a frustrating situation until the organism attains the goal. Such a definition, of course, is so wide as to be of little use since, by definition, any theory of frustration would be a theory

[2] This conclusion will be further modified in this chapter.

covering the whole of psychology.[3] Some delimitation of the field covered by the term 'frustration situation' would therefore seem to be desirable.[4] The problem is essentially a semantic one, i.e. it is one of agreement that some situations will by definition constitute frustrating situations and that the term will be restricted to those situations. It is proposed that the term frustrating situation should be restricted to those situations in which *an organism is prevented, by a physical barrier, from attaining a physical goal by the performance of responses which previously led to the attainment of that goal.* It is recognized that the concept of physical barriers and goals is a very restrictive one. For example, Lewin has argued that 'an individual is in a state of frustration only if, and as long as, the inaccessible goal (G) is a part of his life space . . . the amount of frustration depends upon the degree to which the inaccessible goal is kept alive or present within the life space of the individual' (Barker, Dembo, and Lewin, 1941, pp. 58–9). It is realized that any complete theory of frustration will ultimately have to account for the presence and effects of internalized goals and barriers, and indeed these will be considered shortly. It is, however, entirely legitimate to formally restrict our definition of a frustrating situation in this way, just as it is legitimate to concern oneself only with the T-maze as a learning situation. One would even be justified in restricting one's definition of a frustrating situation to a single standard barrier situation. The definition given above has the further advantage of distinguishing clearly between learning and frustrating situations;[5] and also distinguishes between frustrating situations (which involve the *presence* of the goal) and deprivation conditions (in which the goal is *absent*).

b) FRUSTRATED ORGANISM

It is here argued that the frustrating situation, as defined above, gives rise to differential responses in the organism indicative of a state of frustration, and in particular that *organisms will differ in the extent to which they are frustrated by a standard frustrating situation.* These

---

[3] It is, of course, a tenable point of view that concepts such as frustration and conflict are superfluous, the appropriate behaviour being accounted for in terms, say, of the constructs of learning theory.

[4] The review of the literature on frustration by Lawson and Marx (1958a) includes under frustrating situations such variables as hypothetical situations, altered reward conditions, delayed reward, extinction, failure with possibility of success implied, prevention of completion of a response sequence, interruption of a response aroused by goal stimuli, failure on a task on which the subject has previously succeeded, punishment, any combination of the above, and conflict.

[5] It should be noted, however, that the frustrating situation, as defined, may prevent the completion of *unlearned* as well as learned responses.

differences will arise in a number of ways. They may be a function of basic personality structure or they may arise from differing prior experiences of frustrating situations. These problems will be considered later in this chapter.[6] Here it is merely necessary to recognize that there will not be a perfect correlation between a frustrating situation and frustration state any more than a learning situation leads to equal amounts of learning. The main problem here is the identification of the state of frustration as opposed to the identification of responses to that state. There are a number of ways of doing this, for example, by conceptualizing frustration as a hypothetical response which has stimulus drive and cue properties influencing subsequent behaviour. This aspect of the problem will be dealt with shortly. Here we merely wish to point out that there is a good deal of evidence that physiological indices may be reliably and validly used as indices of a state of frustration, but that psychological indices may also be used.

We need not here review the literature on physiological indices of a state of frustration. The most significant indices have been found to be changes in galvanic skin reflex activity and pulse rate. A study by Thiesen and Meister (1949) will serve as a paradigm. Their frustrating situation involved failure in a maze learning situation following success and where the subject expected to succeed. As measures of frustration state they took pulse rate, galvanic skin reflex, blood pressure, hand tremor, and respiration rate, the frustration index being the change from success to failure. They found that there was significant variability in changes between subjects in the frustrating situation on the physiological measures of galvanic skin reflex and pulse rate[7] and thus confirmed the hypothesis that subjects differ significantly in the extent to which a frustration state is induced in a frustrating situation. Results of this nature have been confirmed in a number of studies, most notably by Freeman and his colleagues (Freeman, 1939, 1940, 1948; Freeman and Giese, 1940).[8]

We may conclude that *the degree to which the organism is in a state of frustration may be measured as a function of the physiological changes which take place when that organism is placed in a standard frustrating situation*, with particular emphasis being placed on changes in the level of activity of the galvanic skin reflex and pulse rate. This is

---

[6] See the section on personality and frustration tolerance.

[7] They examined and rejected the possibility that these might be sheer temporal changes due to factors such as fatigue, etc.

[8] See also Brower (1946), Jost (1941), Sherman (1947), Sherman and Jost (1942).

not, of course, to deny that the galvanic skin reflex and pulse rate may be indices of states other than frustration (e.g. anxiety), but this difficulty is overcome by the restriction of the measurements as indices of frustration to a specific set of situations which we have called frustrating.

c) RESPONSES TO FRUSTRATION STATE

The physiological and psychological responses which constitute the frustration state will themselves serve as stimuli-producing responses. It is argued here, however, that we are not necessarily referring at this point to such phenomena as regression, fixation, and the like, but that before some at least of these types of phenomena are produced by the organism it is necessary to introduce the phenomenon of conflict. We must now turn, therefore, to the relationship between frustration and conflict.


## II. RELATIONSHIP BETWEEN FRUSTRATION AND CONFLICT

As already pointed out, many views have been expressed concerning the relationships between frustration and conflict. Thus, Brown and Farber (1951) argued that 'frustration is the consequence of either (1) the simultaneous activation of two competing excitatory tendencies or (2) the presence of a single excitatory tendency and an opposing inhibitory tendency' (p. 481), and indeed deny that any useful distinction can be made between conflict and frustration. Amsel (1958), working also within the general Hullian framework, adopts a different viewpoint, designating frustration as 'a condition which is the result of the interaction of a single prepotent response tendency with events external to the organism' (p. 103), whereas by conflict he means 'that process which is defined by the presence of two more response tendencies of about equal strength which are incompatible' (pp. 103-4).

We do not wish to deny the validity of either of these points of view but rather would draw attention to a somewhat different formulation, which is implicit in the Yale work on frustration and aggression but has not been explicitly stated by them. In doing so, we propose to show that certain constructs within Hullian theory have been used differently by various authors to conceptualize a state of conflict. Briefly, it is here suggested that approach-avoidance conflict *may* result from frustration, though it is not intended to imply that *all* such conflicts are the result of frustration, nor to deny that a state of conflict may itself induce further frustration. In order to maintain and demonstrate the justification for this point of view we propose to start with a frustrating situation and follow through the development of the situation to the point at which an approach-avoidance conflict state is achieved. We will assume that we are dealing with a naïve organism.

To do this it is necessary to introduce the notion of the fractional anticipatory response, as elaborated by Hull (1952) and Spence (1956). When an organism makes an overt goal-response ($R_g$), covert or fractional components ($r_g$) of that goal-response become classically conditioned to the goal area in which the consummatory responses are made. The strength of $r_g$ will be determined by the same factors that determine the strength of $R_g$, i.e. number of conditioning trials, and so on. The fractional goal-response ($r_g$) will have characteristic stimulus effects ($s_g$) with both motivational and associative properties. Through generalization, these properties will affect the behaviour of the organism at earlier stages of its locomotion towards the goal, and the motivational properties of $r_g — s_g$ will be reflected in the vigour of the behaviour occurring at the time of elicitation of the $r_g — s_g$ sequence. The associative properties of $r_g — s_g$ will be manifested by summation with other stimulus properties of the situation and affect learning.

Now, in Hullian terminology, $r_g$ is a response and hence must have behind it a habit, which we will call $_sH_{r_g}$. In any approach situation, the reaction potential of the organism to approach the goal will be a function[9] of the drive to the goal ($D_g$), the expectancy of attainment of the goal ($_sH_{r_g}$) and the incentive motivation[10] ($K_g$): i.e.

$$_sE_{r_g} = D_g \times {}_sH_{r_g} \times K_g$$

It will be noted that we have called the $_sH_{r_g}$ component of the equation the expectancy of attainment of the goal. The word is not used anthropomorphically, but can be defined operationally. It is, in fact, an 'expectancy' or 'cognitive' habit underlying $r_g — s_g$, which is the covert (but measurable) anticipatory response.

We are now ready to consider the sequence of events linking frustration and conflict. Let us suppose that we have established a reaction

---

[9] We are deliberately simplifying the situation for the sake of clarity.

[10] Incentive motivation as a determiner of reaction potential is not crucial to the argument but is included here because of certain comparisons between the Hullian system and those of Amsel and Atkinson which will be made later.

potential to approach a particular goal through training. Then the strength of that approach reaction potential may be represented (as we have seen) by the equation:

$$_sE_{r_g} = D_g \times {_sH_{r_g}} \times K_g$$

Supposing now we place a barrier in front of the goal and prevent the organism from attaining the goal-object. This will by definition constitute a frustrating situation. This frustrating situation will in some organisms lead to a state of frustration, which will on subsequent occasions when the organism is faced by the same or similar situations produce fractional anticipatory frustration responses $(r_f - s_f)$. Thus, the strength of the frustration potential may be represented as:

$$_sE_{r_f} = D_f \times {_sH_{r_f}} \times K_f$$

Now it is here assumed, on both theoretical and empirical grounds,[11] that the *initial* effect of frustration is to increase the approach tendency to the goal. The immediate effect therefore will be the *summation* of the approach and frustration reaction potentials to produce greater striving towards the blocked goal. Thus:

$$_sE_{r_{g+f}} = {_sE_{r_g}} + {_sE_{r_f}}$$

It is important to notice that the mere induction of a state of frustration in this theory does *not* lead to a state of conflict, but only to increased vigour of response towards the goal.

The effect of this summation of approach and frustration reaction potentials, resulting in a raising of approach strength towards the blocked goal, may be either that the goal is achieved or that punishment is incurred. Let us suppose that the latter is the case. If the renewed approach results in punishment then an inhibitory tendency not to approach (i.e. initially to withdraw from, and subsequently to avoid) the goal will be established. The fractional anticipatory portion of that avoidance response we will call $r_p - s_p$[12] and the avoidance reaction potential will be a function of:

$$_sE_{r_p} = D_p \times {_sH_{r_p}} \times K_p$$

It is here postulated that *conflict arising in this kind of situation repre-*

---

[11] See the later discussion of the work of Amsel and his colleagues.
[12] We use the terminology of Amsel (1958) to indicate the effects of punishment.

*sents the clash between the excitatory and inhibitory components of approach and avoidance behaviour,* i.e.

$$\text{Conflict} = ({}_sE_{r_{g+1}} - {}_sE_{r_p})$$

This general theoretical statement may be clearer if we take a concrete example. Let us consider again the frustration-aggression hypothesis. An organism is blocked from the attainment of a familiar goal and experiences frustration. The goal-potential summates with the frustration-potential to produce increased striving towards the goal and this increased striving *may* take the form of aggression (e.g. trying to remove the physical barrier). If this increased striving is severely punished, however, the organism will develop an avoidance-potential and when placed in similar situations or the same situation again will be in a state of conflict.

Several points should be noted about the model. In the first place it does not regard conflict as an inevitable consequence of frustration but only as a possible consequence. Whether or not conflict arises depends on what happens when the increased reaction potential leads the organism to try and overcome the barrier. Secondly, conflict refers to a clash of excitatory and inhibitory *potentials*, not to a clash of drives, or habits alone. This is an important point. Practically all workers in this field consider conflict to refer to conflict between *drives*. But, as Haner and Brown (1955) pointed out some time ago, this is quite illogical. Clearly, incompatible drives conflict only under appropriate environmental circumstances and where the possibility of action arises. Conflict therefore must refer to the potential for action of the organism. Thirdly, conflict arises from the clash of aversive and approach tendencies but frustration is an approach, not an aversive tendency. This, as we shall see, is in direct contrast to some workers who regard conflict as arising from approach-frustration clashes.

## III. FRUSTRATION AND LEARNING THEORY

We have attempted here to set up a limited theory of frustration and approach-avoidance conflict in terms of general learning theory. We must now look at some experimental work which has recently been carried out in the area of frustration by learning theorists. In recent years, the notion that frustration may be conceptualized as an intervening variable within the Hullian system has received a good deal of attention, although the formulations have been somewhat different from the theory presented above. The work in question received its main impetus from a paper by Brown and Farber (1951) and has been mainly carried out by Amsel and his colleagues.

Brown and Farber (1951) argued that the introduction of frustration as an intervening variable involves three major tasks:

1) the denotation of the antecedent conditions that are assumed to lead to frustration;
2) the specification of the functional relations holding between frustration and these conditions;
3) the denotation of ways in which the postulated frustration state might significantly affect behaviour.

Their definition of the antecedent conditions of frustration is a very wide one, including such conditions as the introduction of partial or complete physical barriers, the omission or reduction of reward, delay between initiation and completion of a response sequence, or variations in the organism's condition, environment, or training. Their definition of a frustration state in effect equates it, as we have seen, with a state of conflict.

Brown and Farber suggest two major ways in which frustration may effect overt behaviour. Firstly, they suggest that frustration may increase the general level of motivation, by functioning as an irrelevant drive and summating with relevant drives in a particular situation. Compared with other drives, however, frustration is unique in that it depends upon the arousal of competitive tendencies rather than upon conditions of deprivation, and with respect to the events that result in its diminution. Secondly, they suggest that frustration may serve as an internal cue or stimulus. As such, frustration might serve as a source of new response patterns which will be carried over into other situations in which the subject is frustrated. 'Responses to frustration originally restricted to a single environmental context might thus be elicited by frustration-produced cues in other contexts despite any ostensible inappropriateness that might characterize such appearance' (Brown and Farber, 1951, p. 490).

Both of the suggestions of Brown and Farber concerning the effects of frustration have been experimentally investigated.

a) FRUSTRATION-PRODUCED DRIVE INCREMENT

If frustration acts as irrelevant drive which summates with other relevant drives to influence behaviour, then one consequence of frustration would be that responses performed subsequent to the frustration would be strengthened. Amsel and Roussel (1952) tested two specific predictions from this general hypothesis.

i) When a running response has been maximally elicited under hunger motivation, the addition of frustration to the motivational complex will result in the establishment of a new and higher maximum running speed;

ii) The facilitating effect of frustration on running speed will vary with variation in the amount of time spent in the frustrating situation just preceding that running.

The apparatus they used is shown in Fig. 6.1. Essentially, it consists of two goal-boxes (G1 and G2) connected by two runways, together with a timing system enabling measurement of the time taken

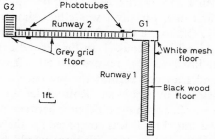

Fig. 6.1. Apparatus used in experiments by Amsel. (Source: Amsel, A., and Hancock, W. 'Motivational properties of frustration: III. Relation of frustration effect to antedating goal factors'. *J. exp. Psychol.*, 1957, 53, 126–31.)

to traverse part of runway 2. The rats were initially trained to run to goal-box 1 to find food, thence to goal-box 2, where they also found food. It was predicted that subsequent failure to find food in goal-box 1 would lead to an increase in general drive-level which would speed up running to goal-box 2. The longer they were detained in goal-box 1, the faster their running should be. The measures used were latency of response time for leaving goal-box 1 when the door leading to runway 2 was raised; and speed of running over a measured stretch of runway 2. The hypothesis that frustration would increase drive-level was supported, both latency and running time significantly decreasing following frustration; but increased delay had no effect on these measures. This may have been either because increased drive reaches its maximum very rapidly and then remains steady or even decreases; or (more probably) because the delay periods were very short.

N

In a subsequent experiment, Amsel and Hancock (1957) developed their interpretation further. Pointing out that 'only after some minimal number of rewards will non-reward of a response be frustrating', they attempted to account for this fact by conceptualizing frustration as 'the failure of an expectation' from being realized. 'The "expectancy" construct in the Hullian system is the fractional antedating (anticipatory) goal reaction ($r_g - s_g$). Presumably, then, not rewarding a response will elicit frustration to the degree that earlier rewards of that response have led to the conditioning of $r_g$ to cues in an instrumental response sequence' (p. 126). Now one set of conditions favouring elicitation of $r_g$ is an approach to the goal which is as similar to the goal itself as possible. Under these conditions the frustration effect should be greater.

Two experiments were carried out, using the apparatus described earlier. In the first one, runway 1 was either similar to or different from goal-box 1. Otherwise the experiment was identical with that carried out by Amsel and Roussel. In the second experiment, however, *all* training involved 50% reward and 50% frustration in goal-box 1. Amsel and Hancock verified the presence of the frustration effect as demonstrated by Amsel and Roussel, i.e. an increase in running time in runway 2. When the difference between running time for rewarded and frustrated trials was compared for the white and black runways the hypothesis that the difference would be greater when runway 1 and goal-box 1 were similar was confirmed. In experiment 2, however, this difference was found only after the first block of 18 trials. Amsel and Hancock conclude that 'there is a positive relationship between the frustrating effect of non-reward and the strength of an ante-dating goal reaction preceding the non-reward' (p. 131).

Evidence supporting the drive-increment theory of frustration has been reported by Marx (1956). Thus Bernstein (1957) established a strong wheel-turning escape response in rats, using Miller's (1948a) experimental method. The rats were then divided into four groups, which were extinguished under four times of delay of escape following wheel-turning – 0, 2, 4, and 8 seconds delay. The results supported the drive-increment theory in that rats whose wheel-turning responses were blocked for 2 or 4 seconds showed greater resistance to extinction of the responses than rats suffering no delay of escape. Similarly, an experiment by Holder *et al.* (1957) interfered with a learned response half-way to the goal, the animal being delayed in a runway for 0, 15, or 45 seconds. Response strength (as measured by starting time and running time) increased following removal of the barrier as a direct function of the delay.

An alternative explanation for the results obtained by Amsel and his colleagues was put forward by Seward *et al.* (1957), who argued that the increased running speed found in the second runway after non-reinforcement in the first goal-box was an artefact of the experimental situation. Reinforcement in the first goal-box might just as well produce a decrease in running speed, thus erroneously suggesting an increase following non-reinforcement. They showed experimentally that feeding the animals before placing them in the starting box produced a decrease in running speed in both runways. However, Wagner (1959) has effectively refuted this alternative explanation. If the hypothesis of Seward *et al.* is correct, then a control group of rats who are never fed in the first goal-box should run faster in the second runway than the experimental group who are fed, since their motivational level would be higher. If the hypothesis of Amsel is correct, on the other hand the control group should run more slowly than the experimental group in the second runway, since the former animals have never been frustrated in the first goal-box. Replicating the studies of Amsel and Roussel (1952) and of Amsel and Hancock (1957), with the addition of the appropriate control group, Wagner showed clearly that Amsel's hypothesis was supported rather than that of Seward *et al.*

This experimental evidence is congruent with earlier observations, e.g. Finch (1942), that chimpanzees which had learned to pump a spigot to obtain a reward would (when frustrated) show significantly increased vigour of response. Haner and Brown (1955) showed that vigour of pressing a plunger increased significantly the closer the subject was to his goal when he was frustrated.

b) FRUSTRATION-PRODUCED DRIVE-INCREMENT AS CUE

The argument here is that disruption of a learned sequence, e.g. omission of food where previously present as a reward, blocking of an instrumental response, etc., will produce frustration stimulation ($S_f$), which will elicit a characteristic class of responses ($R_{s_f}$). Hence a new habit of responding to the cues of the previously rewarded situation will begin to build up, which will interact or interfere with the old habit (Adelman and Maatsch, 1955). It has been suggested by these authors that since $S_f$ will elicit a number of responses, that one will be strengthened which removes S from the frustrating situation.

This general hypothesis was tested by Amsel and Ward (1954), using the apparatus previously described. After the initial procedure, also previously described, the first part of the maze was converted into a simple T-maze, with goal-box 1 serving as choice-point. After initial training on right and left turning, intermittent frustration and reward was given in goal-box 1. It was predicted that the rats would learn to discriminate the new reward-boxes on the basis of reward/no reward patterns in goal-box 1. Amsel and Ward found that the animals learned the correct discrimination to a criterion of 75% correct responses in about 85 trials, but that this learning proved to be highly unstable and quickly dropped to chance level again. They also

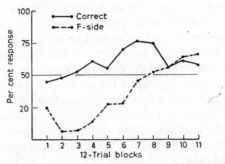

Fig. 6.2. Learning curve and curve of responses of the frustration (white) side for five rats. (Source: Amsel, A., and Ward, J. S. 'Motivational properties of frustration: II. Frustration drive stimulus and frustration reduction in selective learning'. *J. exp. Psychol.*, 1954, **48**, 37–47.)

found a tendency for the rats to respond increasingly to the side correct following frustration, i.e. 'a mild fixation of F-side response develops' (p. 40). Fig. 6.2 shows the curve of learning and the curve of response to the side correct following frustration. 'This mild fixation might be attributed to double reinforcement on frustration trials: hunger reduction and frustration reduction' (p. 40).

More significant findings for this hypothesis were provided by an experiment of Bernstein (1957). After extinguishing the wheel-turning response in the experiment described earlier, he ran the same animals in a straight runway to food reward and then extinguished this new habit, under the assumption that this new extinction would have stimulus ('frustration') properties in common with the first extinction. Greater resistance to extinction was apparent for the

2- and 4-second animals of the original experiment as compared with the 0-second animals, the hypothesis thus being supported.[13]

The hypothesis that frustration-stimulation has both drive and cue properties has been further developed in a series of ingenious experiments. Thus, it has been argued that frustration-produced cues may facilitate extinction. Rohrer (1949) argued that decline of a bar-pressing response under conditions of massed practice could be attributed to a frustration drive, which would interfere with the on-going response more in massed trials than in spaced, since it would dissipate more slowly in the former.[14] Adelman and Maatsch (1955) argued that frustration as a drive-stimulus ($S_f$) will elicit a number of responses, the one which is strengthened being that which removes S from the frustrating situation. Thus they predicted that extinction would proceed at a different rate if removal from the frustrating situation is consistently associated with a particular $S_f$ (e.g. jumping) as compared with the normal extinction procedure of lifting the animal out of the box. Specifically, they argued:

i) Extinction would be most rapid, if the $S_f$ was specific and incompatible with the originally rewarded response;

ii) extinction would be slowest if the $S_f$ was specific and compatible with the repetition of the originally rewarded response;

iii) extinction would proceed at a rate intermediate between (i) and (ii) if removal from the box were associated with a random array of $S_f$s, i.e. the $S_f$ on each occasion would be different.

To test these hypotheses, they trained rats to run a simple straight-way to food and then extinguished them in three ways:

i) The rat was allowed to withdraw from the box immediately after finding no food there (specific/incompatible response).

ii) the rat was allowed to jump on to the top of the box immediately after finding no food there (specific/compatible response);

[13] The 0-second delay group did not differ from a new group run only in the straight runway, so Bernstein rejected any explanation in terms of fear from the earlier shock experiences generalizing differentially.

[14] Amsel and Roussel (1952) criticize Rohrer's experiments on the grounds that his results can be more readily explainable in terms of reactive and conditioned inhibition, and that 'in order to show that frustration is a motivating condition, it would seem necessary to demonstrate that its presence increases some aspect of behaviour. It is not sufficient simply to show a decrease in strength of the response leading to frustration' (Amsel and Roussel, 1952, p. 363).

iii) the rat was removed from the box manually (general/incompatible response).[15]

All three predictions were verified and it therefore seems clear that frustration-produced responses will interfere with the ongoing habit (i.e. lead to their extinction) to the extent that they are incompatible with these responses.

Highly relevant to the Adelman and Maatsch work is an experiment by Hulse and Stanley (1956). They trained rats under conditions of partial or continuous reinforcement to find food in a goal-box. At the far end of the goal-box was a small food-box which was either open or closed on each trial and thus served as a present or absent secondary reinforcement. Now Hulse and Stanley found that rats trained under conditions of partial reinforcement extinguished more slowly than rats trained under conditions of continuous reinforcement, only if secondary reinforcement were present continuously during acquisition of the response. In terms of the formulation of Adelman and Maatsch, this finding would be interpretable as evidence that when secondary reinforcement is present on nonreinforced trials the animal is able to make a response which is both specific and not incompatible with the primary response of eating. Hence extinction will be slow compared with the continuously reinforced group of rats which will not have learned such alternative compatible responses. Hulse and Stanley's own explanation is close to this.

> During partially reinforced training S learns to eat food in the goal-box when food is present, but learns to do something else when food is absent . . . Partially reinforced Ss thus enter extinction proper with something to do in the empty goal-box, while continuously reinforced Ss have learned only to eat there. This, in turn, means that during extinction, the partially reinforced S, by making these other responses, is quickly removed from cues stimulating eating for a longer time. Thus conditioned eating should extinguish more quickly (p. 226),

Hulse and Stanley relate these results to the frustration-generated excitement theory of food reinforcement (Sheffield and Campbell, 1954) but they are clearly compatible with the interpretation of Adelman and Maatsch.

---

[15] Time spent in the box was controlled.

The results of the experiments described above pose some interesting conundrums. They may be classified into those experiments dealing with frustration as drive and those dealing with frustration as cue.

### a) FRUSTRATION AS DRIVE

It has been argued that frustration as drive *strengthens* ongoing responses (Amsel and Roussel, 1952; Amsel and Hancock, 1957); on the other hand, it has been argued that frustration as drive weakens ongoing responses (Rohrer, 1949).

### b) FRUSTRATION AS CUE

It has been argued that frustration as cue helps in the learning of new discriminations (Amsel and Ward, 1954); on the other hand, it has been argued that frustration as cue brings about extinction (Adelman and Maatsch, 1955).

Fortunately, a good deal of the confusion may be resolved fairly easily by reference to a number of other considerations. Let us consider first the alleged contradiction between the finding that either increased vigour of response, or extinction may follow frustrating events. Schlosberg and Pratt (1956) showed that hungry rats will return repeatedly to a source of food, provided the food can be seen and smelled, but is inaccessible, and these results were confirmed by Lawson and Marx (1958b). On the other hand, as we have seen, Rohrer (1949) found extinction following frustration under conditions of massed practice. The contradiction between these findings is, however, more apparent than real. In the first place, it is necessary to distinguish clearly between the effect of frustration on responses which *follow* the frustrating events, and those which *precede* it. Thus, Amsel and his colleagues have concerned themselves with what happens in the second runway following frustration in the first goal-box. They do not report in these studies what happens to the rat's response in the first runway. It is at least possible that the animals will begin to extinguish their responses in the first runway and would eventually fail to reach the first goal-box (because, until they reach the first goal-box, there is no way of avoiding or escaping frustration). Provided they reach the first goal-box, however, then their subsequent response will be intensified. Indeed, Amsel (1958), although not citing any evidence, has argued that

> frustrative-non-reward events determine activating (drive) effects, which can be measured as an increase in the vigour of behaviour

which immediately follows the frustrative events, and *are also responsible for inhibitory effects, which are at least partly responsible for decreases in strength of the instrumental behaviour which is terminated by the frustrative event* (p. 102; italics not in original).

Secondly, it should be noted that the secondary reward effects found by Schlosberg and Pratt (1956) are not incompatible with the extinction effects postulated by Amsel (1958) as a result of frustration, for the two authors are clearly referring to quite different classes of frustrating event. This brings us to an important point which concerns Amsel's definition of a frustrating situation. Amsel himself is quite clear about his definitions of frustration and frustrating situations which refer to 'a hypothetical, implicit reaction elicited by non-reward after a number of prior rewards' (Amsel, 1958, p. 103). By non-reward, Amsel explicitly means absence of reward. The study of Schlosberg and Pratt (1956), on the other hand, clearly uses frustration to refer, not to absence of reward, but to *inaccessibility* of a reward which is still present. That is, the definition of Schlosberg and Pratt involves essentially the introduction of a barrier, whereas the definition of Amsel does not. It is clear, therefore, that secondary reinforcement effects would be likely to be more prominent in the former than in the latter case. It will be apparent that our own definition of a frustrating situation coincides with that of Schlosberg and Pratt and not with that of Amsel.

There is also no necessary difficulty involved in the findings that frustration stimuli acting as cues produce both learning and extinction effects, provided we regard extinction as being brought about by the replacement of one response by another, and not just a function of repetition without reinforcement. Hence, the results of Amsel and Ward (1954) and of Adelman and Maatsch (1955) are complementary rather than contradictory.

Three further points should be noted. Firstly, as both Brown and Farber (1951) and Marx (1956) have pointed out, the experimental facts *may* be interpretable within the general Hullian framework without the introduction of the new construct of frustration, and that weighty evidence is required before such additional constructs may be admitted. In this connection, Marx and his colleagues have produced experimental evidence (Lawson and Marx, 1958b; Tyler *et al.*, 1959) which at least suggests the need for caution in so far as some of the data may be interpreted in conventional discrimination terms without recourse to the concept of frustration. On the other hand, it may be pointed out that acceptance of the concept of fractional anticipatory goal-responses ($r_g - s_g$) as a necessary construct within the Hullian framework logically would seem to demand a complementary construct of fractional anticipatory frustration responses ($r_f - s_f$) and hence Amsel (1958) may be regarded merely as filling a gap in Hull's system, rather than modifying it. Furthermore, it is clear that Hull (1952) himself was willing to incorporate such a construct into his system.

Secondly, and more importantly, although Amsel (1958) carefully distinguishes between the three kinds of fractional anticipatory mechanisms (reward, frustration, and anxiety) we have mentioned earlier, it is by no means certain that either he, or Brown and Farber, have made a satisfactory case for clearly distinguishing between frustration and anxiety as intervening variables within the Hullian system.

We have already outlined the conditions required to be satisfied before frustration can be accepted as a legitimate intervening variable within the Hullian framework, viz. the specification of the antecedent conditions and consequent behaviour; the specification of the relationships existing between the antecedents and frustration, and between frustration and the consequents; and (as a result of the previous specifications) the demonstration that frustration is a necessary intervening variable.

Now it is uncertain whether a satisfactory justification in these terms has yet been put forward for the concept of frustration. Brown and Farber were at pains to show that frustration had different antecedents and consequents from other drives, such as hunger and thirst. But such a demonstration does not settle the crucial point that it is necessary in particular that the antecedents and consequents are different for frustration as compared with *anxiety*. If the results of the experiments can all be adequately accounted for in terms of this intervening variable, then the postulation of a new variable will be unnecessary. Indeed anxiety has been conceptualized in an almost identical fashion with frustration. Thus anxiety is considered to have both drive properties and cue properties. It can either facilitate performance (where competing responses are absent) or interfere with performance (where the learning situation is more complex). The evidence for the interference effects of frustration has been shown above to be very strong, and where it served as a cue to facilitate new learning it should be noted that the learning situation was still a very simple one (as compared with complex maze learning) and that the learned response was very unstable. Finally, Amsel and Ward (1954) in their study actually refer to frustration reduction as a reinforcing state of affairs. It is difficult to avoid the translation of this sentence into 'anxiety reduction as a reinforcing state of affairs'.

Thirdly, it will be apparent that conflict is conceptualized by Amsel as arising from a clash of frustration-motivated responses and goal-motivated responses. Thus, he explicitly indicates that 'one of the incompatible response tendencies in an approach-avoidance competition may be frustration motivated, or, to be more exact, motivated by conditioned (anticipatory) frustration'. He does not indicate the role of fractional anticipatory anxiety in producing conflict.

## IV. FRUSTRATION AND ACHIEVEMENT

By contrast with Amsel's position, we turn now to some important formulations of Atkinson and his colleagues in which approach-avoidance conflict is conceptualized in terms of the clash of goal- and anxiety-responses, but there is no incorporation within the system of frustration as yet.

The most important constructs in Atkinson's theoretical system are those of motive (or need), motivation, expectancy, and incentive. Atkinson defines a motive as '. . . a disposition to strive for a certain kind of satisfaction, as a capacity for satisfaction in the attainment of a certain class of incentives' (Atkinson, 1957, p. 360). Thus the achievement motive is defined as a disposition to approach success, and the motive to avoid failure as a disposition to avoid failure or a capacity for experiencing shame and humiliation as a consequence of failure. Motives, it should be noted carefully, are stable dispositions learned early in life, and have no specific reference, i.e. they do not themselves dictate which particular responses will occur.

The second construct, expectancy, is defined as 'a cognitive anticipation, usually aroused by cues in a situation, that performance of some act will be followed by a particular consequence. The strength of an expectancy can be represented as the subjective probability of the consequence, given the act' (Atkinson, 1957, p. 360).

The third construct, incentive, is defined as '. . . the relative attractiveness of a specific goal that is offered in a situation or the

relative unattractiveness of an event that might occur as a consequence of some act' (Atkinson, 1957, p. 360).

Atkinson makes a clear distinction between the relatively permanent motives of a person and his momentary motivational state.
The momentary strength of motivation is determined by the multi-
plicative interaction of motive (M) with expectancy of success or
failure (P) and amount of incentive (I), i.e.

$$\text{Strength of motivation} = f(M \times P \times I)$$

One of Atkinson's most important contributions has been the
construction of separate measures for motive and motivation. This
was accomplished by standardizing the procedures for administering
the Thematic Apperception Test (TAT) and by using pictures with
neutral content. Under these conditions, the individual differences
observed in thematic content (scored for achievement, or failure-
avoidance) should reflect only fundamental or permanent differences
in motive. Such scores can then be used as a baseline from which to
measure the effect of situational and picture content cues in non-
neutral conditions upon motivation.

The particular form of expectancy with which Atkinson has concerned himself is the subjective probability of success ($P_s$). If we
assume that the degree of difficulty of a task can be inferred from the
subjective probability of success, and if we further assume that the
incentive value of success ($I_s$) is a positive linear function of difficulty, then:

$$I_s = 1 - P_s$$

It also follows that if the incentive value of failure ($I_f$) is a negative
linear function of difficulty, then:

$$I_f = - P_s$$

Now, suppose we hold strength of motive (M) constant and assign
arbitrary values for the subjective probability of success ($P_s$) and
failure ($P_f$) for a number of different tasks (A to I), as shown in
Table 6.1. We can then calculate the strength of motivation to avoid
failure for each task separately, with the results shown. One interesting feature of this theoretical analysis is that, in a constrained
situation (i.e. where the subject is not allowed to choose the task
he will attempt), similar behaviour may be expected both of subjects
with motivation to achieve success and those with motivation to avoid
failure, in that in both cases, the subject will try hardest on tasks of

## TABLE 6.1

AROUSED MOTIVATION TO ACHIEVE (APPROACH) AND TO AVOID
FAILURE (AVOIDANCE) AS A JOINT FUNCTION OF MOTIVE
(M), EXPECTANCY (P), AND INCENTIVE (I), WHERE
$I_s = (1 - P_s)$ AND $I_f = (-P_s)$

| | Motivation to achieve | | | Motivation to avoid failure | | | Resultant motivation |
|---|---|---|---|---|---|---|---|
| | $M_s \times P_s \times I_s$ = Approach | | | $M_f \times P_f \times I_f$ = | | Avoidance | (Approach-avoidance) |
| Task A | 1 | ·10 | ·90 | ·09 | 1 | ·90–·10 | −·09 | 0 |
| Task B | 1 | ·20 | ·80 | ·16 | 1 | ·80–·20 | −·16 | 0 |
| Task C | 1 | ·30 | ·70 | ·21 | 1 | ·70–·30 | −·21 | 0 |
| Task D | 1 | ·40 | ·60 | ·24 | 1 | ·60–·40 | −·24 | 0 |
| Task E | 1 | ·50 | ·50 | ·25 | 1 | ·50–·50 | −·25 | 0 |
| Task F | 1 | ·60 | ·40 | ·24 | 1 | ·40–·60 | −·24 | 0 |
| Task G | 1 | ·70 | ·30 | ·21 | 1 | ·30–·70 | −·21 | 0 |
| Task H | 1 | ·80 | ·20 | ·16 | 1 | ·20–·80 | −·16 | 0 |
| Task I | 1 | ·90 | ·10 | ·09 | 1 | ·10–·90 | −·09 | 0 |

Source: Atkinson, J. W. 'Motivational determinants of risk-taking behaviour'. *Psychol. Rev.*, 1957, **64**, 359–72

intermediate difficulty. In a free situation, where the subject is allowed to choose the level of difficulty, a person with high motivation to avoid failure will avoid tasks of intermediate difficulty (because failure is most likely here) and choose either very easy tasks (where success is assured) or exceptionally difficult tasks (where failure is assured, but does not produce emotional disturbance). Results in accordance with this theoretical model were obtained in a study by Atkinson *et al.* (1960). Using subjects with high and low achievement motives they found that in a free situation (involving a shuffleboard game in which the subject could choose the position from which he aimed at the target) 64% of subjects with high need for achievement chose to aim from intermediate distances from the goal, whereas this was the case with only 39% of subjects with low need for achievement scores.

It will be noted that even in this recent study by Atkinson *et al.* (1960) high and low need for achievement is contrasted, the assumption being that 'there is considerable presumptive evidence that the motive to avoid failure is likely to be stronger than the achievement motive in many persons having low achievement scores' (Atkinson *et al.* 1960, p. 27). Atkinson appears to have been uncertain as to whether to postulate one or two dimensions in connection with achievement and failure avoidance. A paper published simultaneously, however (Atkinson and Litwin, 1960), suggests that Atkinson now prefers to regard need for achievement and need to avoid failure as orthogonal dimensions. Thus, the two needs are in this paper for the first time assessed by separate measures: need for achievement by the French Test of Insight, and need to avoid failure by the Test Anxiety Questionnaire of Mandler and Sarason. It is hypothesized that need for achievement scores should show a positive, and need to avoid failure scores a negative, correlation with preference for intermediate risk, persistence, and efficiency of performance. In the experiment, a modified Ring Toss game was used to measure preference for risk. A distance of 15 feet was marked out in 1-foot sections from the ring, and the subject allowed to choose the position from which he would throw. The results indicated that subjects with high need achievement and low need to avoid failure tended to throw from an intermediate position and also showed more persistence and higher scores on an examination. Furthermore, scores on the French Test of Insight and the Mandler/Sarason Anxiety Questionnaire correlated —·15.

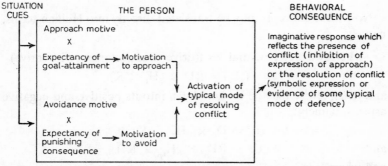

Fig. 6.3. A conception of approach-avoidance conflict as it affects the attempt to assess the strength of an approach motive from manifest motive-related imagery in thematic apperception. (Source: Atkinson, J. W., ed., Chapter 42 in *Motives in Fantasy, Action, and Society.* Princeton: Van Nostrand, 1958.)

The orthogonality of the two dimensions allows Atkinson to introduce the notion of conflict in situations involving risk-taking behaviour. The present position may be summarized in Fig. 6.3. Situational cues (i.e. expectancies of success and failure) arouse the approach and avoidance motives which interact with the expectancies of goal-attainment and failure respectively to produce motivation to approach and avoid. These simultaneously aroused motivations will produce a state of conflict if they are approximately equal in strength. The conflict may be resolved either by the inhibition of behaviour or by the activation of characteristic defence mechanisms.

It should be clear from the foregoing account that Atkinson's terms may be readily translated into those used by Hull. Thus the fundamental equation for behaviour in Atkinson's system is:

$$\text{Motivation} = f(\text{motive} \times \text{expectancy} \times \text{incentive})$$

and this may be broken down into its positive and negative aspects, namely:

| | |
|---|---|
| Positive motivation = (i.e. achievement) | f(achievement motive × subjective probability of success × incentive value of success) |
| and Negative motivation = (i.e. failure avoidance) | f(failure avoidance motive × subjective probability of failure × incentive value of failure) |

and where

Conflict = the extent to which positive and negative motivations approach equality

Now these concepts may be translated directly into Hullian terms, namely:

$$\text{Performance potential} = f(\text{drive} \times \text{expectancy} \times \text{incentive})$$
$$(_sE_r) = f(D \times {}_sH_r \times K)$$

and this likewise may be broken down into its positive and negative aspects, namely:

$${}_sE_{r_g} = D_g \times {}_sH_{r_g} \times K_g$$
and
$${}_sE_{r_g} = f(D_p \times {}_sH_{r_p} \times K_p)$$

and where

Conflict = the extent to which $_sE_{r_g}$ and $_sE_{r_p}$ approach equality

Now it will be noticed that no mention has been made in this comparison of the construct of fractional anticipatory frustration, as used by Amsel. This has been deliberately omitted in the above comparison because Atkinson himself has conceptualized the need to avoid failure as involving fractional anticipatory punishment (i.e. anxiety) rather than frustration. On the other hand, of course, it is possible that Atkinson may find it necessary to introduce some kind of frustration concept, in addition to his anxiety concept. It should also be noted that no mention has been made of the inhibitory constructs ($I_r$ and $_sI_r$) of Hull's system. It may well be that Atkinson will eventually need to take these into consideration also.

It should be noted in fairness that Atkinson would almost certainly reject the comparisons made above between his system and that of Hull. Although he has explicitly acknowledged the similarity between his own formulation of conflict and that of Miller (Atkinson, 1958), he has equally explicitly denied that his concept of motive is identical with that of drive as an energizing factor (Atkinson, 1957). None the less, it seems apparent from the comparisons made above that the similarities between the two systems are very close. The comparisons are not intended in any way to detract from Atkinson's achievement, nor to suggest that he should have employed Hull's terminology rather than his own. It seems highly likely that Atkinson's terminology is preferable in the field of human behaviour, whereas Hull's is preferable in the field of animal behaviour. The similarities between the systems of Miller, Amsel, and Atkinson, however, do suggest very strongly that variables basic to the explanation of human behaviour have been formulated in a rigorous fashion and should lead to a substantial body of knowledge in this area of study.

To summarize: our own formulation has indicated that approach-avoidance conflict may result from the clash between anticipatory anxiety on the one hand, and anticipatory frustration summating with anticipatory reward on the other. Amsel has conceptualized conflict as resulting from the clash of anticipatory frustration and reward; Atkinson as resulting from the clash of anticipatory reward and anxiety. It may well be that under certain conditions Amsel may need to consider the incorporation of anxiety within his system; whereas Atkinson may need to incorporate anticipatory frustration within his. At present, no more than this can be said.[16]

[16] It may be noted in passing that Feather (1959), in his penetrating review of the similarities between Atkinson's system and that of four other workers in the field of decision-making, did not consider the similarities between Atkinson and Hull.

## V. FRUSTRATION TOLERANCE AND PERSONALITY

Finally, we must consider briefly the relationship of frustration tolerance and personality to the concepts already introduced. Here again, terminological difficulties have caused confusion. Thus, when referring to frustration tolerance, it is rarely clear whether authors are referring to tolerance of a frustration situation (in which case frustration tolerance could probably be used synonymously with frustration state); or whether they are referring to the individual's ability to withstand a particular degree of frustration (in which case frustration state and frustration tolerance could be regarded as independent dimensions). The view taken here is that the latter formulation is probably to be preferred. Thus, it is possible to imagine two individuals, placed in identical frustrating situations, and manifesting the same degree of frustration state (as measured, say physiologically), but showing unequal amounts of ability to tolerate that state of frustration. On the other hand, it may be that frustration tolerance will turn out eventually to be indistinguishable from responses to the frustration state. For example, of two individuals with identical amounts of frustration, one may show high frustration tolerance because he has learned not to respond inadequately to such states, whereas the other individual has learned characteristic unadaptive responses to frustration, such as aggression.

The notion of frustration threshold was first systematically formulated by Rosenzweig (1944), who defined it as 'an individual's capacity to withstand frustration without failure of psychobiological adjustment, i.e., without resorting to inadequate modes of response' (p. 385). The reader will again notice the ambiguous use of the term 'frustration' in the quotation, though it seems reasonably clear from the general context that by this term Rosenzweig intends to refer to the state of the individual, not to the frustrating situation as such.

In developing his ideas about the nature of frustration tolerance, Rosenzweig likens it to the analytic concept of ego weakness, which itself he regards as defined by the ability to delay gratification. In other words frustration tolerance is equivalent to the development of the reality principle, where behaviour is guided by an appraisal of possible future consequences of action.

It is interesting to notice that in another paper, Rosenzweig (1945) virtually gives an operational definition of frustration tolerance as the extent to which the organism prefers to return to tasks at which he has been unsuccessful rather than successful. Using this measure of frustration tolerance, Rosenzweig was able to show that the choice of failure rather than success for repetition was a function of mental age level. Thus, when normal children were allowed to fail on one jigsaw puzzle, and succeed on another, and were then asked which one they preferred to repeat, there was a difference of nearly four years in mental age between those who preferred to repeat the unsuccessful and those who preferred to repeat the successful puzzle. And this difference was confirmed when spontaneous resumption was allowed.[17]

These findings are of considerable interest for two reasons. In the first place, they provide a link with Atkinson's work on the motivation to approach success and avoid failure; and secondly, they suggest that frustration tolerance may be a rather basic personality variable. The possible links are indicated in an important paper by Gewirtz (1959). She constructed a set of five formboard puzzle boxes constructed so as to represent a similarity dimension of shape. The two extreme puzzles (each of which could be made either easy or difficult to solve) served as training stimuli. Two groups of children received initial positive reinforcement (one group to each extreme puzzle); and two groups negative reinforcement, where positive reinforcement refers to successful solution of the problem, approval of the experimenter, and a material reward; and negative reinforcement refers to the reverse. The subjects were then presented with all possible pairs of the five puzzles and asked to indicate which one they would prefer to play with. The results indicated that both the negative reinforcement groups showed a reliable avoidance gradient, i.e. they preferred puzzles which were dissimilar to those on which they had failed. The results for the positive reinforcement groups were quite different, however. The effect of success in training on subsequent preference for one of a pair depended on the level of achievement motivation of the subject. Subjects *low* on achievement motivation tended to choose puzzles which were *similar* to those on which they had been allowed to succeed; whereas subjects *high* on achievement motivation tended to choose puzzles which were *different* (i.e. more difficult in this context) from those on which they had been allowed to succeed. This is an important finding because it

[17] This finding has been confirmed and extended more recently by Crandall and Rabson (1960).

O

indicates quite clearly that reinforcement may not always produce a gradient of approach, but may sometimes produce a gradient of avoidance, dependent significantly upon personality factors. As Gewirtz points out, there is a terminological difficulty here. Two kinds of gradient may be produced by success: 'one by the less achievement-motivated subjects, directed towards the goal of easy and safe success (the approach gradient); and the other by the highly achievement-motivated subjects, directed towards the goal of outstanding achievement in terms of solving the most difficult appearing task (the avoidance-like gradient)' (Gewirtz, 1959, p. 116). Gewirtz used the term 'avoidance-like' undoubtedly to point up the fact that the avoidance-of-success gradient is quite different conceptually from the avoidance gradient produced by failure. It is, in fact, a gradient of approach in the sense that some subjects will have a tendency to approach difficulty, as it were.

It is here suggested that Gewirtz's measure of the gradient to avoid success and approach difficulty may serve as an objective measure of degree of frustration tolerance (provided degree of frustration is controlled).

The relationship between *degree of frustration* and *frustration tolerance* is by no means clear. It is possible that these factors are independent of each other, as suggested here, or that they are related to each other, e.g. that frustration tolerance is inversely related to degree of frustration in any particular situation. It is also quite probable, as Rosenzweig (1944) suggested some time ago, that frustration tolerance is not a unitary variable. Until basic problems of this kind are experimentally and theoretically resolved, it would be a fruitless endeavour to attempt to discuss systematically the large number of studies on 'frustration' in relation to abnormal groups and no attempt will be made to do so here. The difficulties may be highlighted by briefly returning to a point made earlier in this chapter. There it was pointed out that in many of the studies reviewed in earlier chapters it was often unclear whether regression, aggression, fixation, etc., was intended to refer to a response to a frustrating situation, or to a state of frustration in the organism. It will now be clear that such responses never refer to the frustrating situation as such, but it should also by now be apparent that it is not even clear whether such responses are being made to a state of frustration *or* to a state of conflict resulting from frustration. Thus, in the case of the Yale studies on frustration and aggression, *direct* aggression will usually be a response to the state of frustration, whereas indirect aggression (i.e. displacement of aggression) will be a response to the state of conflict resulting from punishment of the original direct form of aggression. Regression, on the other hand, may turn out always to result from a state of conflict.

A few remarks may be made, however, in relation to future work on the relationship between frustration, conflict, and personality. In the past, progress has been impeded by a lack of any adequate dimensional personality framework, within which to work. Thus, studies by Wilensky (1952), Hybl and Stagner (1952), Brown (1939), and others are difficult to relate to each other because of their reliance on unsatisfactory diagnostic psychiatric categories. Such difficulties have now largely been overcome and it should be possible to relate the main dimensional systems of personality in a more rigorous fashion to predictions concerning behaviour in frustrating and conflict situations. The principal personality systems referred to here are, of course, those of Cattell (1957) and Eysenck (1947b, 1952, 1957). Although Cattell has thrown out some suggestions concerning the relationship between frustration and personality structure[18] we shall here consider very briefly the possible directions which the linking of Eysenck's personality theory with frustration and conflict theory might take. Of the four main dimensions adumbrated by Eysenck (intelligence, neuroticism, psychoticism, and introversion-extraversion) we shall consider only neuroticism and introversion-extraversion.

As we have already seen in a frustrating situation, it is necessary to distinguish between indices of the state of frustration of the organism, indices of his frustration tolerance level, and indices of his reactions to the state of frustration. In relation to Eysenck's personality system, it would be necessary to discover (or, in relation to his theories of neuroticism and introversion-extraversion, to predict) in what way neurotics will differ from normals, and introverts from extraverts, on these three variables.

It is hypothesized that *in a standard frustrating situation the amount of frustration manifested will be a positive function of the amount of neuroticism*. Now, since neurotics are commonly supposed to be characterized by high (autonomic) drive states, and since we have previously postulated that a frustration state involves essentially

---

[18] He has suggested, for instance (Cattell, 1957), that the source trait cyclothymia-schizothymia may be interpreted in terms of 'general frustration level'.

a state of increased drive, it follows that in a frustrating situation neurotics will *initially* show a greater striving towards the blocked goal, i.e. their approach tendency will be increased. And this conclusion is, of course, in agreement with the experimental finding that increased drive level raises the entire approach gradient.

With respect to frustration tolerance (if this is conceptualized as a variable separate from frustration state) it is hypothesized that *neurotics will be less able to tolerate a given level of frustration state than will matched normal controls.* The testing of this hypothesis will depend upon the development of separate measures of frustration state and frustration tolerance.

Similar speculations may, of course, be made about behaviour under states of conflict. Thus it would be expected that both approach and avoidance gradients in a conflict situation would be raised for neurotics as compared with normals placed in the same situation, because the increased drive level of neurotics should operate equally on approach and avoidance tendencies. From this it follows, for example, that displacement phenomena should show predictable differences for neurotics as compared with normals. Furthermore, the point of maximal conflict (using Miller's model) should occur further away from the goal for neurotics. The most important point here, however, concerns differential expectations concerning the behaviour in frustrating and conflict situations, of introverts and extraverts (or their neurotic prototypes – dysthymics and hysterics). It is hypothesized that *the principal differences between introverts and extraverts would relate to the rate of development of conflict and the techniques resorted to in order to resolve conflict.* Thus, if, as Eysenck (1957) suggests, extraverts are characterized by a more rapid growth, a higher asymptotic value, and a slower dissipation of reactive inhibition than are introverts, then in a situation involving the learning of incompatible responses and the subsequent resolution of the ensuing conflict state, there would be characteristic differences in mode of resolution as between introverts and extraverts. The integration of personality theory with frustration and conflict theory thus opens the way to the solution of the problem of how it is that conflicts resulting from frustration are resolved in different ways by different individuals. Such work, however, lies in the future.

Finally, mention must be made of the position of Maier in relation to the material of this chapter. It must be quite frankly admitted that the ideas discussed in this chapter cannot be integrated in such a way as satisfactorily to account for Maier's work at present. In view of the fact that it has been clearly shown that Maier's work is of far greater complexity than he seems to have appreciated, judgement on this point must be suspended.

# BIBLIOGRAPHY

ADELMAN, H. M., and MAATSCH, J. L. (1955) 'Resistance to extinction as a function of the type of response elicited by frustration'. *J. exp. Psychol.*, **50**, 61–5.

ADER, R., and CLINK, D. W. (1957) 'Effects of chlorpromazine on the acquisition and extinction of an avoidance response in the rat'. *J. Pharmacol. exp. Ther.*, **121**, 144–8.

AEBLI, H. (1952) 'Regression toward an unlearned preference in the rat'. *J. comp. physiol. Psychol.*, **45**, 258–63.

ALLISON, J., and HUNT, D. E. (1959) 'Social desirability and the expression of aggression under varying conditions of frustration'. *J. consult. Psychol.*, **23**, 528–32.

ALLPORT, G. W., and KRAMER, B. M. (1946) 'Some roots of prejudice'. *J. Psychol.*, **22**, 9–39.

AMMONS, C. H., and AMMONS, R. B. (1953) 'Aggression in doll-play: interviews of two- to six-year-old white males'. *J. genet. Psychol.*, **82**, 205–13.

AMSEL, A. (1958) 'The role of frustrative non-reward in non-continuous reward situations'. *Psychol. Bull.*, **55**, 102–19.

AMSEL, A., and HANCOCK, W. (1957) 'Motivational properties of frustration. III. Relation of frustration effect to antedating goal factors'. *J. exp. Psychol.*, **53**, 126–31.

AMSEL, A., and ROUSSEL, J. (1952) 'Motivational properties of frustration. I. Effect on a running response of the addition of frustration to the motivational complex'. *J. exp. Psychol.*, **43**, 363–8.

AMSEL, A., and WARD, J. S. (1954) 'Motivational properties of frustration. II. Frustration drive stimulus and frustration reduction in selective learning'. *J. exp. Psychol.*, **48**, 37–47.

ANDREAS, B. G. (1950) 'Motor responses as a function of type of conflict'. *Proc. Ia. Acad. Sci.*, **57**, 361–5.

ANDREAS, B. G. (1954) 'Empirical gradients of generalization in a perceptual motor task'. *J. exp. Psychol.*, **48**, 119–22.

ANDREAS, B. G. (1958) 'Motor conflict behavior as a function of motivation and amount of training'. *J. exp. Psychol.*, **55**, 173–8.

ANTONITIS, J. J., and SHER, A. J. (1952) 'Social regression in the white rat'. *J. Psychol.*, **33**, 99–111.

APPEL, M. H. (1942) 'Aggressive behaviour of nursery school children and adult procedures in dealing with such children'. *J. exp. educ.*, **11**, 185–199.

ARKOFF, A. (1957) 'Resolution of approach-approach and avoidance-avoidance conflicts'. *J. abnorm. soc. Psychol.*, **55**, 402–4.

ATKINSON, J. W. (1957) 'Motivational determinants of risk-taking behaviour'. *Psychol. Rev.*, **64**, 359–72.

ATKINSON, J. W. (Ed.) (1958) *Motives in Fantasy, Action, and Society*. Princeton: Van Nostrand.

ATKINSON, J. W., BASTIAN, J. R., EARL, R. W., and LITWIN, G. H. (1960) 'The achievement motive, goal setting, and probability preferences'. *J. abnorm. soc. Psychol.*, **60**, 27–36.

ATKINSON, J. W. and LITWIN, G. H. (1960) 'Achievement motive and test anxiety conceived as motive to approach success and motive to avoid failure'. *J. abnorm. soc. Psychol.*, **60**, 52–63.

BACH, G. R. (1945) 'Young children's play fantasies'. *Psychol. Monogr.*, **59** (No. 2), (pp. 69).

BAILEY, C. J., and MILLER, N. E. (1952) 'Effect of sodium amytal on behavior of cats in an approach-avoidance conflict'. *J. comp. physiol., Psychol.*, **45**, 205–8.

BARKER, R. G. (1938) 'Frustration as an experimental problem. V. The effect of frustration upon cognitive ability'. *Charact. & Pers.*, **7**, 145–50.

BARKER, R. G. (1942) 'An experimental study of the resolution of conflict by children; time elapsing and amount of vicarious trial-and-error behavior occurring'. In McNemar, Q., and Merrill, M. A. *Studies in Personality*, New York: McGraw-Hill (pp. 13–34).

BARKER, R. C ., DEMBO, T., and LEWIN, K. (1941) 'Frustration and regression: an experiment with young children'. *Studies in Topological and Vector Psychology II*. Univ. of Iowa Studies: *Studies in Child Welfare*, Vol. 18, No. 1.

BARKER, R. G., DEMBO, T., and LEWIN, K. (1943) 'Frustration and regression'. In Barker R. G., Kounin, J. S., and Wright, H. F. (Eds) *Child Behavior and Development*. New York: McGraw-Hill (pp. 441–58).

BARTHOL, R. P., and KU, N. D. (1959) 'Regression under stress to first learned behaviour'. *J. abnorm. soc. Psychol.*, **59**, 134–6.

BARUCH, D. W. (1941) 'Aggression during doll-play in a pre-school'. *Amer J. Orthopsychiat.*, **11**, 252–60.

BENDER, L., KEISER, S., and SCHILDER, P. (1936) 'Studies in aggressiveness'. *Genet. Psychol. Monogr.*, **18**, 357–564.

BENDIG, A. W. (1961a) 'A factor analysis of scales of emotionality and hostility'. *J. clin. Psychol.*, **17**, 189–92.

BENDIG, A. W. (1961b) 'A factor analysis of personality scales including the Buss-Durkee Hostility Inventory'. *J. gen. Psychol.* (in press)

BERGMAN, M. S., GRAHAM, H., and LEAVITT, H. C. (1947) 'Rorschach exploration of consecutive hypnotic chronological age level regressions'. *Psychosom. Med.*, **9**, 20–8.

BERKOWITZ, L. (1958) 'The expression and reduction of hostility'. *Psychol. Bull.*, **55**, 257–83.

BERKOWITZ, L. (1959) 'Anti-Semitism and the displacement of aggression'. *J. abnorm. soc. Psychol.*, **59**, 182–7.

BERKOWITZ, L. (1960a) 'Some factors affecting the reduction of overt hostility'. *J. abnorm. soc. Psychol.*, **60**, 14–21.

BERKOWITZ, L. (1960b) 'Repeated frustrations and expectations in hostility arousal'. *J. abnorm. soc. Psychol.*, **60**, 422–9.

BERKOWITZ, L. (1960c) 'The judgmental process in personality functioning'. *Psychol. Rev.*, **67**, 130–42.

BERKOWITZ, L., and HOLMES, D. S. (1959) 'The generalization of hostility to disliked objects'. *J. Person.*, **27**, 565–77.

BERKUN, M. M. (1957) 'Factors in the recovery from approach-avoidance conflict'. *J. exp. Psychol.*, **54**, 65–73.

BERNSTEIN, B. B. (1957) 'Extinction as a function of frustration drive and frustration-drive stimulus'. *J. exp. Psychol.*, **54**, 89–95.

BODY, M. K. (1955) 'Patterns of aggression in the nursery school'. *Child Developmt*, **26**, 1–11.

BORNSTON, F. L., and COLEMAN, J. C. (1956) 'The relationship between certain parents' attitudes toward child rearing and the direction of aggression of their young adult offspring'. *J. clin. Psychol.*, **12**, 41–4.

BRADY, J. V. (1951) 'The effect of electroconvulsive shock on a conditioned emotional response: the permanence of the effect'. *J. comp. physiol. Psychol.*, **44**, 507–11.

BRIDGES, K. M. B. (1931) *The Social and Emotional Development of the Pre-school Child*. London: Kegan Paul.

BROWER, D. (1946) 'Respiration and blood pressure in sensory motor conflict'. *J. gen. Psychol.*, **34**, 47–58.

BROWN, J. F. (1939) 'Reactions of psychiatric patients in a frustrating situation'. *Bull. Menninger Clin.*, **3**, 44–64.

BROWN, J. S. (1942a) 'The generalization of approach responses as a function of stimulus intensity and strength of motivation'. *J. comp. Psychol.*, **33**, 209–26.

BROWN, J. S. (1942b) 'Factors determining conflict reactions in difficult discriminations'. *J. exp. Psychol.*, **31**, 272–92.

BROWN, J. S. (1948) 'Gradients of approach and avoidance responses and their relation to motivation'. *J. comp. physiol. Psychol.*, **41**, 450–65.

BROWN, J. S., and FARBER, I. E. (1951) 'Emotions conceptualized as intervening variables – with suggestions toward a theory of frustration'. *Psychol. Bull.*, **48**, 465–95.

BUGELSKI, B. R., and MILLER, N. E. (1938) 'A spatial gradient in the strength of avoidance responses'. *J. exp. Psychol.*, **23**, 494–505.

BUGELSKI, B. R., and WOODWARD, D. P. (1951) 'The effect of distinctive cues on the spatial gradient of avoidance'. *J. comp. physiol. Psychol.*, **44**, 450–6.

BURTON, A. (1941) 'The influence of social factors upon the persistence of satiation in pre-school children'. *Child Developmt*, **12**, 121–9.

BURTON, A. (1942) 'The aggression of young children following satiation'. *Amer. J. Orthopsychiat.*, **12**, 262–7.

BUSS, A. H. and DURKEE, A. (1957) 'An inventory for assessing different kinds of hostility'. *J. consult. Psychol.*, **21**, 343–9.

CATTELL, R. B. (1950) *Personality: A Systematic Theoretical and Factual Study*. New York: McGraw-Hill.

CATTELL, R. B. (1951) 'P-technique: a new method for analyzing the structure of personal motivation'. *Trans. New York Acad. Sci.*, **14**, 29–34.

CATTELL, R. B. (1957) *Personality and Motivation Structure and Measurement*. New York: World Book Co.

CHASDI, E. H., and LAWRENCE, M. S. (1955) 'Some antecedents of aggression and effects of frustration in doll-play'. In McClelland, D. C. (Ed.) *Studies in Motivation*. New York: Appleton-Century-Crofts (pp. 517–28).

CHILD, I. L., FRANK, K. F., and STORM, T. (1956) 'Self-ratings and

TAT: Their relations to each other and to childhood background'. *J. Person.*, **25**, 98–114.

CHILD, I. L., and WATERHOUSE, I. K. (1952) 'Frustration and the quality of performance: I. A critique of the Barker, Dembo, and Lewin experiment'. *Psychol. Rev.*, **59**, 351–62.

COGHILL, G. E. (1929) *Anatomy and the Problem of Behaviour.* London: Cambridge Univ. Press.

COHEN, A. R. (1955) 'Social norms. arbitrariness of frustration, and status of the agent of frustration in the frustration-aggression hypothesis'. *J. abnorm. soc. Psychol.*, **51**, 222–6.

CONGER, J. J. (1951) 'The effects of alcohol on conflict behaviour in the albino rat'. *Quart. J. Stud. Alcohol.*, **12**, 1–29.

COWEN, E. L., LANDES, J., and SCHAET, D. E. (1959) 'The effects of mild frustration on the expression of prejudiced attitudes'. *J. abnorm. soc. Psychol.*, **58**, 33–8.

CRANDALL, V. J. (1951) 'Induced frustration and punishment-reward expectancy in thematic apperception stories'. *J. consult. Psychol.*, **15**, 400–4.

CRANDALL, V. J., and RABSON, A. (1960) 'Children's repetition choices in an intellectual achievement situation following success and failure'. *J. genet. Psychol.*, **97**, 161–8.

CRASILNECK, H. B., and MICHAEL, C. M. (1957) 'Performance on the Bender under hypnotic age regression'. *J. abnorm. soc. Psychol.*, **54**, 319–22.

DAVIS, J. M. (1958) 'A reinterpretation of the Barker, Dembo, and Lewin study of frustration and regression'. *Child Developmt*, **29**, 503–6.

DAVITZ, J. R. (1952) 'The effects of previous training on post frustration behavior'. *J. abnorm. soc. Psychol.*, **47**, 309–15.

DE VALOIS, R. L. (1954) 'The relation of different levels and kinds of motivation to variability of behavior'. *J. exp. Psychol.*, **47**, 392–8.

DINWIDDIE, F. M. (1955) *An Application of the Principle of Response Generalization to the Prediction of Displacement of Aggressive Responses.* Washington: The Catholic Univ. of America Press.

DOLLARD, J., MILLER, N. E., DOOB, L. W., MOWRER, O. H., and SEARS, R. R. (1944) *Frustration and Aggression.* London: Kegan Paul, Trench, Trubner and Co. Ltd.

DOOB, L. W., and SEARS, R. R. (1939) 'Factors determining substitute behavior and the overt expression of aggression'. *J. abnorm. soc. Psychol.*, **34**, 292–313.

DUNCAN, C. P. (1948) 'Habit reversal induced by electroshock in the rat'. *J. comp. physiol. Psychol.*, **41**, 11–16.

EDWARDS, A. L. (1953) 'The relationship between the judged desirability of a trait and the probability that the trait will be endorsed'. *J. appl. Psychol.*, **37**, 90–3.

EDWARDS, A. L. (1957) *The Social Desirability Variable in Personality Assessment and Research*. New York: Dryden.

EGLASH, A. (1951) 'Perception, association, and reasoning in animal fixations'. *Psychol. Rev.*, **58**, 424–34.

EGLASH, A. (1954) 'Fixation and inhibition'. *J. abnorm. soc. Psychol.*, **49**, 241–5.

ELDER, S. T., NOBLIN, C. D., and MAHER, B. A. (1961) 'The extinction of fear as a function of distance versus dissimilarity from the original conflict situation'. *J. abnorm. soc. Psychol.* (in press).

ELIZUR, A. (1949) 'Content analysis of the Rorschach with regard to anxiety and hostility'. *J. proj. Tech.*, **13**, 247–84.

ELLEN, P. (1956) 'The compulsive nature of abnormal fixations'. *J. comp. physiol. Psychol.*, **49**, 309–17.

EVERALL, E. E. (1935) 'Perseveration in the rat'. *J. comp. Psychol.*, **19**, 343–69.

EYSENCK, H. J. (1944) 'General social attitudes'. *J. soc. Psychol.*, **19**, 207–27.

EYSENCK, H. J. (1947a) 'Primary social attitudes: I. The organization and measurement of social attitudes'. *Internat. J. Opin. Attit. Res.*, **1**, 49–84.

EYSENCK, H. J. (1947b) *Dimensions of Personality*. London: Routledge & Kegan Paul.

EYSENCK, H. J. (1950) 'War and aggressiveness: A survey of social attitude studies'. In T. H. Pear (Ed.) *Psychological Factors of Peace and War*. London: Hutchinson & Co. (pp. 49–81).

EYSENCK, H. J. (1952) *The Scientific Study of Personality*. London: Routledge & Kegan Paul.

EYSENCK, H. J. (1954) *The Psychology of Politics*. London: Routledge & Kegan Paul.

EYSENCK, H. J. (1957) *The Dynamics of Anxiety and Hysteria*. London: Routledge & Kegan Paul.

FARBER, I. E. (1948) 'Response fixation under anxiety and non-anxiety conditions'. *J. exp. Psychol.*, **38**, 111–31.

FARBER, I. E. (1954) 'Anxiety as a drive state'. In M. R. Jones (Ed.)

*Nebraska Symposium on Motivation*. Lincoln, Nebraska: Nebraska Univ. Press (pp. 1–55).

FEATHER, N. T. (1959) 'Subjective probability and decision under uncertainty'. *Psychol. Rev.*, **66**, 150–64.

FELDMAN, R. S. (1953) 'The specificity of the fixated response in the rat'. *J. comp. physiol. Psychol.*, **46**, 487–92.

FELDMAN, R. S. (1957) 'The role of primary drive reduction in fixations'. *Psychol. Rev.*, **64**, 85–90.

FELDMAN, R. S., ELLEN, P., LIBERSON, N. T., and ROBINS, J. (1959) 'The effect of chlorpromazine on the brightness discrimination of rats with habits and fixations'. *J. comp. physiol. Psychol.*, **52**, 322–6.

FELDMAN, R. S., and LIBERSON, W. T. (1960) 'The effects of reserpine on behaviour fixations in rats'. *J. comp. physiol. Psychol.*, **53**, 483–7.

FELDMAN, R. S., and NEET, C. C. (1954) 'The effect of electroconvulsive shock on fixated behaviour in the rat. II. The effect of ECS supplemented by guidance'. *J. comp. physiol. Psychol.*, **47**, 210–12.

FELDMAN, R. S., and NEET, C. C. (1957) 'The effect of electroconvulsive shock on fixated behaviour of the rat: III. The effect of ECS as a function of the duration of conflict'. *J. comp. physiol. Psychol.*, **50**, 97–9.

FELDMAN, R. S., and NEET, C. C. (1960) 'The effect of electroconvulsive shock on fixated behaviour in the rat: IV. The prevention of fixations with ECS'. *J. comp. physiol. Psychol.*, **53**, 532–4.

FELDMAN, R. S., and WAITE, R. R. (1957) 'The role of the sequential cue in behavior fixation. *J. comp. physiol. Psychol.*, **50**, 567–70.

FERGUSON, L. W. (1939) 'Primary social attitudes'. *J. Psychol.*, **8**, 217–23.

FESHBACH, S. (1955) 'The drive-reducing function of fantasy behaviour'. *J. abnorm. soc. Psychol.*, **50**, 3–11.

FESHBACH, S. (1956) 'The catharsis hypothesis and some consequences of interaction with aggressive and neutral play objects'. *J. Person.*, **24**, 449–62.

FESHBACH, S., and SINGER, R. (1957) 'The effects of personal and shared threats upon social prejudice'. *J. abnorm. soc. Psychol.*, **54**, 411–16.

FINCH, G. (1942) 'Chimpanzee frustration responses'. *Psychosom. Med.*, **4**, 233–51.

FITE, M. D. (1940) 'Aggressive behaviour in young children and children's attitudes toward aggression'. *Genet. Psychol. Monogr.*, **22**, 151–319.

FREDERICKSEN, N. (1942) 'The effects of frustration on negativistic behavior of young children'. *J. genet. Psychol.*, **61**, 203–26.

FREDERICSON, E. (1950) 'The effects of food deprivation upon competitive and spontaneous combat in C57 black mice'. *J. Psychol.*, **29**, 89–100.

FREDERICSON, E. (1952) 'Aggressiveness in female mice'. *J. comp. physiol. Psychol.*, **45**, 254–7.

FREEMAN, G. L. (1939) 'Toward a psychiatric plimsoll mark: physiological recovery quotients in experimentally induced frustration'. *J. Psychol.*, **8**, 247–52.

FREEMAN, G. L. (1940) 'A method of inducing frustration in human subjects and its influence on palmar skin resistance'. *Amer. J. Psychol.*, **53**, 117–20.

FREEMAN, G. L. (1948) *The Energetics of Human Behaviour*. Ithaca: Cornell Univ. Press.

FREEMAN, G. L., and GIESE, W. J. (1940) 'The relationship between task difficulty and palmar skin resistance'. *J. gen. Psychol.*, **23**, 217–20.

FRENCH, J. R. P. (1944) 'Organized and unorganized groups under fear and frustration'. *Univ. Ia. Stud. Child Welf.*, **20**, 229–308.

FREUD, S. (1920) *A General Introduction to Psychoanalysis*. New York: Boni & Liveright.

FRY, F. D. (1952) 'A normative study of the reactions manifested by college students and by state prison inmates in response to the Minnesota Multiphasic Personality Inventory, the Rosenzweig Picture-Frustration study, and the Thematic Apperception Test'. *J. Psychol.*, **34**, 27–30.

GEWIRTZ, H. B. (1959) 'Generalization of children's preferences as a function of reinforcement and task similarity'. *J. abnorm. soc. Psychol.*, **58**, 111–18.

GIDRO-FRANK, L., and BOWERSBUCH, M. K. (1948) 'A study of the plantar response in hypnotic age regression'. *J. nerv. ment. Dis.*, **107**, 443–58.

GLADIN, L. L., and DENNY, M. K. (1955) 'A sequential cue and fixation in the rat'. *J. comp. physiol. Psychol.*, **48**, 94–6.

GLUCK, M. R. (1955a) 'Rorschach content and hostile behaviour'. *J. consult. Psychol.*, **19**, 475–8.

212 BIBLIOGRAPHY

GLUCK, M. R. (1955b) 'The relationship between hostility in the TAT and behavioural hostility'. *J. proj. Tech.*, **19**, 21–6.

GOLDSTEIN, A. P., and RAWN, M. L. (1957) 'The validity of interpretive signs of aggression in the drawing of the human figure'. *J. clin. Psychol.*, **13**, 169–71.

GOUGH, H. G. (1951) 'Studies of social intolerance: I. Some psychological and sociological correlates of anti-Semitism'. *J. soc. Psychol.*, **33**, 237–46.

GRAHAM, F. K., CHARWAT, W. A., HONIG, A. S., and WELTZ, P. C. (1951) 'Aggression as a function of the attack and the attacker'. *J. abnorm. soc. Psychol.*, **46**, 512–20.

GREEN, E. H. (1933) 'Group play and quarrelling among pre-school children'. *Child Developmt*, **4**, 302–7.

GUTTMAN, L. (1950) 'The basis for scalogram analysis'. In S. A. Stouffer *et al. Studies in Social Psychology in World War II.* Vol. IV. *Measurement and Prediction.* Princeton: Princeton Univ. Press (pp. 60–90).

HALL, C. S. (1941) 'Temperament: a survey of animal studies'. *Psychol. Bull.*, **38**, 909–43.

HALL, C. S., and KLEIN, S. J. (1942) 'Individual differences in aggressiveness in rats'. *J. comp. Psychol.*, **33**, 371–83.

HAMILTON, G. V. (1916) 'A study of perseverance reactions in primates and rodents'. *Behav. Monogr.*, **3**, No. 13.

HAMILTON, J. A., and KRECHEVSKY, I. (1933) 'Studies in the effect of shock upon behavior plasticity in the rat'. *J. comp. Psychol.*, **16**, 237–53.

HANER, C. F., and BROWN, P. A. (1955) 'Clarification of the instigation to action concept in the frustration-aggression hypothesis'. *J. abnorm. soc. Psychol.*, **51**, 204–6.

HARTUP, W. W., and HIMENO, Y. (1959) 'Social isolation vs. interaction with adults in relation to aggression in pre-school children'. *J. abnorm. soc. Psychol.*, **59**, 17–22.

HASLERUD, G. M., BRADBARD, L., and JOHNSTONE, R. P. (1954) 'Pure guidance and handling as components of the Maier technique for breaking abnormal fixations'. *J. Psychol.*, **37**, 27–30.

HAYES, J. R. (1958) 'The maintenance of play in young children'. *J. comp. physiol. Psychol.*, **51**, 788–94.

HESS, R. D., and HANDEL, G. (1956) 'Patterns of aggression in parents and their children'. *J. genet. Psychol.*, **89**, 199–212.

BIBLIOGRAPHY 213

HILGARD, E. R. (1956) *Theories of Learning* (2nd ed.). New York: Appleton-Century-Crofts.

HIMMELWEIT, H. T. (1950) 'Frustration and aggression: a review of recent experimental work. In: Pear, T. H. *Psychological Factors of Peace and War*. New York: Philosophical Library (pp. 161–91).

HOKANSON, J. E. (1961) 'Vascular and psychogalvanic effects of experimentally aroused anger'. *J. Person.*, **29**, 30–9.

HOLDER, W. B., MARX, M. H., HOLDER, E. E., and COLLIER, G. (1957) 'Response strength as a function of delay of reward in a runway'. *J. exp. Psychol.*, **53**, 316–23.

HOVLAND, C. I., and SEARS, R. R. (1938) 'Experiments on motor conflict. I. Types of conflict and their modes of resolution'. *J. exp. Psychol.*, **23**, 477–93.

HOVLAND, C. I., and SEARS, R. R. (1940) 'Minor studies of aggression: VI. Correlation of lynchings with economic indices'. *J. Psychol.*, **9**, 301–10.

HULL, C. L. (1934a) 'The rat's speed-of-locomotion gradient in the approach to food'. *J. comp. Psychol.*, **17**, 393–422.

HULL, C. L. (1934b) 'The concept of the habit-family hierarchy and maze learning'. *Psychol. Rev.*, **41**, 33–54 and 134–52.

HULL, C. L. (1938) 'The goal-gradient hypothesis applied to some "Field-force" problems in the behaviour of young children'. *Psychol. Rev.*, **45**, 271–99.

HULL, C. L. (1943) *Principles of Behaviour*. New York: Appleton-Century-Crofts.

HULL, C. L. (1952) *A Behaviour System*. New Haven: Yale Univ. Press.

HULSE, S. H., and STANLEY, W. C. (1956) 'Extinction by omission of food as related to partial and secondary reinforcement'. *J. exp. Psychol.*, **52**, 221–7.

HUNT, H. F., and BRADY, J. V. (1951) 'Some effects of electroconvulsive shock on a conditioned emotional response ("anxiety")'. *J. comp. physiol. Psychol.*, **41**, 348–63.

HYBL, A. R., and STAGNER, R. (1952) 'Frustration tolerance in relation to diagnosis and therapy'. *J. consult. Psychol.*, **16**, 163–70.

ICHHEISER, G. (1950) 'Frustration and aggression or frustration and defence: a counter-hypothesis'. *J. gen. Psychol.*, **43**, 125–9.

JENKINS, W. O., and STANLEY, J. C. (1950) 'Partial reinforcement: a review and a critique'. *Psychol. Bull.*, **47**, 193–234.

JENSEN, A. R. (1957) 'Aggression in fantasy and overt behaviour'. *Psychol. Mongr.*, **71** (No. 16), Whole No. 445.

JERSILD, A. T., and MARKEY, F. V. (1935) 'Conflicts between preschool children'. *Child Developmt Monogr.*, No. 21 (pp. 181). New York City, Teachers' College, Columbia University.

JONES, L. C. T. (1954) 'Frustration and stereotyped behavior in human subjects'. *Quart. J. exp. Psychol.*, **6**, 12–20.

JOST, H. (1941) 'Some physiological changes during frustration'. *Child Developmt*, **12**, 9–15.

KAGAN, J. (1956) 'The measurement of overt aggression from fantasy'. *J. abnorm. soc. Psychol.*, **52**, 390–3.

KAPLAN, D. M., and GOODRICH, D. W. (1957) 'A formulation for interpersonal anger'. *Amer. J. Orthopsychiat.*, **27**, 387–95.

KAUFMAN, E. L., and MILLER, N. E. (1949) 'Effect of number of reinforcements on strength of approach in an approach-avoidance conflict'. *J. comp. physiol. Psychol.*, **42**, 65–74.

KLEE, J. B. (1944) 'The relation of frustration and motivation to the production of abnormal fixations in the rat'. *Psychol. Monogr.*, **56** (No. 4), Whole No. 257 (pp. 45).

KLEEMEIER, R. W. (1942) 'Fixation and regression in the rat'. *Psychol. Monogr.*, **54** (No. 4), Whole No. 246 (pp. 34).

KLINE, M. V. (1950) 'Hypnotic age regression and intelligence'. *J. genet. Psychol.*, **77**, 129–32.

KLINE, M. V. (1951) 'Hypnosis and age progression: a case report'. *J. genet. Psychol.*, **78**, 195–206.

KLINE, M. V. (1953) 'Hypnotic retrogression: a neuropsychological theory of age regression and progression'. *J. clin. exp. Hypnosis*, **1**, 21–8.

KLINE, M. V. (1954) 'Living out "future" experience under hypnosis'. *Science*, **120**, 1076–7.

KNOPFELMACHER, F. (1952) 'Some effects of reward on the strength of position stereotypes in the white rat'. *Quart. J. exp. Psychol.*, **4**, 78–86.

KNOPFELMACHER, F. (1953a) 'Fixations, position stereotypes, and their relation to the degree and pattern of stress'. *Quart J. exp. Psychol.*, **5**, 108–27.

KNOPFELMACHER, F. (1953b) 'Fixations, position stereotypes and their relation to the degree and pattern of stress. Part II'. *Quart. J. exp. Psychol.*, **5**, 150–8.

KOCH, S. (Ed.) (1954) *Modern Learning Theory.* New York: Appleton-Century-Crofts.

KRECH, D., and CRUTCHFIELD, R. S. (1948) *Theory and Problems of Social Psychology.* New York: McGraw-Hill.

LAMBERT, W. W., and SOLOMON, R. L. (1952) 'Extinction of a running response as a function of distance of block point from the goal'. *J. comp. physiol. Psychol.,* 45, 269-79.

LANIER, L. H. (1941). An experimental study of "affective conflict" '. *J. Psychol.,* 11, 199-217.

LANZETTA, J. T. (1955) 'Group behaviour under stress'. *Hum. Relat.,* 8, 29-52.

LASHLEY, K. S. 'The mechanism of vision: I. A method for rapid analysis of pattern vision in the rat'. *J. genet. Psychol.,* 1930, 37, 453-60.

LAWSON, R., and MARX, M. H. (1958a) 'Frustration: theory and experiment'. *Genet. Psychol. Monogr.,* 57, 393-464.

LAWSON, R., and MARX, M. H. (1958b) 'A comparison of some presumed frustrating and secondary-reinforcing operations'. *J. comp. physiol. Psychol.,* 51, 742-6.

LEBO, D., and LEBO, E. (1957) 'Aggression and age in relation to verbal expression in non-directive play therapy'. *Psychol. Monogr.,* 71 (No. 20), Whole No. 449.

LESSER, G. S. (1957) 'The relationship between overt and fantasy aggression as a function of maternal response to aggression'. *J. abnorm. soc. Psychol.,* 55, 218-21.

LESSER, G. S. (1958a) 'Application of Guttman's scaling method to aggressive fantasy in children'. *Educ. Psychol. Measmt,* 18, 543-551.

LESSER, G. S. (1958b) 'Extrapunitiveness and ethnic attitude'. *J. abnorm. soc. Psychol.,* 56, 281-2.

LEVIN, H., and SEARS, R. R. (1956) 'Identification with parents as a determinant of doll-play aggression'. *Child Developmt,* 27, 135-53.

LEVIN, H., and TURGEON, V. F. (1957) 'The influence of mother's presence on children's doll-play aggression'. *J. abnorm. soc. Psychol.,* 55, 304-8.

LEVY, D. M. (1937) 'Studies in sibling rivalry'. *Res. Monogr. Amer. Orthopsychiat. Ass.,* No. 2.

LEVY, D. M. (1941) 'The hostile act'. *Psychol. Rev.,* 48, 356-61.
P

LEWIN, K. (1935) *A Dynamic Theory of Personality*. New York: McGraw-Hill.

LEWIN, K. (1954) 'Behaviour and development as a function of the total situation'. In L. Carmichael (Ed.) *Manual of Child Psychology*. New York: Wiley.

LEWIN, K., LIPPITT, R., AND WHITE, R. K. (1939) 'Patterns of aggressive behaviour in experimentally-created "social climates"'. *J. soc. Psychol.*, **10**, 271–99.

LIBERSON, W. T., FELDMAN, R. S., and ELLEN, P. (1959) 'The behavioural analysis of the effects of meprobamate as compared with other tranquilizers and ECS'. In: P. B. Bradley, P. Deniker, and C. Radouco-Thomas (Eds) *Neuropsychopharmacology*. New York: Elsevier (pp. 351–7).

LINDZEY, G. (1950) 'An experimental examination of the scapegoat theory of prejudice'. *J. abnorm. soc. Psychol.*, **45**, 296–309.

LINDZEY, G., and TEJESSY, C. (1956) 'Thematic apperception test: indices of aggression in relation to measures of overt and covert behaviour'. *Amer. J. Orthopsychiat.*, **26**, 567–76.

LIVSON, N., and MUSSEN, P. H. (1957) 'The relation of ego control to overt aggression and dependency'. *J. abnorm. soc. Psychol.*, **55**, 66–71.

LOVAAS, O. I. (1961) 'Effect of exposure to symbolic aggression on aggressive behaviour'. *Child Developmt*, **32**, 37–44.

LURIA, A. R. (1932) *The Nature of Human Conflicts*. New York: Liveright.

McCLELLAND, D. C. (1950) 'Review of "N. R. F. Maier. Frustration: The Study of Behaviour Without a Goal"'. *J. abnorm. soc. Psychol.*, **45**, 564–6.

McCLELLAND, D. C., and APICELLA, F. S. (1945) 'A functional classification of verbal reactions to experimentally induced failure'. *J. abnorm. soc. Psychol.*, **40**, 376–90.

McCRANIE, E. J., CRASILNECK, H. B., and TETER, H. P. (1955) 'The electroencephalogram in hypnotic age regression'. *Psychiat. Quart.*, **29**, 85–8.

McDOUGALL, W. (1923) *Outline of Psychology*. London: Methuen.

McKEE, J. P., and LEADER, F. B. (1955) 'The relationship of socio-enonomic status and aggression to the competitive behaviour of pre-school children'. *Child Developmt*, **26**, 135–42.

McKELLAR, P. (1949) 'The emotion of anger in the expression of human aggressiveness'. *Brit. J. Psychol.*, **39**, 148–55.

McKELLAR, P. (1950) 'Provocation to anger and the development of attitudes of hostility'. *Brit. J. Psychol.*, **40**, 104–14.

MAHER, B. A. (1961) 'Approach-avoidance conflict and behaviour near the point of reinforcement'. Mimeographed manuscript, Harvard University.

MAHER, B. A., NOBLIN, C. D., and ELDER, S. T. (1961) 'Hyperactivity versus avoidance reduction following frontal lobe ablation'. *J. comp. physiol. Psychol.* (in press).

MAIER, N. R. F. (1932) 'The effect of cerebral destruction on reasoning and learning in rats'. *J. comp. Neurol.*, **54**, 45–75.

MAIER, N. R. F. (1949) *Frustration: The Study of Behavior Without a Goal.* New York: McGraw-Hill.

MAIER, N. R. F. (1956) 'Frustration theory: restatement and extension'. *Psychol. Rev.*, **63**, 370–88.

MAIER, N. R. F., and ELLEN, P. (1951) 'Can the anxiety-reduction theory explain abnormal fixations?' *Psychol. Rev.*, **58**, 435–55.

MAIER, N. R. F., and ELLEN, P. (1952) 'Studies of abnormal behavior in the rat. XXIII. The prophylactic effects of "guidance" in reducing rigid behavior'. *J. abnorm. soc. Psychol.*, **47**, 109–16.

MAIER, N. R. F., and ELLEN, P. (1954) 'Reinforcement vs. consistency of effect in habit modification'. *J. comp. physiol. Psychol.*, **47**, 364–9.

MAIER, N. R. F., and ELLEN, P. (1955) 'The effect of three reinforcement patterns on positional stereotypes'. *Amer. J. Psychol.*, **68**, 83–95.

MAIER, N. R. F., and ELLEN, P. (1956) 'Studies of abnormal behavior in the rat. XXIV. Position habits, position stereotypes, and abortive behavior'. *J. genet. Psychol.*, **89**, 35–49.

MAIER, N. R. F., and ELLEN, P. (1959) 'The integrative value of concepts in frustration theory'. *J. consult. Psychol.*, **23**, 195–206.

MAIER, N. R. F., and FELDMAN, R. S. (1948) 'Studies of abnormal behavior in the rat. XXII. Strength of fixation and duration of frustration'. *J. comp. physiol. Psychol.*, **41**, 348–63.

MAIER, N. R. F., GLASER, N. M., and KLEE, J. B. (1940) 'Studies of abnormal behavior in the rat: III. The development of behavior fixations through frustration'. *J. exp. Psychol.*, **26**, 521–46.

MAIER, N. R. F., and KLEE, J. B. (1941) 'Studies of abnormal behaviour in the rat. VII. The permanent nature of abnormal fixations and their relation to convulsive tendencies'. *J. exp. Psychol.*, **29**, 380–9.

MAIER, N. R. F., and KLEE, J. B. (1943) 'Studies of abnormal behaviour in the rat: XII. The pattern of punishment and its relation to abnormal fixations'. *J. exp. Psychol.*, **32**, 377–98.

MAIER, N. R. F., and KLEE, J. B. (1945) 'Studies of abnormal behavior in the rat. XVII. Guidance versus trial and error in the alteration of habits and fixations'. *J. Psychol.*, **19**, 133–163.

MAIER, N. R. F., and SCHNEIRLA, T. C. (1942) 'Mechanisms in conditioning'. *Psychol. Rev.*, **49**, 117–34.

MARQUART, D. I. (1948) 'The pattern of punishment and its relation to abnormal fixation in adult human subjects'. *J. gen. Psychol.*, **39**, 107–44.

MARQUART, D. I., and ARNOLD, L. P. (1952) 'A study in the frustration of human adults'. *J. gen. Psychol.*, **47**, 43–63.

MARTIN, R. F. (1940) ' "Native traits" and regression in rats'. *J. comp. Psychol.*, **30**, 1–16.

MARX, M. H. (1956) 'Some relations between frustration and drive'. In M. R. Jones (Ed.) *Nebraska Symposium on Motivation.* Nebraska: Univ. of Nebraska Press (pp. 92–130).

MASLOW, A. H. (1941) 'Deprivation, threat, and frustration'. *Psychol. Rev.*, **48**, 364–6.

MASSERMAN, J. H., and SIEVER, P. W. (1944) 'Dominance, neurosis, and aggression: an experimental study'. *Psychosom. Med.*, **6**, 7–16.

MAY, M. A. (1948) 'Experimentally acquired drive'. *J. exp. Psychol.*, **38**, 66–77.

MILLER, N. E. (1941) 'The frustration-aggression hypothesis'. *Psychol. Rev.*, **48**, 337–42.

MILLER, N. E. (1944) 'Experimental studies of conflict'. In J. McV. Hunt (Ed.) *Personality and the Behaviour Disorders.* New York: Ronald Press (pp. 431–65).

MILLER, N. E. (1948a) 'Studies of fear as an acquirable drive: I. Fear as motivation and fear-reduction as reinforcement in the learning of new responses'. *J. exp. Psychol.*, **38**, 89–101.

MILLER, N. E. (1948b) 'Theory and experiment relating psychoanalytic displacement to stimulus-response generalization'. *J. abnorm. soc. Psychol.*, **43**, 155–78.

MILLER, N. E. (1951) 'Learnable drives and rewards'. In S. S. Stevens (Ed.) *Handbook of Experimental Psychology.* New York: Wiley (pp. 435–72).

MILLER, N. E. (1959) 'Liberalization of basic S-R concepts: extensions to conflict behaviour, motivation, and social learning'. In S. Koch (Ed.) *Psychology: A Study of a Science.* New York: McGraw-Hill (Study I, Vol. 2, pp. 196–292).

MILLER, N. E., and BUGELSKI, R. (1948) 'Minor studies of aggression. II. The influence of frustrations imposed by the in-group on attitudes expressed toward out-groups'. *J. Psychol.,* 25, 437–42.

MILLER, N. E., and KRAELING, D. (1952) 'Displacement: greater generalization of approach than avoidance in a generalized approach-avoidance conflict'. *J. exp. Psychol.,* 43, 217–21.

MILLER, N. E., and MURRAY, E. J. (1952) 'Conflict and displacement: learnable drive as a basis for the steeper gradient of avoidance than of approach'. *J. exp. Psychol.,* 43, 227–31.

MINTZ, A. (1946) 'A re-examination of correlations between lynchings and economic indices'. *J. abnorm. soc. Psychol.,* 41, 154–60.

MOLTZ, H. (1954) 'Resistance to extinction as a function of variations in stimuli associated with shock'. *J. exp. Psychol.,* 47, 418–24.

MORGAN, P. K., and GAIER, E. L. (1956) 'The direction of aggression in the mother-child punishment situation'. *Child Developmt,* 27, 447–57.

MORLAN, G. K. (1949) 'A note on the frustration-aggression theories of Dollard and his associates'. *Psychol. Rev.,* 56, 1–8.

MORSE, N. C., and ALLPORT, F. H. (1952) 'The causation of anti-Semitism: An investigation of seven hypotheses'. *J. Psychol.,* 34, 197–233.

MOWRER, O. H. (1940) 'An experimental analogue of "regression" with incidental observations on "reaction formation" '. *J. abnorm. soc. Psychol.,* 35, 56–87.

MOWRER, O. H. (1949) 'Frustration and aggression'. In Branham, V. C., and Kutash, S. B. *Encyclopaedia of Criminology.* New York: Philosophical Library (pp. 176–86).

MOWRER, O. H. (1950) *Learning Theory and Personality Dynamics.* New York: Ronald Press.

MOWRER, O. H. (1956) 'Two-factor learning theory reconsidered, with special reference to secondary reinforcement and the concept of habit'. *Psychol. Rev.,* 63, 114–28.

MUENZINGER, K. F., and WOOD, A. (1935) 'Motivation in learning: IV. The function of punishment as determined by its temporal relation to the act of choice in the visual discrimination habit'. *J. comp. Psychol.,* 20, 95–106.

MURNEY, R. G. (1955) *An Application of the Principle of Stimulus Generalization to the Prediction of Object Displacement.* Washington, D.C.: Catholic Univ. of America Press.

MURPHREE, O. D., and PETERS, J. E. (1956) 'The effect of electroconvulsions, insulin comas, and certain chemical agents on fixations in the rat'. *J. nerv. ment. Dis.*, **124**, 78–83.

MURRAY, E. J., and BERKUN, M. M. (1955) 'Displacement as a function of conflict'. *J. abnorm. soc. Psychol.*, **51**, 47–56.

MURRAY, E. J., and MILLER, N. E. (1952) 'Displacement: steeper gradient of generalization of avoidance than of approach with age of habit controlled'. *J. exp. Psychol.*, **43**, 222–6.

MUSSEN, P. H. (1950) 'Some personality and social factors related to changes in children's attitudes towards Negroes'. *J. abnorm. soc. Psychol.*, **45**, 423–41.

MUSSEN, P. H., and NAYLOR, H. K. (1954) 'The relationship between overt and fantasy aggression'. *J. abnorm. soc. Psychol.*, **49**, 235–40.

MUSTE, M. J., and SHARPE, D. F. (1947) 'Some influential factors in the determination of aggressive behaviour in pre-school children'. *Child Developmt*, **18**, 11–28.

NEET, C. C., and FELDMAN, R. S. (1954) 'The effect of electroconvulsive shock on fixated behaviour of the rat: I. The effect of a ten- and of a twenty-five-day series of ECS on the stability of the fixated response'. *J. comp. physiol. Psychol.*, **47**, 124–9.

NEWCOMB, T. M. (1947) 'Autistic hostility and social reality'. *Hum. Relat.*, **1**, 69–86.

NISSEN, H. W. (1950) 'Description of learned responses in discrimination behavior'. *Psychol. Rev.*, **57**, 121–31.

NOBLIN, C. D., and MAHER, B. A. (1961) 'Temporal and physical factors in conflict reduction'. *J. comp. physiol. Psychol.* (in press).

O'KELLY, L. I. (1940a) 'An experimental study of regression: I. Behaviour characteristics of the regressive response'. *J. comp. Psychol.*, **30**, 41–53.

O'KELLY, L. I. (1940b) 'An experimental study of regression. II. Some motivational determinants of regression and perseveration'. *J. comp. Psychol.*, **30**, 55–95.

O'KELLY, L. I., and BIEL, W. C. (1940) 'The effect of cortical lesions on emotional and regressive behavior in the rat. II. Regressive behavior'. *J. comp. Psychol.*, **30**, 241–54.

ORNE, M. T. (1951) 'The mechanisms of hypnotic age regression'. *J. abnorm. soc. Psychol.*, **46**, 213–25.

OSGOOD, C. E. (1953) *Method and Theory in Experimental Psychology*. New York: Oxford Univ. Press.

OTIS, N. B., and McCANDLESS, B. (1955) 'Responses to repeated frustrations of young children differentiated according to need area'. *J. abnorm. soc. Psychol.*, 50, 349–53.

PALMER, S. (1960) 'Frustration, aggression, and murder'. *J. abnorm. soc. Psychol.*, 60, 430–2.

PASTORE, N. (1950) 'A neglected factor in the frustration-aggression hypothesis: A comment'. *J. Psychol.*, 29, 271–9.

PASTORE, N. (1952) 'The role of arbitrariness in the frustration aggression hypothesis'. *J. abnorm. soc. Psychol.*, 47, 728–32.

PATRICK, J. B. (1934) 'Studies in rational behavior and emotional excitement. II. The effect of emotional excitement on rational behavior in human subjects'. *J. comp. Psychol.*, 18, 153–95.

PATTERSON, G. (1960) 'A non-verbal technique for the assessment of aggression in children'. *Child Developmt*, 31, 643–53.

PEPITONE, A., and REICHLING, G. (1955) 'Group cohesiveness and the expression of hostility'. *Hum. Relat.*, 8, 327–37.

PHILLIPS, R. (1945) 'Doll-play as a function of the realism of the materials and the length of the experimental session'. *Child Developmt*, 16, 123–43.

PINTLER, M. H. (1945) 'Doll-play as a function of experimenter-child interaction and initial organization of materials'. *Child Developmt*, 16, 145–66.

PLATONOW, K. I. (1933) 'On the objective proof of the experimental personality age regression'. *J. gen. Psychol.*, 9, 190–209.

POSCHEL, P. H. (1957) 'Proactive and retroactive effects of electro-convulsive shock on approach-avoidance conflict'. *J. comp. physiol. Psychol.*, 50, 392–6.

REIFF, R., and SCHEERER, M. (1959) *Memory and Hypnotic Age Regression*. New York: International Univ. Press Inc.

ROGERS, C. R. (1939) *Counseling and Psychotherapy*. Cambridge, Mass.: Harvard Univ. Press.

ROHRER, J. H. (1949) 'A motivational state resulting from non-reward'. *J. comp. physiol. Psychol.*, 42, 476–85.

ROSENBAUM, M. E., and DECHARMS, R. (1960) 'Direct and vicarious reduction of hostility'. *J. abnorm. soc. Psychol.*, 60, 105–11.

ROSENBLITH, J. F. (1949) 'A replication of "Some roots of prejudice"'. *J. abnorm. soc. Psychol.*, 44, 470–89.

ROSENZWEIG, S. (1944) 'An outline of frustration theory'. In Hunt,

J. McV. (Ed). *Personality and the Behavior Disorders*. New York: Ronald (pp. 379–88).

ROSENZWEIG, S. (1945) 'Further comparative data on repetition-choice after success and failure as related to frustration tolerance'. *J. genet. Psychol.*, **66**, 75–81.

ROTHAUS, P., and WORCHEL, P. (1960) 'The inhibition of aggression under non-arbitrary frustration'. *J. Person.*, **28**, 108–17.

RUSSELL, R. W., and PRETTY, R. G. F. (1951) 'A study of position habits induced by reward and "frustration"'. *Quart. J. exp. Psychol.*, **3**, 151–6.

SANDERS, M. J. (1937) 'An experimental demonstration of regression in the rat'. *J. exp. Psychol.*, **21**, 493–510.

SARASON, I. G. (1961) 'Intercorrelations among measures of hostility'. *J. clin. Psychol.*, **17**, 192–5.

SARBIN, T. R. (1950) 'Mental age changes in experimental regression'. *J. Person.*, **19**, 221–8.

SARBIN, T. R., and FABEROW, N. L. (1952) 'Contributions to role-taking theory: a clinical study of self and role'. *J. abnorm. soc. Psychol.*, **47**, 117–25.

SCHLOSBERG, H., and PRATT, C. H. (1956) 'The secondary reward value of inaccessible food for hungry and satiated rats'. *J. comp. physiol. Psychol.*, **49**, 149–52.

SCOTT, J. P. (1958) *Aggression*. Chicago: Univ. of Chicago Press.

SEARS, P. S. (1951) 'Doll-play aggression in normal young children: Influence of sex, age, sibling status, father's absence'. *Psychol. Mongr.*, **65** (No. 6), Whole No. 323.

SEARS, R. R. (1941) 'Non-aggressive reactions to frustration'. *Psychol. Rev.*, **48**, 343–6.

SEARS, R. R. (1943) 'Survey of objective studies of psychoanalytic concepts'. *Soc. Sci. Res. Coun. Bull.*, No. 51.

SEARS, R. R. (1951) 'Effects of frustration and anxiety on fantasy aggression'. *Amer. J. Orthopsychiat.*, **21**, 498–505.

SEARS, R. R., and HOVLAND, C. I. (1941) 'Experiments on motor conflict: II. Determination of mode of resolution by comparative strengths of conflicting responses'. *J. exp. Psychol.*, **28**, 280–6.

SEARS, R. R., HOVLAND, C. I., and MILLER, N. E. (1940) 'Minor studies of aggression: I. Measurement of aggressive behaviour'. *J. Psychol.*, **9**, 275–94.

SEARS, R. R., MACCOBY, E. E., and LEVIN, H. (1957) *Patterns of Child Rearing*. Evanston: Row, Peterson & Co.

SEARS, R. R., and SEARS, P. S. (1940) 'Minor studies of aggression: V. Strength of frustration-reaction as a function of strength of drive'. *J. Psychol.*, **9**, 297–300.

SEWARD, J. P. (1945a) 'Aggressive behaviour in the rat: I. General characteristics; age and sex differences'. *J. comp. Psychol.*, **38**, 175–99.

SEWARD, J. P. (1945b) 'Aggressive behaviour in the rat. III. The role of frustration'. *J. comp. Psychol.*, **38**, 225–38.

SEWARD, J. P., PEREBOOM, A. C., BUTLER, B., and JONES, R. B. (1957) 'The role of prefeeding in an apparent frustration effect'. *J. exp. Psychol.*, **54**, 445–50.

SHAPIRO, D. S. (1957) 'Perceptions of significant family and environmental relationships in aggressive and withdrawn children'. *J. consult. Psychol.*, **21**, 381–5.

SHEFFIELD, F. D., and CAMPBELL, B. A. (1954) 'The role of experience in the "spontaneous" activity of hungry rats'. *J. comp. physiol. Psychol.*, **47**, 97–100.

SHERMAN, M. (1957) 'The frustration threshold'. *Amer. J. Psychiat.*, **104**, 242–6.

SHERMAN, M., and JOST, H. (1942) 'Frustration reactions of normal and neurotic persons'. *J. Psychol.*, **13**, 3–19.

SIEGEL, A. E. (1956). 'Film-mediated fantasy aggression and strength of aggressive drive'. *Child Developmt*, **27**, 365–78.

SIEGEL, P. S. (1943) 'The effect of electroshock convulsions in the acquisition of a simple running response in the rat'. *J. comp. Psychol.*, **36**, 61–5.

SIMKINS, L. (1961) 'Generalization effects of hostile verb reinforcement as a function of stimulus similarity and type of reinforcer'. *J. Person.*, **29**, 64–72.

SMITH, J., and COLEMAN, J. (1956) 'The relationship between manifestations of hostility on projective tests and overt behavior'. *J. proj. Tech.*, **20**, 326–34.

SMITH, N. (1960) 'An empirical determination of an approach gradient'. *J. comp. physiol. Psychol.*, **53**, 63–7.

SOLOMON, R. L., and WYNNE, L. C. (1954) 'Traumatic avoidance learning: the principles of anxiety conservation and partial irreversibility'. *Psychol. Rev.*, **61**, 353–85.

SPENCE, K. W. (1956) *Behavior Theory and Conditioning*. New Haven: Yale Univ. Press.

STAGNER, R. (1944a) 'Studies of aggressive social attitudes: I.

Measurement and interrelation of selected attitudes.' *J. soc. Psychol.*, **20,** 109–20.

STAGNER, R. (1944b) 'Studies of aggressive social attitudes. II. Changes from peace to war'. *J. soc. Psychol.*, **20,** 121–8.

STAGNER, R. (1944c) 'Studies of aggressive social attitudes: III. The role of personal and family scores'. *J. soc. Psychol.*, **20,** 129–40.

STAGNER, R., and CONGDON, C. S. (1955) 'Another failure to demonstrate displacement of aggression'. *J. abnorm. soc. Psychol.*, **51,** 695–6.

STEVENS, S. S. (Ed.) (1951) *Handbook of Experimental Psychology.* New York: Wiley.

TAYLOR, J. A., and MAHER, B. A. (1959) 'Escape and displacement experience as variables in the recovery from approach-avoidance conflict'. *J. comp. physiol. Psychol.*, **52,** 586–90.

THIBAUT, J. (1950) 'An experimental study of the cohesiveness of underprivileged groups'. *Hum. Relat.*, **3,** 251–78.

THIBAUT, J., and COULES, J. (1952) 'The role of communication in the reduction of interpersonal hostility'. *J. abnorm. soc. Psychol.*, **47,** 770–7.

THIBAUT, J., and RIECKEN, H. (1955) 'Authoritarianism, status, and the communication of aggression'. *Hum. Relat.*, **8,** 95–120.

THIESEN, J. W., and MEISTER, R. K. (1949) 'A laboratory investigation of frustration tolerance of pre-adolescent child'. *J. genet. Psychol.*, **75,** 277–91.

TRAPOLD, M. A., MILLER, N. E., and COONS, E. E. (1960) 'All-or-none versus progressive approach in an approach-avoidance conflict'. *J. comp. physiol. Psychol.*, **53,** 293–6.

TRUE, R. M. (1949) 'Experimental control in hypnotic age regression states'. *Science*, **110,** 583–4.

TYLER, D. W., MARX, M. H., and COLLIER, G. (1959) 'Frustration stimuli in discrimination'. *J. exp. Psychol.*, **58,** 295–301.

WAGNER, A. R. (1959) 'The role of reinforcement and non-reinforcement in an "apparent frustration effect" '. *J. exp. Psychol.*, **57,** 130–6.

WALTERS, J., PEARCE, D., and DAHMS, L. (1957) 'Affectional and aggressive behavior of pre-school children'. *Child Developmt*, **28,** 15–26.

WALTERS, R. H., and ZAKS, M. S. (1959) 'Validation studies of an aggression scale'. *J. Psychol.*, **47,** 209–18.

WEISS-FRANKL, A. B. (1941) 'Play interviews with nursery school children'. *Amer. J. Orthopsychiat.*, **11**, 33–40.

WHITE, R. W. (1959) 'Motivation reconsidered: the concept of competence'. *Psychol. Rev.*, **66**, 297–333.

WHITING, J. W. M., and MOWRER, O. H. (1943) 'Habit progression and regression – a laboratory study of some factors relevant to human socialization'. *J. comp. Psychol.*, **36**, 229–53.

WILCOXON, H. C. (1952) ' "Abnormal fixation" and learning'. *J. exp. Psychol.*, **44**, 324–33.

WILENSKY, H. (1952) 'The performance of schizophrenic and normal individuals following frustration'. *Psychol. Mongr.*, **66** (No. 12), Whole No. 344.

WILLIAMS, J. R. (1959) 'A test of the validity of P-technique in the measurement of internal conflict'. *J. Person.*, **27**, 418–37.

WOLPE, J. (1953) 'Learning theory and "abnormal fixations" '. *Psychol. Rev.*, **60**, 111–16.

WORCHEL, P. (1957) 'Catharsis and the relief of hostility'. *J. abnorm. soc. Psychol.*, **55**, 238–43.

WRIGHT, M. E. (1942) 'Constructiveness of play as affected by group organization and frustration'. *Charact. & Pers.*, **11**, 40–9.

WRIGHT, M. E. (1943) 'The influence of frustration upon the social relations of young children'. *Charact. & Pers.*, **12**, 111–22.

WURTZ, K. R. (1960) 'Some theory and data concerning the attenuation of aggression'. *J. abnorm. soc. Psychol.*, **60**, 134–6.

YARROW, L. J. (1948) 'The effect of antecedent frustration on projective play'. *Psychol. Monogr.*, **62** (No. 6), Whole No. 293.

YATES, A. J. (1960) 'Abnormalities of psychomotor functions'. In H. J. Eysenck (Ed.) *Handbook of Abnormal Psychology*. London: Pitman Medical Publishing Co. Ltd (pp. 32–61).

YATES, A. J. (1961) 'Hypnotic age regression'. *Psychol. Bull.*, **58**, 429–40.

YOUNG, P. T. (1959) 'The role of affective processes in learning and motivation'. *Psychol. Rev.*, **66**, 104–25.

ZAKS, M., and WALTERS, R. H. (1959) 'First steps in the construction of a scale for the measurement of aggression'. *J. Psychol.*, **47**, 199–208.

ZAWADSKI, B. (1948) 'Limitations of the scapegoat theory of prejudice'. *J. abnorm. soc. Psychol.*, **43**, 127–41.

# NAME INDEX

Adelman, H. M., 185, 187, 189, 190
Ader, R., 163
Aebli, H., 131
Allison, J., 98
Allport, F. H., 93
Allport, G. W., 94
Ammons, C. H., 79, 103, 105
Ammons, R. B., 79, 103, 105
Amsel, A., 178, 180, 183, 184, 185, 186, 187, 189, 190, 191, 192
Andreas, B. G., 149, 164, 165, 166, 167
Antonitis, J. J., 134
Apicella, F. S., 70
Appel, M. H., 86
Arkoff, A., 167
Arnold, L. P., 55
Atkinson, J. W., 192, 193, 194, 195, 197

Bach, G. R., 79, 86, 103
Bailey, C. J., 163
Barker, R. G., 22, 113–28 passim, 168, 174, 176
Barthol, R. P., 135
Baruch, D. W., 33, 103
Bastian, J. R., 194
Bender, L., 79, 103
Bendig, A. W., 99
Bergman, M. S., 136
Berkowitz, L., 95, 97, 108, 112
Berkun, M. M., 157, 159, 168
Bernstein, B. B., 184, 186
Biel, W. C., 132
Body, M. K., 80
Bornston, F. L., 79, 83
Bowersbuch, M. K., 136
Bradbard, L., 20
Brady, J. V., 163
Bridges, K. M. B., 79, 105
Brower, D., 177
Brown, J. F., 201
Brown, J. S., 147, 148, 149, 150, 151, 152, 153, 155, 161, 165, 178, 182, 190
Brown, P. A., 68, 111, 181, 185
Bugelski, B. R., 91, 107, 149, 150, 151
Burton, A., 127
Buss, A. H., 97, 99, 100
Butler, B., 185

Campbell, B. A., 188
Cattell, R. B., 172, 201
Charwat, W. A., 69, 73, 79, 100
Chasdi, E. H., 72, 73
Child, I. L., 98, 123, 127
Clink, D. W., 163
Coghill, G. E., 64
Cohen, A. R., 73, 107
Coleman, J. C., 79, 83, 98, 101
Collier, G., 184, 190
Congdon, C. S., 91
Conger, J. J., 163
Coons, E. E., 161
Coules, J., 75, 86
Cowen, E. L., 91
Crandall, V. J., 79, 199
Crasilneck, H. B., 136, 137
Crutchfield, R. S., 109

Dahms, L., 104
Davis, J. M., 126
Davitz, J. R., 109
Decharms, R., 88
Dembo, T., 22, 113–28 passim, 174, 176
Denny, M. K., 45, 59
Devalois, R. L., 47
Dinwiddie, F. M., 77, 86, 112
Dollard, J., 67, 174
Doob, L. W., 67, 72, 75, 79, 83, 107, 174
Duncan, C. P., 129
Durkee, A., 97, 99, 100

Earl, R. W., 196
Edwards, A. L., 98
Eglash, A., 55, 56
Elder, S. T., 160
Elizur, A., 98
Ellen, P., 6, 14, 15, 17, 20, 21, 44, 56, 59, 60, 62, 63, 64, 65
Everall, E., 47
Eysenck, H. J., 99, 100, 105, 201, 202

Farber, I. E., 39, 57, 178, 182, 190
Farberow, N. L., 138
Feather, N. T., 197
Feldman, R. S., 13, 15, 16, 17, 18, 19, 20, 56, 59, 60
Ferguson, L. W., 99

227

Feshbach, S., 85, 88, 95, 101, 112
Finch, G., 69, 71, 185
Fite, M. D., 103, 105
Frank, K. F., 98
Fredericksen, N., 82
Fredericson, E., 100, 103
Freeman, G. L., 177
French, J. R. P., 74, 77
Freud, S., 67
Fry, F. D., 79, 83

Gaier, E. L., 105
Gewirtz, H. B., 199, 200
Gidro-Frank, L., 136
Giese, W. J., 177
Gladin, L. L., 45, 59
Glaser, N. M., 6, 8, 13, 17, 44, 60
Gluck, M. R., 98
Goldstein, A. P., 109
Goodrich, D. W., 107
Gough, H. G., 93, 94
Graham, F. K., 69, 73, 79, 100
Graham, H., 136
Green, E. H., 79, 105
Guttman, L., 100

Hall, C. S., 100, 103
Hamilton, G. V., 4
Hamilton, J. A., 47, 128
Hancock, W., 183, 184, 185, 189
Handel, G., 79
Haner, C. F., 68, 111, 181, 185
Hartup, W. W., 104, 111
Haslerud, G. M., 20
Hayes, J. R., 128
Hess, R. D., 79
Hilgard, E. R., 36
Himeno, Y., 104, 111
Himmelweit, H. T., 112
Hokanson, J. E., 72
Holder, E. E., 184
Holder, W. B., 184
Holmes, D. S., 95, 97
Honig, A. S., 69, 73, 79, 100
Hovland, C. I., 69, 98, 107, 164, 165, 166, 168
Hull, C. L., 37, 139, 148, 169, 171, 179, 191
Hulse, S. H., 188
Hunt, D. E., 98
Hunt, H. F., 163
Hybl, A. R., 201

Ichheiser, G., 107

Jenkins, W. O., 42
Jensen, A. R., 101
Jersild, A. T., 79, 105
Johnstone, R. P., 20
Jones, L. C. T., 54

Jones, R. B., 185
Jost, H., 177

Kagan, J., 101
Kaplan, D. M., 107
Kaufman, E. L., 151
Keiser, S., 79, 103
Klee, J. B., 6, 8, 10, 11, 12, 13, 15, 17, 20, 21, 31, 42, 43, 44, 60
Kleemeier, R. W., 47, 48
Klein, S. J., 100, 103
Kline, M. V., 136, 138
Knopfelmacher, F., 49, 50, 54
Koch, S., 97
Kraeling, D., 155
Kramer, B. M., 94
Krech, D., 109
Krechevsky, I., 47, 128
Ku, N. D., 135

Lambert, W. W., 148
Landes, J., 91
Lanier, L. H., 168
Lanzetta, J. T., 74
Lashley, K. S., 6
Lawrence, M. S., 72, 73
Lawson, R., 176, 189, 190
Leader, F. B., 80, 104, 105
Leavitt, H. C., 136
Lebo, D., 104
Lebo, E., 104
Lesser, G. S., 79, 93, 95, 100, 101
Levin, H., 79, 80, 104, 105
Levy, D. M., 103, 110
Lewin, K., 22, 74, 113–28 passim, 139, 142–6 passim, 174, 176
Liberson, W. T., 15, 20
Lindzey, G., 92, 98
Lippitt, R., 74
Litwin, G. H., 194, 195
Livson, N., 79, 80
Lovaas, O. I., 109
Luria, A. R., 139–42 passim

Maatsch, J. L., 185, 187, 189, 190
McCandless, B., 71
McClelland, D. C., 36, 70
Maccoby, E. E., 79
McCranie, E. J., 136
McDougall, W., 67
McKee, J. P., 80, 104, 105
McKellar, P., 73, 78
Maher, B. A., 160, 161, 163
Maier, N. R. F., 4–65 passim, 202, 203
Markey, F. V., 79, 105
Marquart, D. I., 55
Martin, R. F., 130, 132
Marx, M. H., 176, 184, 189, 190
Maslow, A. H., 111
Masserman, J. H., 84

# SUBJECT INDEX

Abortive responses, 7, 45, 59
Achievement motive, 192
  and failure-avoidance, 195
Affective conflict, 168
Affective disturbances, 140, 141
Aggression, 66–112
  against the self, 82–3
  and culture, 79
  and ego-control, 80, 88
  and frustration-arbitrariness, 107, 110
  and group organization, 73–4
  and lynchings, 69
  and social class, 80
  and social isolation, 111
  and theory of prejudice, 89–97
  as a consequence of frustration, 66–70
  as a frustrating situation, 70
  as a function of
    age, 103
    attack, 70
    attacker, 70
    permissiveness, 72–3, 88
    sex, 104
    status of frustrator, 73
  changes in the form of, 105
  child-rearing antecedents, 105–6
  cognitive factors, 106–9, 110
  definition of, dependent, 67
    independent, 67
  displacement of, 69, 76, 77–83, 89–97, 200–1
  experimental induction of, 86
  fantasy, 78–9
  identification and, 105–6
  in doll-play, 73, 98, 103–5
  inhibition of, 71–5, 181
  objects of, 75–84
  parental, 105
  strength of instigation to, 68–71
  towards minority groups, 91–2
  within groups vs. between groups, 74
Aggression-anxiety, 72, 85
  and change in physiological state, 72
Aggressive behaviour,
  measurement, 97–9
  operant conditioning of, 109
  unlearned, 102, 103–5

Aggressiveness,
  and anxiety, 99
  and insult, 112
  and neuroticism, 99
  direct training in, 109
  generality of, 92, 99–103
Alcohol,
  effect on approach-avoidance conflicts, 163
Anti-Semitism,
  and circumstance frustration, 93
  and extrapunitiveness, 93, 95
  and impunitiveness, 94
  and intropunitiveness, 94
  and projected frustration, 93
  and self-frustration, 93
  scales of, 93
Anxiety,
  and aggression, 72
  and frustration, 191, 197
  as secondary drive, 39–40
  elimination of, 40–2
  Maier's treatment of, 35–6
  physiological indices, 72
  reduction as reinforcing, 40
  social, 78
Approach-approach conflict, 142, 146, 152
  and personal characteristics, 167–168
  mode of resolution, 164, 168
Approach-avoidance conflict, 143, 145, 146, 172
  double, 146, 152, 157, 158, 164
  effects of alcohol, 163
  mode of resolution, 164
Approach gradients,
  and distinctive cues, 151
  and intensity of stimulus, 151
  and number of reinforcements, 151
  effects of
    alcohol, 163
    change in drive, 150, 161, 168
    ECS, 163
  in neurotics, 202
  intersection with avoidance gradient, 152–4, 157–9, 168
Approach-reaction potential, 180
Arbitrariness, 107

Attitudes,
    correlates of prejudiced, 92–5
    generality of aggressive, 99
    social aggressive, 99–100
Autistic hostility, 74–5
Availability of response, 24, 31–2, 63,
    64–5
Avoidance-avoidance conflict, 143,
    144, 152
    and personal characteristics, 167–
    168
    mode of resolution, 164, 166, 168
Avoidance gradients,
    and distinctive cues, 151
    and intensity of stimulus, 151
    and number of reinforcements, 151
    effects of
        alcohol, 163
        change in drive, 150, 161, 168
        chlorpromazine, 163
        ECS, 163
        escape, 163
        sodium amytal, 163
    following success, 200
    greater steepness of, 154, 169
    in neurotics, 202
    intersection with approach gradient,
        152, 157–9, 169
    lowered by extinction of fear, 159
Avoidance-of-success gradient, 200

Barrier, 116
    and frustrating situations, 176, 180
    as an adient object, 171
    functional, 142
    in conflict situations, 142
Barrier behaviour, 117, 124
    extinction of, 126
    in free play, 118
    in frustration, 118
    in strong frustration, 120
    in weak frustration, 120
Behaviour deviations, 26–7
Bender-Gestalt test, 138

Catharsis, 29, 84–9, 111
    and fantasy aggression, 101–2
Chain associative series, 140
Combined motor method, 140
Command with prospect of reward,
    145–6
Command with threat of punishment,
    144–5
Conflict, 139–73
    and detour behaviour, 171
    and displacement, 155–63
    and frustration, 174–5, 178–80
    and heterogeneous objects, 170
    and homogeneous objects, 170
    and incentive value, 170

and personal characteristics, 167–8
and sentiment structures, 172
approach-approach, 142–3
approach-avoidance, 143
avoidance-avoidance, 143
confined vs. free space, 169, 170
definitions of, 142, 143, 172, 180–1,
    195–6, 197
ECS, 163
effects of
    alcohol, 163
    factor-analytically defined, 172–3
    in human subjects, 164–8
    in risk-taking situations, 195
    modes of resolution, 164–7
    real vs. hypothetical situations, 168
    three-dimensional model of, 157
    time to resolve, 168
    types of, 141, 142–3
Conflicts of defection, 141
Conflicts of the setting, 141
Conservatism and aggressive attitudes,
    100
Constructiveness
    and developmental maturity, 123
    and mood index, 126
    and training in aggressiveness, 109
    correlation with barrier and escape
        behaviour, 125, 126
    correlation with time spent in other
        activities, 125
    of episodes of behaviour, 120–1
    of primary play, 118, 120
    of secondary play, 118, 120
Constructiveness rating, 117
Constructivity score, 117
    reliability and validity, 117, 123
Criminal behaviour, 27
Culture and aggressiveness, 79

Dedifferentiation, 115
Deprivation and frustration, 110
Destructive behaviour, 27
Detour behaviour, 171
Development,
    and constructiveness of play, 123
    characteristics of behaviour in, 114–
    115
Differentiation, 115
Displacement,
    and conflict, 155–63
    and neuroticism, 202
    and prejudice formation, 90
    and social anxiety, 78
    and substitute responses, 83–4
    as a resolution of conflict, 159
    of aggression, 69, 77–83, 89–97
    therapeutic effect of, 159
    three-dimensional model of, 15
Drive regression, 113

Emotion as a cause of regression, 122
Enuresis, 5
Episodes of behaviour, 117, 120–1
and real vs. irreal substitutes, 122
Escape behaviour, 118, 120, 124
Expectancy, 192–3
Extraversion-introversion, 201–2

Fantasy aggression, 78–9, 88–9, 98–9, 100–3, 112
and catharsis, 101–2
and sex differences, 104
and social class, 80
as an enduring disposition, 100–1
film mediated, 89
inhibition of, 101
relation to overt, 79, 80, 100–3
scalogram analysis of, 100
Fixations,
all-or-nothing character, 17, 36
and human behaviour, 54–5
and intensity of punishment, 53
and learning theory, 31–2
as a cognitive defect, 55–6
as a function of,
hunger drive, 60
partial reinforcement, 42–5, 58–9
problem difficulty, 60
substitute response, 56
as anxiety-reducing responses, 37–42, 53, 57–8
as primary drive-reducing responses, 46–55
as regression, 129
as responses to sequential cues, 46, 59
as strong habits, 45, 59–60
as tension-relieving responses, 16–17, 33, 34
bimodal distribution, 17, 57
breaking of,
role of guidance, 19–21, 33–4, 58
role of punishment, 15, 45, 53
compulsive nature of, 12–15, 63
effects of,
chlorpromazine, 15
convulsions, 15, 16
prior experience, 21–2
punishment, 10–12, 60–4
vacation period, 15
in learning situations, 47–9
permanent nature of, 15–16
prevention of
by ECS, 20
by guidance, 20
reliability of, 30
specificity of, 16, 32–3
variability in strength of, 17–18, 56
Frustrated organism,
and GSR, 177

and pulse rate, 177
components of, 10, 115
definition of, 176–8
physiological indices of, 177–8
Frustrating situation,
and deprivation conditions, 176
and experience of failure, 65
components of, 8–9, 65
definitions of, 115, 175–6, 190
examples of, 176
Frustration,
adaptation to, 54–5
and achievement, 192–7
and aggression, 22, 66–112
and bottle withdrawal, 68
and competing excitatory tendencies, 178
and competing excitatory/inhibitory tendencies, 178
and conflict, 174–5, 178–81
and convicted murderers, 71
and deprivation, 110
and fixation, 4–65
and induced failure, 70
and learning theory, 181–92
and neurosis, 25–6
and neuroticism, 201–2
and privation, 110
and regression, 22–3, 113–38
and resignation, 23
and social attitudes, 91–2
and stereotypes, 10
and submissiveness, 82
antecedent conditions of, 182
as an intervening variable, 182
as internal cue, 182, 185–92
as irrelevant drive, 182–5, 189–92
circumstance, 93
cognitive aspects, 62–4, 184
critique of, 30–56
definitions of, 8–10, 67, 175–8
effect on running speed, 183–5
non-aggressive reactions to, 110
potential, 180
projected, 93
response to, 175
types of response to, 22
Frustration-instigated behaviour,
applications of, 25–30
compared with motivation-instigated behaviour, 24–25
definition of, 25
effect of reward and punishment on, 27
expression of, as catharsis, 29
general characteristics of, 24–5
Frustration-responses, 175
Frustration threshold, 26, 198–201
and fixations, 64
definition, 198, 199

Frustration threshold, effect of reward and punishment on, 28
for aggression, 92
in neurosis, 26
Frustration tolerance, 198–201
and degree of frustration, 200
and neuroticism, 201–2
and reaction to failure, 199
Functional barrier, 142

Galvanic skin reflex (GSR), 177
Generalization,
and displacement, 155
and fixations, 31
and substitution, 76–7
in free space, 170
of approach gradient, 148, 169
of avoidance gradient, 154, 169
response, 75–6, 77–8
spatial, 148
stimulus, 76, 78–83
vs. specificity, 32–3
Goal-attainment expectancy, 179
Goal-gradient hypothesis, 148
Goal-response, 67, 77
Gradients,
intersection of approach and avoidance, 152–4, 155–63
linearity vs. non-linearity, 161–3, 170
of approach, 147
of avoidance, 149
of stimulus generalization of approach, 148
of stimulus generalization of avoidance, 150
Guidance, 19–21, 58
and trial-and-error, 20
in breaking fixations, 19, 33–4
in prevention of fixations, 20, 21
in psychotherapy, 29, 33–4
mechanical, 20

Habit progression, 132–5
Habit regression, 113, 132
Hypnotic age regression, 135–8
accuracy of, 137
and instrumental act regression, 138
and regression, 138
and waking state, 137
as habit-reactivation, 138
direct vs. indirect measures of, 135–6
on Bender-Gestalt test, 138
role-playing in, 136, 138
simulable vs. non-simulable measures of, 136
simulation of, 136, 137
theories of, 138

Identification and aggressive behaviour, 79, 105–6

Incentive motivation, 179
Incentive value of failure, 193
Infants, frustration in, 68
Inhibition of instigation to aggression,
and presence of mother, 80–1
and self-punishment, 79
and social class differences, 80
as a function of,
anticipated punishment, 71–5
permissiveness, 72–3
status of frustrator, 73
as autistic response, 74–5
measurement of, 77–8, 81–2, 112
Instigation to aggression
and overt aggression, 84
and strength of group organization, 73–4, 77
and type of group leadership, 74
and type of instigator, 73
as a function of,
age, 79
degree of interference with frustrated response, 69–71
latency of crying in infants, 68
mother's presence, 80–1
number of alternative extinguished responses, 71
number of frustrated response sequences, 71
parental permissiveness, 78–9
social class, 80
strength of instigation to frustrated response, 68–9
generalization of, 75–84
measurement of, 98, 111–12
strength of, 67, 69
Instigation to self-aggression, 82–3
Instigator, definition of, 66
of high vs. low status, 73
Instrumental act regression, 113, 128–135
in humans, 135
Island behaviour, 118, 120, 125

Judgemental theory and aggression, 108

Lashley jumping apparatus, 5
Latency of responses, 13, 45, 46, 53, 55
Learning theory,
and anxiety reduction, 37–9
and fixations, 31–2, 36–55
and psychotherapy, 32
associationistic tradition, 37
hedonistic tradition, 37
two-factor, 37–9
Level of aspiration, 28
Luria technique, 140
Lynchings and aggression, 69

Minority groups, 91–5, 111
  prejudiced attitudes in, 94–5
Mood index, 121–2
  and constructiveness, 126
Motivation, 192–3
Motivation-instigated behaviour,
  applications of, 25–30
  compared with frustration-instigated
    behaviour, 24–5
  definition of, 25
  effect of reward and punishment on,
    27
  general characteristics of, 24–5
Motive disturbance as conflict indi-
    cator, 141
Motive to achieve success, 192
Motive to avoid failure, 192
Motor impulsiveness, 141

Neurosis,
  as frustration-instigated behaviour,
    25–6
  characteristics of, 25–6
  generalization in, 31
Neuroticism, 201–2
Neurotic paradox, 5, 25

Object regression, 113
Open-field situation, 129

Partial reinforcement, 42–6, 58–9, 160,
    188
Permissiveness and aggression, 72–3,
    101
Personality, frustration, and conflict,
    201–2
Physiological changes,
  in aggression-anxiety, 72
  in frustrated organisms, 177–8
Play,
  constructiveness of, 115
  free, 116, 125
  in frustration period, 116
  in post-frustration period, 116
  in pre-frustration period, 116
  primary, 117, 118, 120
  regression in, 115
  secondary, 117, 118
  total duration of, 117
Play unit,
  duration of, 117
  in frustration, 118
Prejudice, 89–97
  and degree of victimization, 94
  and displacement of aggression,
    92
  and past experience, 95–7
  and personality traits, 92, 95–7
  correlation with aggression, 92
  personal vs. shared threats, 95

rationalization of, 90
  stages in development of, 89–90
Primitivization, 24, 114–28
Privation and frustration, 110
Problem situations,
  insoluble, definition of, 6
  soluble, definition of, 6
Prohibition with threat of punish-
    ment, 146
Psychotherapy, 29–30
  and guidance, 29
  and learning theory, 32
  and trial-and-error, 29
  non-directive, 30
P-technique and conflict, 172–3
Pulse rate, 177
Punishment, 10–12, 27–9, 41, 42–4,
    49–55, 60–4, 143–6, 180
  actual pattern of, 50, 61–2
  and abandonment of initial res-
    ponse, 11, 17–19
  and correct and incorrect responses,
    43
  and number of fixations, 10–11
  and time to learn new response, 11,
    18
  anticipated, 27, 72, 84, 144, 146, 180
  as a frustrating agent, 12, 19, 28, 50,
    64, 79
  as a method of training, 29
  as a negative incentive, 12
  effects contrasted with reward, 27
  fractional anticipatory, 180, 197
  in conflict situations, 144—6
  intensity of, 50–3
  logical combinations of, 60
  random vs. orderly, 10–12, 21
    49–53, 59, 60–4

Quality of performance, 123, 125

Realism, 115
Regression, 113–38
  and emotional behaviour, 120–1,
    128–35
  and interfering responses, 124–5,
    128–35
  and previous learning, 132
  as primitivation, 114–28
  as rational adjustment, 132
  definitions of, 114, 128, 129–32
  drive, 113
  habit, 113
  hypnotic age, 135–8
  instrumental act, 113, 128–35
  in the absence of shock, 132
  object, 113
  'social', 134
  types of, 113
Regulatory systems, 139

Reinforcement,
  and frustration reduction, 192
  continuous, 43, 188
  partial, 43, 58, 160, 188
Resignation, 23
Resolution of conflict, 164–8
Response generalization, 75–6, 77–8
  direct vs. displaced, 75–6
Responses,
  Abortive, definition of, 7
  acquisition of, 43
  displacement of, 69
  effect of rewarding stereotyped, 50
  extinction of, 43
  fixated, definition of, 8
  fractional anticipatory, 179, 180
  goal, definition of, 67
  interfering, 124–5
  latency of, 13, 45, 53
  maintenance of, 43
  motor, 141
  perseverative, 132
  position reward, definition of, 7
  position stereotype, definition of, 7
  preferred, 130, 131
  random, 129, 131
  reversal of, 11
  shift of, 11, 21
  symbol reward, definition of, 7
  symbol stereotype, definition of, 7
Retrogression, 113, 114
Risk-taking and conflict, 195

Satiation, 123, 127–8
Scapegoat theory of prejudice, 84–97
Sentiment structures, 172

Shock,
  and avoidance gradient, 149, 155, 156
  and regression, 129, 130, 131, 132, 134
Social desirability,
  and aggressiveness, 99
  and measurement of aggressiveness, 98
  and prejudice, 92
Stealing, 26
Stimulus generalization, 76, 78–83
  direct vs. displaced, 76
Subjective probability of success, 193
Substitute goals, 9
Substitute responses, 56, 76–7, 83–4
  and displacement, 83–4
  real vs. irreal, 122

Terminology, 175–8
Three-window situation, 14
Tough-mindedness and aggressive attitudes, 100
Traumatic-avoidance learning, 39
Two-factor theory of learning, 36, 37–42
Two-window situation, 14

Units of action, 117
Units of activity, 117

Valence, 142–6
Variability of response, 44, 56
  in human experiments, 54–5
  in non-frustrating situations, 54–5

Word-association as a conflict indicator, 139–41